FINDING FRANKLIN

McGill-Queen's University Press
Montreal & Kingston • London • Chicago

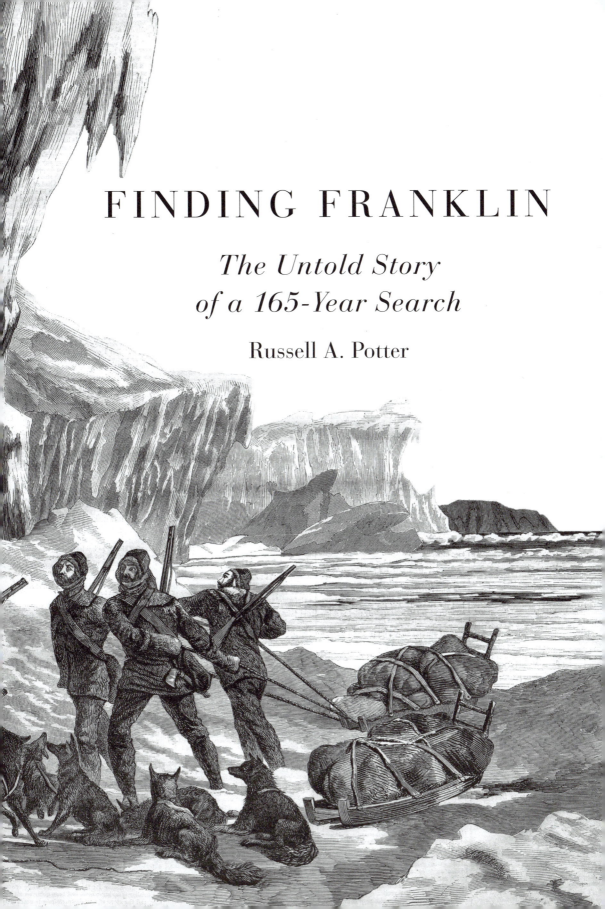

FINDING FRANKLIN

The Untold Story of a 165-Year Search

Russell A. Potter

© McGill-Queen's University Press 2016

ISBN 978-0-7735-4784-1 (cloth)
ISBN 978-0-7735-9961-1 (ePDF)
ISBN 978-0-7735-9962-8 (ePUB)

Legal deposit third quarter 2016
Bibliothèque nationale du Québec

Printed in Canada on acid-free paper

McGill-Queen's University Press acknowledges the support of the Canada
Council for the Arts for our publishing program. We also acknowledge the
financial support of the Government of Canada through the Canada Book
Fund for our publishing activities.

Library and Archives Canada Cataloguing in Publication

Potter, Russell A., 1960–, author
Finding Franklin : the untold story of a 165-year search / Russell A. Potter.

Includes bibliographical references and index.
Issued in print and electronic formats.
ISBN 978-0-7735-4784-1 (cloth). –ISBN 978-0-7735-9961-1 (ePDF).
–ISBN 978-0-7735-9962-8 (ePUB)

1. Franklin, John, Sir, 1786–1847. 2. Erebus (Ship). 3. Shipwrecks –
Canada, Northern. 4. Northwest Passage – Discovery and exploration –
British. 5. Arctic regions – Discovery and exploration – British. I. Title.

G660.P68 2016   919.8   C2016-902075-4
                                      C2016-902076-2

Frontispiece: *Harper's Weekly*, 29 October 1859
(Collection of the author.)

For my children, Brendan, Noah, and Caeli.

Voyagers all.

Contents

CONTENTS

Acknowledgments

It's been said that undertaking historical research is not unlike entering a crowded room where a lively conversation has been carried on since long before one was born. One must catch at a word, a phrase, or a friendly voice, feeling one's way about until it all begins to make sense, before one dares to ask the first question.

The list of voices among which I found my own must begin with Dave Woodman, who – receiving an e-mail from a total stranger some twenty-odd years ago, took care to respond in detail, considering no line of questioning unworthy of consideration; our correspondence in the years since has been invaluable. Early on in my researches, an informal e-mail list of "Franklinites," as we came to call ourselves, began to grow: Margaret Bertulli, Anne Keenleyside, Dave Mullington, Wayne Davidson, John Harrington, Ron Rust, David Meagher, George Hobson, Rebecca Harris, Dorothy Eber, Tom Gross, and Jim Delgado were among that excellent company in those early days. As the web has grown, this list merged into and was subsumed by others, most recently by the "Remembering the Franklin Expedition" Facebook group: Lee Preston, Kristina Gehrmann, Alan Hoch, Louie Kamookak, Ralph Lloyd-Jones, the anonymous "Ship Modeler," Paul Van Peenen, Mechtild Opel, Glenn Marty Stein, Bill Greenwell, Randall Osczevski, Ted Betts, Frank Schuster, Ro Braine, Peter Carney, William Battersby, Chris Valade, the late Garth Walpole, and so many others have taken up the call, and no question or query has arisen among us that hasn't had the benefit of the group's collective wisdom. I owe a special debt to several of its members – Andrés Paredes Salvador, Regina Koellner, Russ Taichman, Wolfgang Opel, Bill Greenwell, and Jonathan Dore – for their assistance with the book's illustrations. It would be a far less colourful book – and world – without them.

ACKNOWLEDGMENTS

Among the friends and kindred spirits who have been especially important to me, I must also mention Doug Wamsley, who has always put his knowledge, and his extraordinary collections, at my disposal; Huw Lewis-Jones, whose keen visual intelligence has been as vital a guidepost to me as the infamous Beechey Island "pointing hand"; and Kenn Harper, whose vast knowledge of Arctic and Inuit history is matched only by his great generosity of spirit. Along my way, I have also been the happy beneficiary of a great many other Arctic encounters and the fine friendships that have ensued. I think here of Kari Herbert, John Wilson, Larry Millman, Pete Capelotti, John Bockstoce, Glyn Williams, John Geiger, Michael Robinson, David and Deirdre Stam, Chip Sheffield, Michael Lapides, Ken McGoogan, Ernie Coleman, Joe O'Farrell, Seamus Taaffe, Doreen Larsen Riedel, Lady Alexandra Shackleton, Nancy Campbell, Andrew Lambert, and all those who have ever clinked a glass at O'Brien's Pub in Athy. *Go raibh maith agaibh!*

I owe, as always, an irreparable debt to the libraries, museums, and archival collections where so much that is a part of these histories is preserved, and whose librarians and curators are the sine qua non in any researcher's work. My thanks especially go to Karen Ryan at the Canadian Museum of History, Claire Warrior at the National Maritime Museum in Greenwich, Willow Silvani at the Scott Polar Research Institute, Amelia Fay at the Manitoba Museum, and Stephen Loring at the Smithsonian Institution. Lastly, to my family, and to those non-Arctic friends who have put up with my obsession for all these years, my deepest thanks for their support and patience.

Editorial Notes

A NOTE ON FRANKLIN SEARCHES

The period of 165 years covered in this book begins in 1849 – the year that the first major search for Franklin launched by the Royal Navy returned home having found no trace of Franklin or his ships. It's then that we can begin to speak of a Franklin "mystery" – then that the key elements that have made this story so fascinating for so long – hope, disappointment, and speculation – first came together. From then until 1859, the search for Franklin's ships and men encompassed – following the criteria of W. Gillies Ross – roughly three dozen organized efforts. Of the other searches in this period, though, only *two* brought back significant Inuit testimony as well as physical relics, those of Dr John Rae and Sir Francis Leopold McClintock; no other searches of that era, however significant in terms of the areas they charted and traversed, added to what was known about Franklin's fate. It's no slight to them – their efforts were no less important – but in retelling the story of the Franklin search, my goal has been to focus on the discoveries of those searchers whose work has contributed to the reconstruction of the movements of Franklin's men and ships, up to and including the discovery of HMS *Erebus* in 2014.

A NOTE ON USAGE AND SPELLING

This book draws on a wide array of historical sources; as a rule, when quoting from printed or manuscript materials, I have reproduced their original spelling. The word "Eskimo," and its earlier variant "Esquimaux," is given in such sources, though its use is considered pejorative today; in my own text, *Inuit* is always used. Some earlier texts spell this word "Innuit" and use it as though it were singular (it is plural) – as above, these spellings are preserved in quotations only. Inuit names and words in the Inuktitut language pose another question; in the original quotations I have likewise preserved the (sometimes idiosyncratic) spellings of names, preferring one such spelling (e.g., "Su-pun-ger") over variants to avoid confusion. Contemporary Inuit names and Inuktitut words are spelled according to modern orthography and given in italics at their first appearance.

Introduction

Is Franklin the only man who is lost, that his wife should be so earnest to find him? Does Mr. Grinnell know where he himself is? Be rather the Mungo Park, the Lewis and Clark and Frobisher, of your own streams and oceans; explore your own higher latitudes – with shiploads of preserved meats to support you, if they be necessary; and pile the empty cans sky-high for a sign.
– Henry David Thoreau, *Walden*

In the long course of human history, there are any number of people who have become lost, whose ships have sunk in uncharted waters, whose tombs have been buried by desert sands or jungle undergrowth, or who, perhaps, just stepped outside one day to take an afternoon walk and never returned. When explorers, themselves charged with venturing into the unknown and unearthing its secrets, become lost, we feel their disappearance more keenly, and if, despite all our efforts, we find no trace of them, our confidence in our human knowledge and capabilities is profoundly shaken. We know we live on the edge of an abyss – of time, of space, of our own all-too-brief individual existence – but we dislike being reminded of it.

And so it is that, long after any hope of relief or recovery has passed, there will still be some who refuse to stop looking for the lost: in the South Pacific, searchers arrive each year to comb the coast of Nikumaroro Island looking for traces of Amelia Earhart and her Lockheed Model 10 Elektra; the Norwegian Navy still trolls the depths of the Barents Sea for Roald Amundsen's Latham 47 seaplane; and amateur scientists pore over Google Earth views of the Amazon rainforest seeking evidence of the Lost City of Z and Percy Fawcett, the man who vanished searching for it. And, of all the explorers who have ever gone missing, none has inspired so long, so

Figure 1 Franklin expedition food tins. Courtesy of Doug Wamsley.

persistent a search as has Sir John Franklin, whose final Arctic expedition was last seen off the coast of Greenland in the summer of 1845.

Thoreau, though he admonishes us to seek rather our own interior "higher latitudes," was doubtless following news of the Franklin search in the Boston *Evening Transcript*; it may be that he also saw an illustration depicting the stack of empty food tins left behind on Beechey Island, the site of Franklin's first winter camp, which had just been discovered. In his journal for 23 March 1852, we can find an earlier draft of the sentiments he expressed in the closing chapter of *Walden*: "As I cannot go upon a Northwest Passage, then I will find a passage round the actual world where I am. Connect the Behring Straits and Lancaster Sounds of thought; winter on Melville Island, and make a chart of Banks Land; explore the northwest-trending Wellington Inlet, where there is said to be a perpetual open sea, cutting my way through floes of ice." From this, we can see that Thoreau *did*, in fact, wish he could go upon an Arctic journey; but since he could not, he sought instead a symbolic voyage through similar straits. His metaphorical map, certainly, demonstrates close familiarity with narratives of Arctic exploration: Melville Island (charted by William Edward Parry in 1819);

Banks Land (first sighted by William Beechey on Parry's expedition); and Wellington Inlet, the channel up which, it was then speculated, Franklin might have sailed in search of an Open Polar Sea (a chimerical but then widely sought goal of Arctic explorers).

And Thoreau was not alone in seeking to travel, mentally and spiritually, alongside Franklin and those who searched for him; Emily Dickinson dubbed a central corridor of her Amherst home the "Northwest Passage"; in her poetic hands a "polar expedition" became a "polar expiation," an "Omen in the bone / of Death's tremendous nearness." Back home in Britain, Charles Dickens, too, closely followed the search for Franklin, leaping to the defence of his widow, Lady Franklin, when stories came home of cannibalism among his men; in 1857 he and his protégé Wilkie Collins produced a play, *The Frozen Deep*, as a memorial to their shared Arctic heroes. In France, Jules Verne based the protagonist of the first of his *Voyages Extraordinaires*, Captain Hatteras, on Franklin, while, a few years later in Poland, young Józef Korzeniowski found in the narrative of Franklin's disappearance – which he read in French – the inspiration for both the literal and figurative voyages that would eventually bring him to England as the novelist Joseph Conrad.

One reason for the fascination of all these writers with Franklin, surely, is simply that it took so long to find any trace of him. Aside from his first winter camp, discovered in 1850, it was not until 1859 – fourteen years after he had sailed down the Thames in command of the *Erebus* and *Terror* – that any definite record was found. And, when even that final note proved inadequate as an explanation for the loss of both his ships and all 128 of the men he had commanded, the air of uncertainty that surrounded his fate settled in as a sort of permanent state. Being lost, it would seem, is not so much a physical condition as a *cultural* one; it's the not knowing that matters. And the longer the public does not know, the greater the aura of uncertainty; at some point, after the practical value of rescue has dwindled to zero, it becomes a mythical quest into the nature of loss itself.

The Arctic has long been a special stage for this kind of loss; its hazards include the freezing not simply of bodies but of time. Arctic snows, like desert sands, are lone, level, and stretch far away, reducing the glory of imperial ambition and human hubris to a small gathering of bones. More than any other sort of disaster, death amidst the ice discloses, in its purest form, the utter indifference of nature to human striving. Tales of such a death possess a terrible beauty that can never quite be contained, resolved, or even represented. And as the search for Franklin has continued over the past century and a half, the scattered artifacts and human remains brought back by searchers have themselves formed, in a mournful and melancholy manner, a kind of strange museum of this loss.

Somehow, without quite realizing why, we've inherited a fixation with this same scene of civilization and its technology come to naught, and it troubles the edge of our sense of ourselves as powerfully as it did our Victorian forebears. As the twenty-first century has dawned, it's brought a renewed fascination with the Franklin story – for in the mirror of his fate we behold our uncanny double, a figure whose motives and gestures darkly figure forth our own, though whether to mock us or to warn us we know not. I think that's the only explanation for the way in which Franklin continues to haunt us, inspiring more than two dozen novels, three documentaries, various plays, poems, and radio dramas, an Australian musical, and a German opera – all within the past twenty-five years. We're looking, collectively, for something we truly *have* lost, and trying to grasp the secret nature of that loss – and the finding of one of Franklin's ships will not dissolve that desire but redouble it.

FINDING FRANKLIN

CAPTAIN SIR JOHN FRANKLIN, K.H.C.

Figure 2 Captain Sir John Franklin, after a daguerreotype by Beard.
Courtesy of Doug Wamsley.

1

The Man Who Ate His Boots

On 29 September 2014 Stephen Harper, the prime minister of Canada, announced at a hastily convened press conference that one of Sir John Franklin's ships, missing since 1845, had been found in the Arctic. Ryan Harris, the man who made this discovery, had been rushed back to Ottawa on a red-eye flight-for-one to be present for the occasion, and, as a large video monitor in the room showed the sonar image of the ship, he was greeted by applause from the assembled ministers and representatives of the press. If anyone present had squinted just a bit, though, they might easily have imagined themselves tossed back in time to Victorian London, where, in the early days of the search for Franklin, similar scenes were unveiled upon screens of a similar size – only these were screens of linen or paper, and the representation of Franklin's ships composed of daubs of paint rather than liquid-crystal-screened pixels. In the 1850s there were dozens of showmen in Britain and the United States who were purveying these "moving panoramas" of the Franklin expedition, in which painted scenes of the lost explorers scrolled by upon an illuminated roll of cloth or paper, while a lecturer in a frock coat pointed out scenes of interest with a long stick.

The search for Franklin had lasted that long – from the age of moving panoramas and daguerreotypes to that of side-scan 3D sonar imaging and high-resolution digital cameras, from the time when current events were sketched by artists and transmitted to the world via woodcuts and engravings to one in which instantaneous digital video links delivered the world into people's living rooms at the speed of light. And, although it might be assumed that it was our superior technological prowess that made the discovery of Franklin's ship possible, this marvel was actually the result of more than a century and a half of repeated searches of a bleak landscape that examined fragmentary clues and collected the oral testimony of generations of caribou-skin-clad Inuit hunters, who had preserved their memories of the final fate of the Franklin expedition long after it had been largely forgotten by the "civilized" world.

But perhaps you may ask: Why was Franklin of such importance that, after more than a century since his disappearance, the government of Canada would consider it worthwhile to spend six years and millions of dollars to locate his ships? After all, "is Franklin the only man who is lost?" There is certainly no shortage of lost explorers, lost cities, and lost civilizations in searching for which, were similar resources to be expended, we might learn more about our shared human history. Franklin's personal character and career, though exemplary, were not so different from those of other men of his background and talents, and his quest – the search for a navigable "Northwest Passage" through the Arctic – is one that, though achieved at last by Roald Amundsen in 1904, was of little use then and may not be for years to come, even in our present age of global warming. So what was it that has made Franklin and his men the subject of song and story, of novels, plays, operas, and musicals, as well as the object of hundreds of searchers travelling with equal alacrity by dogsled and armchair, whose determination has not flagged but rather intensified as a new century – the second since his demise – has dawned?

To answer that question, we must search in two places: first in the nineteenth century, when ships of Britain and other nations were exploring the as-yet-uncharted regions of the terrestrial globe; and then in the twenty-first, when geopolitical and economic pressures are converging on the Arctic to an extraordinary, unprecedented degree. For, just as technology has evolved and grown, so has the human population and its needs, to such an extent that the polar regions in general, and the Northwest Passage in particular, have come to represent the future even more than the past. Franklin's voyage, although its route has not changed, has changed very greatly in its significance; like a long-abandoned mine whose rare earths and metals are suddenly vastly more precious, the route he never lived to chart fully now rings and resonates with the glint of gold. And yet, if we are to understand the present meaning of his passage, we must begin with the earlier one, as well as the ripples of rearward-looking nostalgia and romanticism with which, even more than ice, he and his ships have become quite heavily encrusted.

The story begins when Britain, flush from its victories over Napoleon, found itself a great naval nation with a superabundance of ships and men.

As with other global powers, it had always conducted a course of exploration, though more often in the pursuit of commerce than out of pure exploratory curiosity. Indeed, its original connection with what's now the Canadian Arctic came via the Hudson's Bay Company (HBC), officially known as the Company of Adventurers of England Trading into Hudson's Bay; what was being *ventured*, in the sense of this name, was money, not men. It was not necessarily an insult for Napoleon to call England a "nation of shopkeepers" – for although, certainly, great English navigators such as Drake or Cook did much to explore and chart unknown regions, it was no diminishment of their voyages to note that commerce, and colonization, quickly followed. The long peace after the defeat of France meant demobilization for sailors, decommissioning of ships, and retirement of officers on half-pay, but it also freed up some portion of these excess resources to pursue exploration in parts of the world in which the commercial potential was less, or even none. The pendulum of risk, for these voyages, moved back from money to men, and the absence of any practical value actually ennobled their undertaking.

So it was that 1818 saw the launching of two naval expeditions, one to explore the long-neglected bay charted by William Baffin in 1616, and one to sail straight north to the pole. The first, though successful, was derided as a "pleasure cruise" – the ships commanded by Sir John Ross neither experienced peril nor were required to demonstrate perseverance. The second, turned back after an encounter with masses of floating ice that nearly destroyed the two vessels, causing one – the HMS *Trent* – to toss back and forth so sharply that the ship's bell rang out, failed in its goals but succeeded in its encounter with danger. The vessels eventually retreated to the Spitzbergen islands, where they underwent emergency repairs and then limped back to Britain to nearly universal acclaim. And it was then that the young commander of the *Trent*, Lieutenant John Franklin, first stepped into the public eye.

This was in the age before illustrated newspapers, and so the voyage was first commemorated not in print but in paint. For, in addition to the scrolling imagery of "moving" panoramas, there was also another nineteenth-century documentary medium, the fixed or "great-circle" panorama. Painted on enormous cylinders of canvas, then visited from within by the public, they displayed an uninterrupted 360-degree view of some other place on Earth; for the London Panorama's view of the Arctic explorers, this was to be a scene of the ships at anchor off Spitzbergen, in the company of polar fauna such as seagulls and walruses, with Franklin and his senior officer, John Buchan, in the foreground. Franklin agreed to the proprietor's request to pose for his representation, realizing full well that it could be a first, albeit slight, step into fame. To his sister, he wrote declaring that he would avoid Leicester Square, where the painting was on view, lest some member of the public call him out with "There goes the fellow from the panorama!"

He needn't have worried. His service had been duly noted, and he was made the commander of the next Arctic expedition, one sent overland via trading posts in what are now the Northwest Territories, to seek and map the shores of the "Polar Sea." In the course of polar exploration, the notion that open water of some kind might lie beyond an "ice barrier" had proven a persistent one, making its invitation irresistible for both science and commerce. It was on this expedition that Franklin inadvertently cemented his claim to fame, not with unsullied success, but by an encounter with a hostile landscape (and a hostile native) that affirmed the Arctic's proper position of peril. He had, it was true, managed to map some of the northern coast, but on his return trip he unwisely chose a seemingly more direct route back to his winter encampment, crossing over an unmapped area that turned out to contain difficult-to-ford rivers and a striking absence of game; it would ever after be known as the "Barren Lands." Franklin lost several of his guides, French-speaking voyageurs who had been hired to steer his canoes, and worse: another of his guides, a Mohawk named Michel Terohaute, apparently resorted to cannibalism.

In the British view of the day, this was an act which it was believed that no proper Englishman, or devout Christian, would ever commit, and Michel's deed was blamed on his lack of proper religious instruction. And yet, since the mystery meat he brought was in fact consumed by two of Franklin's officers, the incident can't entirely be blamed on that. When Michel progressed from passive cannibalism – eating the remains of already-dead voyageurs – to apparent murder, killing midshipman Robert Hood as he sat beside a fire – his fate was sealed. At the next opportunity, Franklin's surgeon-naturalist John Richardson shot Michel in the head. Richardson then rejoined Franklin at their winter quarters, where they subsisted on rotten deerskins, pounded bones, and the singed leather of their own shoes. They lived long enough to be rescued, and on Franklin's return he received the sobriquet that he would never lose, becoming the "man who ate his boots."

Franklin returned one more time to lead a land expedition in the Arctic; this one was an unqualified success, mapping hundreds of miles of coastline without losing a single soul. He wrote the expected book about his journeys, was knighted, and remarried (his first wife, the poet Eleanor Porden, having died while he was in the Arctic). His new wife, Jane – a world traveller in her own right – preferred politics to poetry, and quickly set about trying to find a new situation for her husband that would be proportionate to his achievements. The position of governor of a small Caribbean island was turned down, as insufficient to his merits, but before long a proper posting was on offer as governor general of Van Diemen's Land (the modern Australian island state of Tasmania). There was, as it happened, to be one slight difference with this position, which was that Van Diemen's Land was at that time Britain's largest penal colony, to which all manner of petty criminals (including my own great-great-grandfather, William Brunt) were sent for their period of servitude.

It was here that both Sir John and Lady Franklin acquired fresh aspects of their reputations – his as a man too kind-hearted to punish prisoners, and too naive to see the machinations being made against his governorship by other parties; and hers as an ambitious woman, prodding her now-pudgy husband to greater and greater achievements while she herself remained happily ensconced in the shadows. As it turned out, the shadows in Tasmania were rather shorter and fainter than they had been back home, and after a bureaucratic insurrection by Franklin's former colonial secretary, they were sent packing. Thus, at just the moment when, with a young Victoria secure upon the throne, a renewed effort toward the long-elusive goal of finding a Northwest Passage was once more on the national agenda, a perfect convergence of the twain: Franklin was the only man for it. As Sir Roderick Murchison, then president of the Royal Geographical Society, declared, "the name Franklin alone is, indeed, a national guarantee."

A word needs to be said about exactly why the Passage was as important as it was. On one level, it was essentially a quest – a mission upon which "knights-errant of the sea" (as Joseph Conrad later called them) could be dispatched – with the requisite difficulty and uncertainty to ensure that its realization would take a long time. Mark Twain, indeed, in his *A Connecticut Yankee in King Arthur's Court*, explained the Holy Grail itself as but the "Northwest passage of that day." That it was difficult was already well known, and in fact it was a matter of parliamentary record that Sir

John Ross, when asked whether the Passage, if achieved, had any potential value, had declared it "utterly useless." A perverse – but very durable – formula of the day had it that the nobility of an undertaking was in inverse proportion to its usefulness, multiplied by the factor of its difficulty: there could be no better mission for a now-imperial power to dispatch men and ships.

The idea may seem absurd to us today, but we can look to our own more recent history, with the "space race" between the United States and the Soviet Union being another example. The actual utility of putting a man upon the moon was known to be nil, and John F. Kennedy, when he proposed this mission, already anticipated that it would be extraordinarily costly (and, as it turned out, he badly underestimated its cost). The justification for the US space program came in the form of science; after all, in addition to learning something about our "nearest neighbour in space," one was meant to think of all the technical achievements, from Teflon to Tang, that the space program would require and that would thence be made available to grateful civilians. But what the moon mission had, above all, was an enormous element of risk, as the deaths of the Apollo 1 astronauts in 1967 proved. Another case in point might be Apollo 13, which – the moon now achieved – received little fanfare, and not even a live television feed from space, until it was suddenly put in peril by the explosion of one of its oxygen tanks, making it headline news again.

As with the US and Soviet astronauts, the men who sailed with Franklin were largely service veterans, and their vessels – rather like the American Space Shuttles – were reusable vehicles supplied with all the on-board necessities for the anticipated length of the mission, which was three years. Once the ships entered the Passage, they had no direct means to communicate with home; telegraph and wireless were decades in the future. Sir John Ross had tried homing pigeons, with some success, but none were sent with Franklin; instead, he had printed forms, with a space to fill out the expedition's status, asking the finder to please return them to the nearest British consulate. At sea, these were meant to be dropped off inside an empty barrel, for flotation; on land, the usual method was to place them in a tin cylinder inside carefully constructed stone cairn. These cairns were sometimes called the "post offices of the North," but, unlike the penny post back home, the pickup and delivery times were quite hard to foresee – the only way for them to reach the outside world was for some other ship or party of explorers to stumble upon them. All this meant that, for the first two years, at least, no communication was expected; even in the third year, it was quite possible to imagine that any of a number of things might have delayed or prevented a message from being found.

It's this silence – one that, in Franklin's case, was to remain unbroken for fourteen years, well past the date at which survival was imaginable – that was the first harbinger of the haunted nature of his disappearance. Even in a world where news of "current" events could take weeks to reach the papers, three years was a very long time, long enough for the slow burn of apprehension to take hold, for the first rumours and conjectures to gestate, and bureaucratic indifference to turn to national alarm. Lady Franklin had hoped that a mission could be sent in 1847, but it was not until 1848 – three years after the expedition's departure – that two ships, the *Enterprise* and *Investigator* under James Clark Ross, were sent. These, alas, found not a trace of Franklin, which deepened the mystery considerably; their search, too, was documented in the Panorama in Leicester Square, striking a note not of accomplishment but absence. Hopes were still high, and humour still possible – such that in the pages of *Punch*, W.M. Thackeray had the chaperone of three hypothetical young children declare the Panorama's view of the frozen ships more "chilling" than Madame Tussaud's Chamber of Horrors.

But then the horror came home, and by slow degrees. The 1850–51 season saw multiple searches by Britain and the United States; the result was the discovery of Franklin's first winter harbour on Beechey Island, whose chief feature was a row of three forlorn graves, marked with the names of seamen John Torrington and John Hartnell and Royal Marine William Braine. An enormous cairn was found, but – incredibly – it contained no message at all, even though the searchers dismantled it and dug in every direction nearby. The only other feature of the place – the stack of empty food tins that so struck Thoreau – seemed to testify at once to continued progress (after all, the men were well fed, and energetic enough to construct this playful pile) and uncanny absence (here was the meal, but where were the men?). The answer to that question proved a further horror; in 1854 Hudson's Bay surveyor Dr John Rae returned with all manner of relics – chronometers, pencil cases, silverware, and Sir John's own medal of knighthood – and also with accounts, given to him by the Inuit, that in their final desperation Franklin's men had turned to the "last resource" of cannibalism.

Lady Franklin, as may well be imagined, did not take this lightly. She enlisted no less a light than Charles Dickens to take on Rae's report, and Dickens obliged with a long tirade against the lying, savage "Esquimaux" in his own magazine, *Household Words*. She also tried – unsuccessfully – to prevent Rae from being given the £10,000 reward for "ascertaining the fate" of her husband. She then turned her attention to persuading the government to launch another search, in part to attend to the unburied bodies of her husband and his men, in part to determine more fully what had become of them, and not least (she hoped) to disprove Rae's account. Unfortunately for her, British forces were by then engaged in the Crimean peninsula, and the Admiralty, on a war footing, had no resources to devote to such a cause, however noble. Having already expended much of her own resources, she turned to her Arctic friends – officers who had served on previous searches – and in 1857 was able to send Francis Leopold McClintock, aboard the yacht the *Fox*, back to seek the source of those sad artifacts returned by Rae. On the voyage out, the *Fox* was caught in the ice pack in the Davis Strait and carried far from her intended course; even once the Northwest Passage was reached, heavy ice delayed McClintock's arrival in the search area until 1859.

And it was then that scattered bones, abandoned supplies, and the final, fatal, record, deposited in a cairn on the remote shores of King William Island, were recovered. The note offered its own miniature version of hubris before a fall, and desperation after: it had first been filled out in 1847, with a list of the expedition's achievements and the doubly underlined phrase <u>All Well</u>. Yet around the margins of this same note, in a cramped hand, Franklin's second and third in command – Francis Crozier and James Fitzjames – had added a grim codicil. In it, they numbered the dead (seventeen more since the three at Beechey, including nine officers) and noted, without further comment, that "Sir John Franklin died on the 11th of June 1847." The *Erebus* and *Terror* had been abandoned in April 1848 – the same year as the Royal Navy's first, failed search – and the men were departing thence for the Back River, though why that route had been elected was not said. Had they, as it was then assumed, tried to ascend this river to the HBC post on the Great Slave Lake, it would have been an arduous journey of more than six hundred miles.

The note became instantly the most famous "last words" document of its kind; it was reproduced in facsimile in the *Illustrated London News* and *Harper's Weekly*, and a fold-out version was included with every copy of McClintock's book. From one point of view, at least, the Franklin "mystery" had at last been solved, since this note – along with the skeletons, some buried and some not, that McClintock and his men found along the coast of King William Island – told a simple, sad tale, one of abandonment, a long march overland, and eventual death. McClintock spoke, through his interpreter, with several groups of Inuit in the area; they told of men dragging whaleboats mounted on heavy sledges, men who looked weak and sickly. McClintock found one of these boats abandoned on the western shores of the island; in it were two skeletons along with an astonishing array of materials – silver forks and spoons, tea, chocolate, lead sheeting, carpet slippers, dozens of books (including bibles, prayer books, and a copy of *The Vicar of Wakefield*), and much other such bric-a-brac, which McClintock regarded as "a mere accumulation of dead weight" that would have made hauling the oak-and-iron sledge even more exhausting.

It's this discovery that, for many at the time, seemed to mark the end of searching. As the *Times* of London put it, "so far it is satisfactory to know that the 'final search' has proved that SIR JOHN FRANKLIN is dead. Alas! There can be no longer those sad wailings from an imaginary Tintagel to persuade the credulous that ARTHUR still lives." And yet, for others, the story seemed incomplete. Where were the ships? Where was the body of Sir John Franklin? Where were most of his men? – McClintock encountered only a handful of skeletons out of the hundred and nine said to have abandoned the ships. And, most of all, where were the other papers one would expect – ship's logs, officers' journals, magnetic observations, or any account of what transpired after the ships were left behind? The only other document recovered, perversely, was a pocketbook of letters, nearly all of them written backwards, which seemed to rant and rave of tropical climes and festive occasions – an odd thing to find in the coat pocket of a skeleton found face-down in a frozen wilderness.

These questions might have simply faded away had not one person kept asking them. Lady Franklin, though dubbed "our English Penelope" by the *Daily Telegraph,* wanted nothing of weaving, or of widow's weeds. Though grateful to McClintock, she was deeply dissatisfied that he had found no definitive evidence against Rae's stories (indeed, privately, he acknowledged that he, too, had heard tales of cannibalism). One single paper, however poignant, was not enough for Lady Franklin, and she continued to dispatch searches, and to welcome those by others, in pursuit of more. The last of these, commanded by Sir Allen Young in 1874, was explicitly charged to search for papers of any kind, but the ice that year prevented him from reaching the vicinity of King William. On his return, he discovered that Lady Franklin had died while he was away; to the Franklin cenotaph at

Westminster Abbey were now added these few lines: "THIS MONUMENT WAS ERECTED BY JANE, HIS WIDOW, WHO, AFTER LONG WAITING, AND SENDING MANY IN SEARCH OF HIM, HERSELF DEPARTED, TO SEEK AND FIND HIM IN THE REALMS OF LIGHT, JULY 18, 1875, AGED 83 YEARS."

Yet even Lady Franklin's death did not put an end to searching. There was something about the manner of Franklin's disappearance that continued then, and continues now, to haunt the edges of our imagination; like the unfinished scale that Mozart's parents used to play on the pianoforte to get their son out of bed – young Wolfgang could not help but leap up and play the missing note – there is something not merely unresolved but profoundly disturbing about the tantalizing and incomplete nature of the scattered trail of relics left behind by Franklin and his men. The hope that someone could, by more careful procedures, more persistent searching, or some fresh interpretation of the known evidence, provide a solution of some kind to this profound mystery offered one sort of lure – here was a quest even more elusive than the Grail of the Passage itself! And at the same time, like a novel lacking its final chapter, the Franklin story offered up a fertile and nearly infinite palette of possibilities for writers whose imaginations bent northward. This urge has always been particularly strong for Canadians – for Canada is a young nation, one whose most heavily populated areas lie to the south of a vast and trackless north. It's a land held together by stories, whose mythic tales are bound up with strange and terrible deeds done in a great white wilderness. As Margaret Atwood wryly put it, that jagged red shape on its flag isn't a maple leaf, "it's where someone got axed in the snow."

Atwood noted early on the significance of the Franklin story in Canadian culture; her 1991 Oxford lecture "Concerning Franklin and His Gallant Crew" traces its roots from the balladeering northern yarns of Robert W. Service through the poems of E.J. Pratt and Gwendolyn MacEwen, the latter of whose verse drama *Terror and Erebus* was first broadcast on the CBC in 1965. And yet most Canadians would have heard of Franklin by the time of Atwood's lecture not through poetry but via another medium entirely, television: the 1988 broadcast of *Buried in Ice*, a documentary about the exhumation of three of Franklin's men from their icy graves at Beechey Island. Here, it was not a new discovery – the location of these graves had been known since 1850 – but a new approach: Could science solve the mystery of the demise of the expedition? The program offered the possibility that high levels of lead detected in the bodies could give one explanation, but that wasn't why it caught the imagination of Canadian – and American –

viewers. It was the uncanny effect of looking into the face of men – John Torrington, in particular, whose blue eyes seemed almost to look back at you – that brought this haunted story out of the deep freeze and deep into the unconscious minds of its viewers.

We had seen the cans – we had even seen the bones – but now, here were the *men*, the men who had been sleeping in our midst for all these years, beautiful in their stillness, dressed in their shore-going clothes, resting on their beds of wood shavings, their wrists and toes tied together by their shipmates with strips of linen. It was as if time had skipped a beat, and our hearts skipped with it. Torrington, who had actually been exhumed the year before Hartnell and Braine, haunted us not only on our televisions but also in the pages of *National Geographic* and even *People*. The American song-writer James Taylor was so struck by this image that he wrote a song, "The Frozen Man," from Torrington's point of view: "My brothers and the others are lost at sea, / I alone am returned to tell thee. / Hidden in ice for a century / to walk the world again, / Lord have mercy on the frozen man." In Taylor's version, the frozen man, thawed, returns to life, only to discover to his distress that his wife and child had both died of "extreme old age" years ago.

The facts of Torrington's condition, alas, precluded the possibility of a return to life: as the autopsy report noted, most of his internal organs had disintegrated owing to cell *autolysis* – a sort of self-cannibalism that takes place when enzymes in the cells digest their hosts; his brain had been reduced by this process to a "puddle of yellow, granular liquid." His lungs, though much of their tissue was similarly degraded, showed signs of "pleural adhesions" and abscesses that were likely the result of tuberculosis. But it was his hair and fingernails – those unglamorous witnesses – that may have told the most significant tale, one of heightened levels of lead, peaking a couple of weeks before his death. This matched with the theory, advanced by Dr Owen Beattie, the anthropologist who supervised the exhumations, that lead poisoning may have damaged the mental faculties of Franklin and his men; Beattie hypothesized that the lead in Torrington's body had come from that same notorious stack of tins – tins that, when examined, showed unusually large and sloppily applied beads of lead solder down their interior surfaces.

Like the Victorians before us, we saw, and we believed. Television at the time was still a "hot" medium, beamed into homes around the world, offering in its science programs an eye on every question from the origins of the species to the exploration of space. The limited number of broadcast channels ensured that, whatever their inclinations, audiences could choose from among only a few options, giving even the public broadcasters CBC and BBC an extraordinarily large share of the viewership by the standards of twenty-first-century cable and Internet providers. And yet, unlike the Victorians, we did not need to travel to lecture halls or Lyceums or wait for the wagon train of Chautauqua lecturers to erect its tents on the edge of town. These images came to us, into our living rooms and dens, arriving at our eyes almost before our rational faculties could defend against them. And so Torrington, Braine, and Hartnell became our shipmates.

The success of this broadcast was followed up by a book, *Frozen in Time*, written by Dr Beattie along with John Geiger, who had accompanied him to the exhumations to document their progress. The book was an unqualified success, earning endorsements from figures such as Atwood and even a blurb from William S. Burroughs, whose famous line "when you cut into the present, the future leaks out" took on a new and uncomfortable meaning in this context. The book was even published in a version for children, with Torrington's face on one corner of its cover – a book that I vividly recall so frightened my own children that they refused to come into a room if it was on the table. Across Canada and around the world, the mystery of the Franklin expedition received a new transfusion of interest; a public that had, for a long time, forgotten it now remembered it with intense feeling. And with it, a strange and perhaps morbid curiosity: Did the story these bodies told fully resolve the mystery?

Apparently not, for in 1991, with his book *Unravelling the Franklin Mystery: Inuit Testimony*, David C. Woodman broke open a whole new vein of inquiry. Woodman pointed out that the graves exhumed by Beattie accounted for only three casualties out of 129. Where were the other bodies? What routes of escape had they tried, and why were so few human remains ever recovered? And, most significantly, where were Franklin's ships? Woodman believed that the Inuit accounts, many by eyewitnesses who had met with groups of Franklin's men before their deaths, held the answer. From Beechey Island, where the graves were found, attention shifted to King William Island, near the shores of which the final record indicated the ships had been abandoned. So it was here that the next phase of the search began, retracing the steps of nineteenth-century explorers who had passed this way before.

Between 1981 and 2008 – the year that that Parks Canada became in-volved – there were more than thirty organized Franklin searches, including visual searches, ground-penetrating radar, magnetometer surveys (it was hoped that the ships' ex-railway engines could be found this way), and sonar. A 1994 CBC documentary, *Searching for Franklin*, documented two of these, one led by Woodman himself, interspersing footage of skulls and Franklin-era relics with interviews with an all-star parade of Canadian writers, including Margaret Atwood, Rudy Wiebe, and the well-known his-torical writer Pierre Berton. It was in this era, more than any other, that Franklin's connection with Canada was highlighted and, via television, made palpable. And yet nearly all of these searches relied on private funds, which limited the amount and kind of ground they could cover, and the re-sources at their command. The brief season of open water, and the vast area to be surveyed, meant that any substantial search for the ships would in-volve a multi-year commitment.

It's here that a number of additional factors came into play, most notably the anxieties surrounding Arctic sovereignty. It may come as a surprise to many outside Canada that there might be any question as regards its claims to its northern territory, but in reality it's been a source of national anxi-ety for some time. In geopolitical terms, Canada is a relatively young coun-try, first established as a dominion only in 1867, twenty-two years *after* Franklin sailed. Its northern territories were added later, beginning with the surrender of private claims to the subarctic region by the HBC in 1870, followed by the cession of the High Arctic – here defined as the islands north of the Barrow Strait, extending to the pole – in 1895. The British had actually tried on several earlier occasions to transfer responsibility for this territory, but the Canadian government had repeatedly balked at the offer. It was, understandably, concerned about the cost of administering such a vast and empty tract of land, land that – at least at the time – seemed of uncertain value.

Once the legal transfer was complete, these northernmost lands became known as the District of Franklin, a name that served both as a memorial and as a reminder of the line of succession from Britain to Canada. Then, as the chill of the "Cold War" descended in the 1950s, this northern land gained sudden strategic importance, even while becoming the locus of a quite dif-ferent sort of anxiety about foreign incursions. This came in the building of the Distant Early Warning or DEW line in the mid-1950s – a defensive series of radar stations erected at the insistence of the United States to allow the early detection of Soviet inter-continental ballistic missiles (ICBMs) – which made it instantly clear to Canada that, if it did nothing to establish its national presence in the north, American military activity, and potentially commercial activity as well – might render its sovereignty merely symbolic. The increasing exploitation of the region's immense resources of fossil fuels, metals, and minerals made a succession of Canadian governments still more keenly aware of the region's potential value. Yet the underlying problem persisted: a claim of sovereignty required some securing of borders, some population of the land or use of its resources, some sense of presence over an area more than twice the size of Alaska.

And so it was that Canada, throughout the latter half of the twentieth century, made a number of moves to try to secure and enhance its claim to the north. Airbases and airports were built, permanent settlements planned, and the nation's fleet of icebreakers and RCMP vessels expanded, taking the place of the Hudson's Bay ships that had formerly comprised the north's main supply line. In 1958 the establishment of the Polar Continental Shelf lengthened the reach of northern research with air transport and supplies. The Canadian Rangers, self-supporting hunters who were equipped at government expense to patrol Canada's remotest borders, were increasingly deployed into the High Arctic, flying the flag over the farthest, uninhabited reaches of the frozen zone. For, while other countries could maintain their sovereignty claims by settling the land, Canada faced the unique difficulty that much of its northernmost lands were scarcely habitable.

But quite beyond these issues, there was another line that cut across the Canadian landmass in an even more problematic way than the DEW line – the Northwest Passage itself. In the modern era, of course, we know that there's more than one route through these waters – they're officially known as the "Northwestern Passages" – but it's that same fact that poses perhaps the biggest problem for Canadian sovereignty. Since the passage is a natural one, and the only way to travel from one large body of international waters (the Atlantic) to another (the Pacific), it seems to meet the definition of an "international strait" by the terms of current sea law. Canada has long taken a different view, regarding the passages as "Canadian Internal Waters," which would require any ships passing through them to obtain permission from the Canadian government. In practice, cargo ships are still quite rare, and those that have made the voyage have gone through the motions of asking permission, though insisting that this was voluntary on their part.

In terms of sovereignty claims, the possible significance of Franklin's ships is unclear; as British-flagged vessels sailing through what was then British-controlled territory, their connection with Canada is one of later descent. Several factors, however, have begun to change both the legal framework and the public perception of their legacy. First, in 1997, a quietly negotiated "memorandum of agreement" was made with the United Kingdom. Under its terms, the British government assigned "custody and control" of the ships to Canada, effectively granting them exclusive salvage rights to both the *Erebus* and *Terror*, if found. The only provisos to this grant were that the UK government reserved its claim to any gold recovered from the wrecks, and obtained a promise that any artifacts found to be "of outstanding significance to the Royal Navy" would be made available for loan and display in an appropriate British museum. Secondly, in 2006, Canada declared the site of both wrecks to be national historic sites, which further put into place protocols and protections similar to those granted to national parks. The irony of this designation was that neither ship had yet been found, making them the first two national monuments so designated by any country to have no known location.

At around this time, the Canadian government, which had in the past played only a minor, supporting role in Franklin searches, began to take the lead. Under (at first) Robert Grenier, and later Ryan Harris and Marc-André Bernier, a Parks Canada underwater archaeology team was dispatched nearly every summer and given the support of the icebreaker CCGS *Sir Wilfrid Laurier* along with two skiffs, side-scan sonar rigs, and other basic supplies. Over the next few years, this commitment continued, although in one year (2009) no search was mounted. Since then, each year's search has received increased support; in 2010 a team was dispatched to Mercy Bay, where the Franklin search ship HMS *Investigator* had been abandoned. Not surprisingly, it was still there, but the visual impact of images of the ship was nevertheless considerable, lending increased impetus and public interest to the ongoing search.

But here we need to take a step back: Where and how was the search for these ships being conducted? All of the Parks Canada searches relied primarily on side-scan sonar towed by smaller ships and boats. As with the finding of any sunken vessel, a search area had to be defined; side-scan sonar demands a slow process of back-and-forth, and without some limits it would have been a matter of decades rather than years to search every possible waterway. Here, it was David Woodman's work that laid the foundation, by compiling, and placing faith in, Inuit oral histories as to the site where one of the ships, at least, had sunk, a place the Inuit called *Utjulik*. Woodman himself had begun the process, using both sonar and magnetometer searches; since the Inuit told that the ship had sunk in water shallow enough that its masts still showed, he could also eliminate areas where the water was too deep, or too shallow, for that to have happened. Like Robert Grenier before him, Ryan Harris consulted regularly with Woodman, and the area searched was closely based on Woodman's previous surveys; without his work, the undertaking would have simply been too long and costly.

Yet, despite these focused efforts, no sign of either ship was found. By 2014, feeling no doubt that, with so much of the southern search area already covered, a new strategy might be in order, the planners reconsidered: If they couldn't find the ship the Inuit had seen to the south, what about the other, which was said to have sunk farther to the north? And so was born the "Victoria Strait Expedition," whose name announced its plan to move its operations closer to the site of the ships' original abandonment. And yet that year, the weather gods had something else in mind, blocking any search of the strait with a constant flow of heavy, multi-year ice that made searching almost impossible. It was only as a fallback position, hoping to save a disappointing season, that the searchers that year returned to the older southern search area – the one based on Inuit evidence and Woodman's earlier searches – which turned out to be the place where HMS *Erebus* was finally found, nearly a hundred and seventy years after she had last been sighted by a passing whaler. The ship has already given up its iconic bell, along with a small array of artifacts, including china plates, buttons, and one of its cannons, and further searches will doubtless discover further clues.

But at the same time we need to remember that the ships hold only part of the Franklin story. It's a compelling part – one can only wonder what artifacts, perhaps even personal papers or records that could tell us something of what happened after the 1848 abandonment, might be retrieved – but only part. The darker side of the Franklin expedition, including the stories of cannibalism, of small groups of survivors each setting out in its own direction, of hospital camps, of overturned boats, graves and caches of records on land – is still largely unknown, and all of it took place after the ships had been left behind. Here too, the way has been led in recent decades by amateur searchers, of whom Woodman is just one; in this book, the story of many of these others who came before and after will be told. And today, even the "armchair" explorers have new technological tools – better publicly accessible satellite imagery, the ability to search millions of books and manuscripts online, and the power of crowds to decipher difficult documents or collate ones separated by time and distance. There's every possibility, indeed, that the next vital discovery relating to the fate of Franklin's men will be made by a lone searcher equipped only with a laptop, in the comfort of his or her own study at home.

And what, then, does the finding of Franklin's ship, HMS *Erebus*, mean? What if we find the *Terror* as well? And what if, against all odds, someone were to locate Franklin's tomb, or unearth a hitherto-unknown cache of records documenting what happened after the ships were left behind? Even then, there would doubtless be plenty of unanswered questions, but that's not the real reason we would still care. No, nor just the strange, vaguely guilty knowledge that these men, for whom so many searched for so long, in the end died desperately, unaware of the effort expended to reach and relieve them. Their bones, though they may be recruited to serve some nation's purpose, or studied to disclose their sufferings, their struggles, or even their names, must someday be put back to rest. In the end, Thoreau was right: it's ourselves, not Franklin, that we're really searching for, and those latitudes know no pole. As Gwendolyn MacEwen put it, "The earth insists / There is but one geography, but then / There is another still – / The complex, crushed geography of men."

2

Bones

"Bones – no need to ask which bones," remarked the *Times* drily, barely concealing its distaste. The great artist Sir Edwin Landseer, painter of innumerable aristocrats' horses and dogs, who had recently finished a commission to sculpt the lions of Trafalgar Square, had clearly lost his mind. He had depicted something so horrid that the national gorge rose up against it: a scene of two ravenous polar bears, arrayed on either side of a broken mast from which the tatters of a naval ensign still hung, one of them chomping away happily on the rib cage of an unfortunate explorer. And *which* bones they were was instantly evident to everyone who saw the painting: those of one of Sir John Franklin's men, all 128 of whom had died, unsuccoured, in the vast and thrilling (and deadly) regions of thick-ribbed ice, despite a decade of efforts to relieve them by the greatest naval nation the world had ever seen.

The year was 1864. Five years earlier, the last of the searchers to seek after Franklin, Sir Francis Leopold McClintock, had returned with the most dismal imaginable news: he had reached the farthest shore where Franklin's men had perished, and found only heaps of abandoned supplies, among them chocolate, silver spoons, carpet slippers, and a copy of the *Vicar of Wakefield*. And amidst this wreckage, skeletons: two in the boat, their lower jaws open to the sky (some man or animal having carried off the crania), two on a low hill, given only the grace of a scattering of gravel, and one on the shore, face down, left where he lay, a pocketbook of cryptic writing and doggerel verses in his vest, a clothes brush by his side. And lastly, that key element in any noble downfall: a final note, concealed in a cairn, in which the last survivors left the only indication ever found of their demise: they had abandoned their ships and taken to the land in a vain attempt to find their way out of a maze of ice and ice-scoured stones.

Last notes were all well and good – but bones, no matter how they got there, were not. And these particular bones had already been the subject of considerable anxiety: ten years earlier, an intrepid Arctic surveyor, Dr John Rae of the HBC, had been the first to bring back intelligence of Franklin's fate to Britain. He had recovered many relics of these men – their clay pipes, their hat bands, bits of their sleeves, their pocketknives, their watches, and chronometers – he had even retrieved Sir John Franklin's medal, a Guelphic Order of Hanover. But along with these almost sacred objects, he brought back stories from the Inuit – then referred to as "Esquimaux" – that chilled the hearts of all who heard them: Franklin's men, in their desperation, had turned to the "last resource" – cannibalism – in a vain attempt to prolong their lives. The Inuit told of bones broken open, of legs cooked in boots, of metal cases in which human body parts had been stowed as though meant for a portable food supply.

Rae's report was roundly rejected by (among other luminaries) Charles Dickens, who took up several issues of his own magazine *Household Words* to deprecate its reliance upon the "vague babble of savages" who knew only a "domesticity of blood and blubber." To Dickens it hardly seemed likely that such seasoned men, Franklin among them, would resort to something repugnant to the conscience of any civilized Christian man; a far more probable scenario was that the Esquimaux had attacked a band of weakened British sailors and officers. In making this argument Dickens sought not only to redeem his Arctic heroes – of whom he was enormously fond – but also to support the efforts of Franklin's widow, Jane, to clear her husband's name. It was Lady Franklin's later efforts along these lines that had sent McClintock on the voyage that uncovered the final evidence, that fatal note. And in it, indeed, was given the death date of only one man: her husband, who had died in June 1847, a year before any anxiety about the missing expedition had been felt at home.

And yet Dickens, even as he exhausted every argument against Rae, may have been to double business bound. As he wrote to his friend W.H. Wills, when setting out to take up the subject, he had long been "rather strong on voyages and cannibalism" – ever since, in fact, he was a child: "I used, when I was at school, to take in the *Terrific Register*, making myself unspeakably miserable, and frightening my very wits out of my head, for the small charge of a penny weekly; which, considering that there was an illustration to every number, in which there was always a pool of blood, and at least one body, was cheap." This magazine was a fertile source of imagery for a young writer-to-be; among its many illustrations was one depicting a miser who, having locked himself in his storeroom of gold, was found dead weeks later, fork in hand, endeavouring to make a morsel of himself – an image linked by some to Dickens's creation of Ebenezer Scrooge. And, over his lifetime, Dickens devoured many other tales of man eating man: the raft of the *Medusa*, the wreck of the *Thomas*, and that of the *St Lawrence*, all of which, perversely, he cited in his defence of Franklin, as evidence that, although foreigners and "persons of an inferior class" might indulge in such horrors, such a thing was impossible for well-trained British sailors and officers.

Dickens believed he had one other ace up his sleeve: the fact that Franklin had already, on a previous expedition, demonstrated his immunity to the cannibalistic urge. As recounted in the previous chapter, one native guide, Michel Terohaute – vilified by Dickens as a "devil" given to "wolfish devices" – cannibalized the bodies of stragglers and offered this meat – which was *eaten*! – to Dr John Richardson, the expedition's naturalist, as well as midshipman Robert Hood and seaman John Hepburn. Not long after, Terohaute shot Hood, and Richardson responded by shooting and killing Terohaute. It makes for a grim recitation, one that does little to suggest that the culinary virtues of a commanding officer will redound to every man under his authority. Nonetheless, Dickens read these events as proof positive that no men under Franklin's leadership would ever resort to such a thing.

Figure 3 Sir Edwin Landseer, *Man Proposes, God Disposes*, 1864.
1909 mezzotint, collection of the author.

A few years later, in *The Frozen Deep*, a play he produced with his protégé Wilkie Collins, Dickens helped stage a scene based on this very moment, set at an isolated Arctic encampment where a cook with the rather pointed name of "John Want" is pounding bones – no need to ask which bones! – while all around him his starving comrades chatter on, unaware (as was Richardson in Franklin's own account of their privations) of the "sepulchral" tone of their own voices:

> *Lieutenant Crayford.* You are the only cheerful man of the ship's company. Look here. Are these bones pounded small enough?
> *John Want* (*Taking the pestle and mortar*). You'll excuse me, sir, but how very hollow your voice sounds this morning.
> *Lieutenant Crayford.* Keep your remarks about my voice to yourself, and answer my question about the bones.
> *John Want.* Well, sir, they'll take a trifle more pounding. I'll do my best with them to-day, Sir, for your sake.
> *Lieutenant Crayford.* What do you mean?
> *John Want.* I don't think I shall have the honour of making much more bone soup for you, sir. Do you think yourself you'll last long, sir? I don't, saving your presence. I think about another week or ten days will do for us all.

Dickens himself played one of the explorers, Richard Wardour, who in the end dies on stage just after rescuing Crayford, his rival, and delivering him to the arms of his true love. The effect on audiences was profound; not only they but the cast, stagehands, and carpenters were unable to keep from weeping, and Dickens wrote delightedly to an old friend of the nightly "crying of two thousand people."

In this, as in so many of his other writings, Dickens displayed a talent for both embracing and repressing what critic Harry Stone has called his "night side" – a lifelong fascination not only with cannibalism but with death, delirium, and dismemberment, with cruelty and disaster and demise, with the wretched state of people so desperate that no act could bring them succour. It's a talent we've inherited, in this age of voyeuristic video and CGI-enhanced gore: we pretend to abhor the knowledge, the sight of the terrible, as much as we abhor the thing itself. But we don't, and for us, as much as our Victorian forebears, the retch in our throats that the idea of "the last resource" elicits is quickly followed – perhaps even accompanied – by a secretive, eager appetite for more.

Dickens was wrong, as it turned out. In fact, at very nearly the same time that the press was denouncing Landseer's carnivorous bears – beneath whose animal guises a subtext of human cannibalism lurked, and lurks – an American journalist-turned-explorer, Charles Francis Hall, was hearing an even more detailed version of the scenes described to John Rae a decade earlier; indeed, he was hearing it from the same man, one "In-nook-poo-zhee-jook." At the time he had talked to Rae, this Inuk had not yet been to the place where the "Kabloonas" (*Qallunaat*, white men) had died, but in the time since, eager for some of the wealth of wood and metal that was sure to be found, he had gone there himself. He discovered a boat, the contents of which he described to Hall in excruciating detail:

> Six paddles; many table-knives, white handles; one watch; a spyglass … something like my [Hall's] compass, but no glass about it; tobacco that had been wet and was in flakes or thin pieces; very many tin dishes; one whole skeleton with clothes on, – the flesh all on, but dried; many skeleton bones; three skulls. Alongside of the boat a big pile of skeleton bones that had been broken up for the marrow in them; they were near a fire-place; skulls among these. The number of them ama-su-ad-loo (a great many) – cannot tell how many. It is certain that some of the men lived on human flesh, for alongside of the boat were some large boots with cooked human flesh in them.

Everywhere Hall went, he heard more such stories: of bodies with their hands sawed off at the wrists, of a "box filled with bones," of "a great many skeleton bones, the flesh all off, nothing except sinews attached to them," of "a tent filled with frozen corpses, some entire and some mutilated by their starving companions, who had cut off much of the flesh with their knives and hatchets and eaten it." There could no longer be any question of *whether* cannibalism had taken place, the only uncertainty was how widespread it had been. There was one camp, certainly, on the western shores of King William Island, where In-nook-poo-zhee-jook and many other witnesses all agreed they had seen bones in great quantity, many broken open, and skulls with holes in them. Hall had to turn back before reaching this place, for the season for sledging was growing short and his Inuit guides needed to return to their seasonal hunting grounds; he contented himself with bringing back just one skeleton that he had found at the southern tip of the island; perhaps, he thought, there might be some way to identify whose it was, and this man, at least, could be given a decent burial.

+ + + +

It was to be a long journey. Hall originally consigned the bones to his friend and patron, J. Carson Brevoort, of Brooklyn, New York. Brevoort, in his efforts to repatriate them, contacted Rear-Admiral Edward Inglefield, an old Arctic hand, who was then serving as naval attaché in Washington, DC. Inglefield, uncertain of how best to proceed, wrote to his old friend George Henry Richards, hydrographer of the Navy, who in turn wrote to Lady Franklin: "He has had a complete skeleton presented to him, which was found by Hall on King William's Land, of an officer – the remains of a silk undervest were on it – and one of the teeth stuffed with gold – all the other perfect. Aged between 35 and 40. My advice will be to put it in a box and bury it – for it could not be certainly identified – and would be no use to anyone – probably, if the skeleton was married – his widow has taken another skeleton before this."

Married or not, this "skellington" arrived in England a few months later, and Richards gave it a cursory examination, which convinced him that "there would be little difficulty indeed in identifying it – there cannot be more than four or five to choose from, the age cannot be much over 30." Nevertheless, to be on the safe side, he entrusted the task to Thomas Henry Huxley, the pre-eminent comparative anatomist of the age, a man known as "Darwin's Bulldog" for his defence of the theory of evolution by natural selection. After a delay of several months, Huxley inspected the bones, consulted with the family, and wrote back that he "had little doubt that it is Le Vesconte." The age would have been about right – Le Vesconte had been thirty-two at the time the expedition sailed – but whatever other evidence was decisive, he did not specify.

Henry Thomas Dundas Le Vesconte had been a lieutenant aboard Franklin's ship of command, HMS *Erebus*, and was by all measures a capable, high-spirited officer. A daguerreotype of Le Vesconte, sporting the same sort of "silk undervest" the tatters of which Richards had noted on the skeleton, survives among those taken before the ships' departure; unlike the other officers with their plain-cloth backdrops, he chose to be photographed at the ship's wheel, a copy of Frederick Marryat's *A Code of Signals, for Use of Vessels Employed in the Merchant Service* in his hand. The bones were placed at first under the floor in the vestibule of the Painted Hall at Greenwich; in 1938 they were reinterred in a hidden recess that was built into the pedestal of a large marble monument dedicated to Franklin and his men at the chapel of the Royal Naval Hospital nearby. And so, at least for a time, Hall's hope – that at least one of the men whose fate he sought would repose within an honoured tomb – was fulfilled.

In 2008, after due consideration, a decision was made that this monument – which, in the course of various modifications to the structure had ended up in a back stairwell of the chapel, inaccessible to the public and largely neglected – should be moved to the front of the building, near the entrance. The marble work was to be restored and reset, and quite naturally the sarcophagus, since it too would have to be moved, was for a time the object of care and study. Within the marble, conservators found a wooden coffin, to which was affixed a small engraved plaque, which read as follows:

THIS BOX CONTAINS HUMAN BONES, CONJECTURED TO HAVE BEEN THE SKELETON OF THE BODY OF LIEUT HENRY TD LE VESCONTE OF HM SHIP EREBUS, WHO PERISHED WITH MANY OTHERS, ABOUT THE YEAR 1848, IN THE EXPEDITION TO THE ARCTIC REGIONS COMMANDED BY SIR JOHN FRANKLIN. THE BONES WERE FOUND BY CAPT HALL, THE AMERICAN EXPLORER, IN KING WILLIAM'S LAND; AND TAKEN BY HIM TO NEW YORK IN 1869, WHENCE THEY WERE BROUGHT TO ENGLAND BY ADMIRAL INGLEFIELD. THEY WERE DEPOSITED HERE BY ORDER OF THE LORDS OF THE ADMIRALTY IN 1873.

The coffin was opened, and several touching yet curious items found within: a pasteboard cross, decorated with small flowers, a map of "Discoveries in the Arctic Seas," and an envelope that contained three of the skeleton's teeth, including the one with the tell-tale filling. The skeleton itself resided in an inner coffin, wrapped in a large Admiralty chart of New Guinea; it appeared to be mainly intact, although both feet were missing. In the hopes that these remains might tell something about the demise of Franklin's men, the historians and conservators present arranged for tests to be made on the teeth, and carefully examined and photographed the bones. All were then returned, with their original wrapping and tokens of esteem, and placed in the base of the restored monument at its new, public location.

++++

On 29 October 2009 a Special Service of Thanksgiving and rededication of the Franklin Memorial was held at the Chapel of Saints Peter and Paul at the Old Royal Naval College. I was there, as were a number of other Arctic scholars from around the world, including Glyn Williams, Huw Lewis-Jones, Kari Herbert, Andrew Lambert, and Kenn Harper. Seated in the pew next to Kenn, I listened as he introduced himself to a gray-bearded fellow adjacent – a man we both assumed must be some unknown polar historian – adding with some pride that, unlike most of the others present, he actually *lived* in the Arctic.

"Oh you *do*, do you?" the man replied.

"Yes, I live in Iqaluit, in Nunavut," said Kenn.

"Well, you clean up pretty well, I guess," returned the man with a laugh. We never did find out who he was.

Having attended a number of Franklin memorials and commemorative events over the years, I can say that this was, by far, the most solemn and moving service of all, and the most beautifully conceived and presented. Of course, it had one distinction that every other such service lacked: the bones of one of Franklin's men. The service, presided over by the Reverend Christopher Chessun, bishop of Woolwich, along with the Reverend Jeremy Frost, chaplain to the Greenwich Foundation, opened with Beethoven's "Funeral March on the Death of a Hero," beautifully played on the chapel organ. The clergy and choir then entered and took their places about the altar. Throughout the service, the choir was magnificent, singing both traditional hymns and more complex modern choral works with a rare combination of verve and purity of tone. At last, the service was opened by the Reverend Frost, who welcomed all present with these words: "We gather on this solemn occasion to give renewed thanks for the life of Lieutenant Henry Thomas Dundas Le Vesconte, and to re-inter his mortal remains in the vestibule of this Chapel. In this the one hundred and fiftieth anniversary year of the discovery of Sir John Franklin's death, we pray that peoples from across the world who visit this holy and historic place may hereafter pause, and remember all those who lost their lives alongside Franklin." The reading, appropriately enough for a man who had suffered much, was from the Book of Job. Afterwards, Bishop Chessun ascended to the pulpit and delivered his address, in which he extolled the urge to explore, to risk life and limb in the pursuit of expanding geographical and scientific knowledge. The Canadian high commissioner, James R. Wright, offered a poignant excerpt from Canadian poet Gwendolyn MacEwen's *Terror and Erebus*.

The congregation then turned, en masse, to face the rear of the chapel, where the clerics and descendants of Franklin's men witnessed the monument's rededication. Holy water was sprinkled upon the marble, and a lovely hymn, "Take Him, Earth for Cherishing," was intoned by the choir. It was a deeply moving moment, and I could not help but think how much easier Le Vesconte's bones would rest now that they were ensconced in a far more visible and honoured location and reinterred with all the rich ceremony omitted on earlier such occasions.

There was only one problem: the bones over whom all these obsequies had been made were not those of Le Vesconte.

++++

It turned out to be the teeth. Teeth can be remarkably eloquent as to the environment in which a person has grown up; the isotopes of strontium and oxygen absorbed by the body and deposited in tooth enamel are retained through adulthood. A person's enamel thus preserves the isotopic fingerprint of the place where the individual spent their first two decades. This technique has even been used on Ötzi – the infamous "Ice Man" whose remains have been dated to about 3300 BCE; it revealed that he had grown up near the present village of Feldthurns in northern Italy. Not every place on earth, of course, has an absolutely distinct isotopic signature, but, at the very least, one can say with a high degree of confidence where someone was *not* from.

And this turned out to be the case with this skeleton. Le Vesconte grew up in Devon, whose chalky soil, grassy hills, and sea exposure would have left a very distinctive isotope ratio indeed – and this tooth did not have it. Instead, the ratio suggested someone who grew up in central or eastern Scotland or England. Since a number of Franklin's men hailed from these very areas, this might not have seemed especially useful evidence – but then there was that filling. Gold fillings, back in 1845, were relatively uncommon and tended to appear only in the remains of high-status individuals, which made it likely that the remains were those of an officer. This led the researchers to consider Harry Goodsir, scion of a distinguished family of Edinburgh surgeons and anatomists. And Goodsir's father, as it turned out, was a close acquaintance of Robert Nasmyth, sometimes known as the "Father of Scottish Dentistry," a man who pioneered the use of gold in filling teeth – circumstantial evidence, at least, that the body might be Goodsir's.

The final step in identifying these remains was a facial reconstruction, and in this case the researchers were fortunate in that Goodsir, as had many of Franklin's other officers, posed for a daguerreotype portrait before the ships sailed; the reconstruction could be compared with this photograph. But how accurate is a facial reconstruction, especially after such a length of time? As with the Ice Man, there are precedents; one particularly well-publicized case was that of German forensic scientist Richard Helmer's identification of the skull of Nazi "Angel of Death" Josef Mengele in 1985. Helmer looked at photographs of a cross-section of the skull and compared them with known photos of Mengele while alive; by "merging" these two images and looking at specific points and proportions, Helmer felt that he could identify the individual with a high degree of certainty. A more recent technique, building up the muscles and skin tissue on a cast of the skull – first used to reconstruct the probable appearance of primitive humans, and later extended to modern remains – was used in this case. This technique depends upon the reconstructor's knowing something of the age, race, and gender of the subject, and involves a certain degree of interpretation.

The photograph distributed with the news of this fresh view of the remains brought back by Hall suggests a blend of both techniques: a facial-reconstruction model superimposed on a photograph of the candidate. There are questions. Given that we only have photographs of just over half of Franklin's officers, and none of his men, there might be matches that could be missed. The tooth enamel is telling, and the gold filling offers potential supporting evidence, but so far it has not proven possible to obtain DNA from a suitable descendant of the Goodsir family. And so, for now at least, the identification shows a high degree of likelihood but not certainty.

Nonetheless, not knowing whose bones these are doesn't mean we can't learn something from them. The examination showed that the skeleton is definitively male, and was that of a Caucasian man between twenty-three and fifty-nine years of age; he was probably tall and slender, which matches a crewmate's description of Goodsir as "long and straight." Intriguingly, there was no sign of scurvy in these bones; perhaps Goodsir, as a surgeon-naturalist with a scientific background, was especially assiduous in taking his daily dram of lemon juice, or his diet included more of fresh meat or mustard-greens, which were sometimes cultivated aboard ships as an anti-scorbutic. Beyond that, it was clear that this individual, at least, was not the victim of his comrade's appetites; none of the bones showed any signs of the defleshing and dismemberment described by the Inuit. Whether Goodsir's or Le Vesconte's, these bones were unmolested, and could now reasonably be described as "resting in peace."

++++

The same could not be said for the bones at the site on the western coast of King William Island. Although testified about by In-nook-poo-zhee-jook and many other Inuit, they had been hidden by snow when McClintock passed through the area, and by the time of Schwatka's search more than a decade later, the boat that had marked the spot had been disassembled by the Inuit and turned into sledge-runners, blubber trays, and fishing spears. He reburied three skeletons he found there, but these graves were soon disturbed by animals, the bones scattered once more. The low, stony ground, which in the few weeks of summer when exposed shows a lively coat of coloured lichens, along with mosses, small flowers, and lemming holes, effectively concealed all that remained for more than a hundred and forty years. It wasn't until the late 1980s, when researcher David Woodman examined Hall's original field notes at the Smithsonian Institution, that the various Inuit accounts of the place, not all of which had been published in Hall's lifetime, were compared and cross-referenced. It was Woodman's 1991 book, *Unravelling the Franklin Mystery: Inuit Testimony*, which led to the identification of this place, although ironically it was not Woodman himself who made the discovery.

Barry Ranford, a photographer and high school teacher from Ontario with a deep Franklin obsession, was not the sort of explorer who could sit happily in an armchair. In 1992, Woodman's book in hand, he managed to reach the western coast of King William Island, searching the area near Erebus Bay, trolling back and forth across the rocky scree, hauling his supplies in a garden cart. And it was then, the day before he was scheduled to fly home, that he saw it: a skull, weathered and whitened to such a degree that at first he thought it could be a bleach bottle. Nearby, as he focused his attention on the first find, he saw other bones, along with bits of blue Navy broadcloth, rope, and leather. Although he had no training as an archaeologist, he knew enough to realize that such a find needed to be examined carefully by specialists if the secrets it had to tell were to be patiently and properly revealed.

The next year, he returned, accompanied by Margaret Bertulli, an archaeologist from the Prince of Wales Northern Heritage Centre in Yellowknife, along with Anne Keenleyside, a forensic anthropologist, and a field team of four other volunteers. The site was mapped out with a grid, and each artifact and bone was carefully mapped and catalogued. Among the material remains were a lens fragment and bits of wire gauze from the improvised snow goggles worn by Franklin's men, a cylinder thought to be a pen shaft, a broken clay-pipe bowl, a comb fragment with eleven spines, three metal grommets, a buckle possibly from a sledge-hauling strap, three weathered lumps of wax, twelve copper rivets, shoe heels fixed with copper tacks, fifty-four fragments of leather, two pieces of thin copper sheeting, a tin-can fragment, and numerous bits of cloth. Many of the cloth fragments were of blue serge, the typical stuff of naval uniforms; there were also bits of flax, blanket cloth, and cotton. Among the more numerous items were buttons, including four of black bone, which help date the site since buttons from only a decade or so after Franklin sailed tended to be made with vegetable ivory rather than bone; similarly, several "Dorset" or thread buttons, which declined in use after 1841, were found.

All of these testified to there having been a copper-fitted boat at the site, and suggested the everyday items and clothing sailors might have carried or worn as the expedition's survivors struggled southward; indeed, there were two boot heels that had been modified for sledge-hauling, as shown by a concentration of tacks nearby, along with a buckle from a sledge harness – the British preferred to haul their sleds not with dogs but with men. But most significantly of all, there were bones – nearly four hundred of them.

The bones were removed for further study, and Keenleyside later conducted a series of laboratory studies upon them. And it was these nameless bones that had the most terrible story to tell: here were the remains of between eleven and fifteen individuals, with the oldest in their forties and the youngest estimated at fifteen years old. Was this last a cabin boy? – and was he, as so often seems to be the case with narratives of cannibalism at sea, the first to be eaten? For there was no question as to that: nearly a quarter of the bones recovered showed cut-marks, marks that under magnification by electron microscopy could be seen to be clean-edged, characteristic of those made by sharpened metal blades. And a great many of these marks were located at sites where major skeletal elements met, or near where ligaments and tendons held muscle to bone. Keenleyside concluded that the number and location of cut-marks was "consistent with defleshing or removal of muscle tissue," noting also that "the fracturing of long bones to facilitate marrow extraction" was another likely sign of cannibalism. The array of cut-marks were mapped onto a skeleton, and a particular concentration was found on the bones of the hands. As Keenleyside later noted, "the hands, next to the face … are among the most recognizably *human* parts of the body" – and they may well have been removed to make eating the flesh more "palatable."

A few years after completing her study of these bones, Dr Keenleyside had a residency at the Royal Holloway College of the University of London. Her daily trek from the car park to her office and classrooms regularly took her through the Picture Gallery, home to a collection of famous Victorian paintings amassed by Thomas Holloway, the patent medicine magnate who had founded the college in 1879. And among those paintings, of all things, was Landseer's depiction of those carnivorous polar bears, "Man Proposes, God Disposes," the same one that had horrified those who saw it in 1864. Indeed, its aura of disaster remained so strong that, during times when exams were held in the Picture Gallery, the painting was covered with the Union Jack, lest bad luck befall the students who sat near it.

Here, indeed, one might say, there was a depiction of the very bones that Keenleyside had studied, though the marks upon them were of animal not man. When I realized that, given its location, she must have passed the painting nearly every day, I asked her what she had thought about the connection – in her reply, she confessed her astonishment. She had never realized it was there.

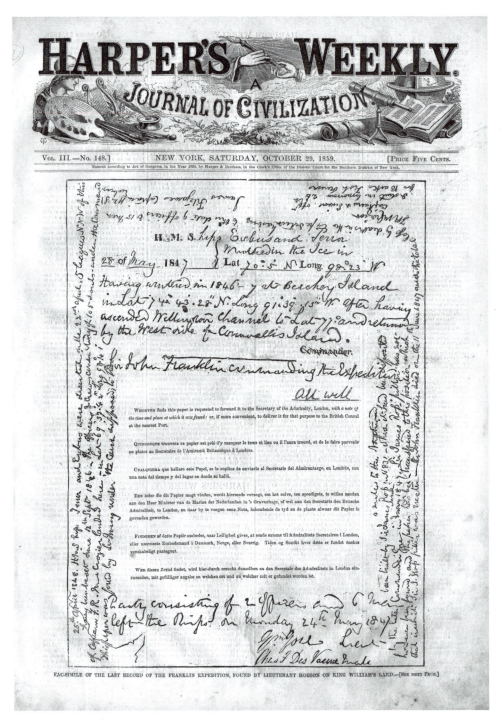

Figure 4 Facsimile of the "Victory Point" record, *Harper's Weekly*,
29 October 1859. Collection of the author.

3

Papers

I THE VICTORY POINT RECORD

It is perhaps the most evocative document in the long history of the Western exploration of the Arctic regions: a single sheet of paper, a pre-printed form with two handwritten messages written not quite a year apart. The first, full of pride and high spirits, describes the Franklin expedition's achievements through May 1847, including its circumnavigation of Cornwallis Island, and ends with the forceful line "Sir John Franklin commanding the Expedition. <u>All Well</u>." The second, written in a tight scrawl around the margins, tells of the death of Franklin (only weeks after the first record was made) and many other officers and men, the abandonment of his ships, and a desperate plan to trek overland to the Back River.

A facsimile of this record, brought back from the Arctic by Sir Francis Leopold McClintock, was reproduced in the *Illustrated London News* and *Harper's Weekly*, and a fold-out facsimile was included in all early printed editions of his book, *The Voyage of the 'Fox' in the Arctic Seas*, in 1859. A few years later, this book reached the hands of a ten-year-old boy by the name of Józef Teodor Konrad Korzeniowski – a boy who would grow up to be the novelist Joseph Conrad. Late in life, he vividly recalled this book, and this document, as the spark that launched his career, both as navigator and writer:

The last words unveiling the mystery of the *Erebus* and *Terror* expedition were brought home and disclosed to the world by Sir Leopold M'Clintock in his book, *The Voyage of the Fox in the Arctic Seas*. It is a little book, but it records with manly simplicity the tragic ending of a great tale. It so happened that I was born in the year of its publication. Therefore I may be excused for not getting hold of it till ten years afterward. I can only account for it falling into my hands by the fact that the fate of Sir John Franklin was a matter of European interest, and that Sir Leopold M'Clintock's book was translated into every language of the white races. My copy was probably in French. But I have read the book many times since. I have now on my shelves a copy of a popular edition got up exactly as I remember my first one. It contains a touching facsimile of the printed form filled in with a summary record of the two ships' work, the name of "Sir John Franklin, commanding the expedition," written in ink, and the pathetic underlined entry "All Well." It was found by Sir Leopold M'Clintock under a cairn, and is dated just a year before the two ships had to be abandoned in their deadly ice-trap and their crews' long and desperate struggle for life began. There could hardly have been imagined a better book for letting in the breath of the stern romance of polar exploration into the existence of a boy whose knowledge of the poles of the earth had been till then of an abstract, formal kind, as the imaginary ends of the imaginary axis upon which the earth turns. The great spirit of the realities of the story sent me off on the romantic explorations of my inner self; to the discovery of the taste for poring over land and sea maps; revealed to me the existence of a latent devotion to geography which interfered with my devotion (such as it was) to my other school work.

For those who read it – and McClintock's book was an instant best-seller, far outpacing rivals such as George Eliot's *The Mill on the Floss* – it was conceived of as the end of the story. As things turned out, it was only to be the beginning.

✦✦✦✦

In the years since it was first published for all the world to see in 1859, this single document has been the subject of more speculation and analysis than any other piece of documentary evidence this side of the Zapruder film, and yet it is far from yielding up all its secrets. With its ambiguities and contradictions, and its encapsulation of the pride that goeth before a fall, it has come to represent – depending on the reader – the very essence of Arctic heroism in the face of extraordinary odds, or a sad and pathetic commentary on the ill-preparedness of Franklin's men to endure the environment that awaited them outside the shelter of their ships.

So what can we learn from this record? Well, we can learn the direct information it conveys as to the location of the ships and the disposition of the crew, and so forth. But we can also glean a great deal more. Just two examples will suffice. First, as William Battersby has noted, the note is entirely in the handwriting of James Fitzjames; this is unusual, since Franklin would ordinarily have written – or at least signed – such notes himself; a note tossed overboard earlier in the expedition was signed by him. We may infer from this that, for some reason, Franklin must have been unable to sign the note himself; that he died only a few weeks later suggests that illness may have been the cause. Second, the years of the expedition's wintering at Beechey Island are given as 1846–47, which is certainly in error; from the headboards of the graves at Beechey we know it was the winter of 1845–46. Why would Fitzjames have made such an elementary mistake, and made it in both the Victory Point document and in a second, identical form left a few miles away at Back Bay? This suggests that Fitzjames's memory was clouded, which has been seen by some as a potential sign of lead poisoning. Those in the early stages of this condition have problems with forming lasting short-term memories, which progresses to difficulty with accurate recollection of the mid-range past. As Colin Field, an Australian pathologist with whom I've consulted on this problem, notes:

> I can imagine a situation where members of the expedition, and in particular the officers, will begin to show gradual problems with memory for recent information, as well as subtle but progressive deficits of organizational function. They begin to make subtle errors; forgetting where they have put things, or whether or not they have issued certain orders. As things progress they become more and more forgetful for events of the recent past. One of the earliest signs of memory deficit is the loss of ability to update, on a daily basis, the current day and date. Failure to be able to name the current day, month and year, and in some cases the current whereabouts, is one of the most telling early signs of all organic dementias, and it is for this reason that mental status examinations always include these orientation questions.

At the same time, lead poisoning would have no immediate effect on what's known as "habitual" memory, including things such as how to tie one's shoes or ascertain one's position with a sextant. And, in fact, we find in the second part of the note that the location where the record was deposited – "Lat. 69°37′42″ Long. 98°41′″ – is reasonably accurate.

But it's the second, marginal note that gives us some of the most suggestive information about the fate of the crews, and the cause of their distress. There is a lengthy aside about how Sir James Clark Ross's cairn was not found where it was thought to be, and a new cairn erected at the site – a curious waste of precious ink and time – perhaps another possible sign of mental difficulties. The date of death of Franklin, 11 June 1847, is given, but no cause of death or indication of his burial site – another odd omission. For the rest of the officers, we hear only of John Irving and Graham Gore; Gore we now know to have received a field promotion, since he is referred to as "Commander" – and also to have died, being referred to as "late." This has given rise to speculation that Gore, who was in command of the party that left the original paper, must have reached Simpson's cairn at Cape Herschel, returning with the news just in time to be promoted by Franklin as a reward. Of course, it is entirely possible that he was simply promoted as a matter of course after Franklin's death when Fitzjames became captain. With Lieutenant Irving, his name comes up only in the context of the description of the search for Ross's cairn – and yet here lies a further mystery, for a body believed to be Irving's was found not far from this very spot by Lieutenant Schawtka's searching expedition years later. How could Irving, who was well enough to be scouting about in 1848 at the start of the southward march, have died near the very place where it began? Could it be a sign of an attempted return to the ships at a later date?

Next, there are the overall casualty figures for the crews: 9 officers and 15 men. There were 24 officers on the two vessels, including the ice masters, and 105 men; this gives an officer casualty rate of 37 per cent as opposed to only 14 per cent among the ordinary seamen and marines – a remarkable ratio. Why did more than twice as large a proportion of officers die? If we assume that lead poisoning was a key factor, we may attribute this to the officers' consuming *more* of something – tinned food, or the water distilled aboard ship – which impaired their health significantly. Alternatively, it's been proposed that a large party rich in officers – perhaps a burial detail – was lost in some accident, skewing the overall ratio. Whatever the cause, the difference seems far too large to be accounted for by random chance.

Finally, we have the enigmatic, and entirely unsatisfactory addendum in Crozier's hand – "and start on tomorrow 26th for Back's Fish River." Was this the destination of the entire body of men who abandoned the ships? Or was it, as David Woodman has argued, simply a large detachment of men gone in search of food and possible Inuit contact to aid their less able comrades? Having reached that area, was the plan to ascend the river – a perilous journey filled with rough portages that Back, a famously able Arctic traveller, condemned as one of the most difficult journeys of its kind – or rather to track to the southeast in the direction of Repulse Bay, in hopes of meeting with Inuit or whalers? On this, the record is silent.

These, then, are the central questions raised by the Victory Point record, and which may never be completely resolved until some further record or evidence is found. Even in all its ambiguity, it continues to be a rich source of fascination, and the terrible irony between its two messages will always evoke what Conrad called "the tragic ending of a great tale."

There was, it turns out, a second record found on King William, one similar in every respect (save the fateful addendum in the margins) to its brother. Both had been filled out by James Fitzjames aboard HMS *Erebus*, and both repeated the same mistake (the year of the ships' wintering there is misstated as 1846–47 rather than 1845–46). This other record was recovered at what became known as "Gore Point," the tip of the peninsula that forms the western side of Collinson Inlet. The location is consistent with the idea of Gore having commanded a party sent out to survey the western coast of King William Island, with the presumed goal of reaching Simpson's cairn on the shores of Washington Bay; such a party would have skirted the coast, taking advantage of the still land-fast new ice for smooth travel. On the Gore Point record, the only significant difference is that the phrase "All Well" was not underlined.

At first glance, this second record adds little to our understanding. Yet, having been deposited just eight miles – possibly one day's march – south of the Victory Point record, it strongly suggests that Gore had been instructed to leave a record frequently, perhaps daily, on his southward trek. One might reasonably expect, then, that several other such records were left along the coast, and might yet be recovered. The most important of these, of course, would have been at Simpson's cairn, but, since by the time McClintock reached it, it had been opened, this record will probably never be found. It would certainly be worth looking for the others – a surviving record would be far more significant than, say, a toothbrush.

It is tantalizing to think that Gore may have achieved the long-sought dream of linking the eastern and western surveys of the Northwest Passage –

it seems hard to imagine he would have missed his goal, only a few days' march south of where he deposited the record. We know that he must have returned alive to the ships, since his promotion to commander could not have been made after his death. We also know that, at some point between his return to the ships in 1847 and the depositing of the 1848 record, he died, but of the cause of his death, or the unusual casualty rate among officers generally, the note is mute. For now, unless some new documents are recovered from the Franklin ship discovered by Parks Canada in 2014, we have only one other documentary source written by a member of the Franklin expedition – a packet of papers so strange, so inscrutable, and so singular that they make the "Victory Point" record seem as plain and unambiguous as a grocery-store receipt.

2 THE "PEGLAR" PAPERS: DEAD SEA SCROLLS
OF THE NORTH

The sight was truly a melancholy one. In the words of Francis Leopold McClintock: "Shortly after midnight of the 25th May, when slowly walking along a gravel ridge which the winds kept partially bare of snow, I came upon a human skeleton, partly exposed, with here and there a few fragments of clothing appearing through the snow. The skeleton, now perfectly bleached, was lying upon its face; and it was a melancholy truth that the old Esquimaux woman spoke when she said, that they fell down and died as they walked along."

This skeleton bore with it one of the most enigmatic documents in the whole Franklin mystery. In the words of Allen Young, who published his separate account in the *Cornhill Magazine* in 1860, "the Captain's party found a human skeleton upon the beach as the man had fallen down and died, with his face to the ground; and a pocket-book, containing letters in German which have not yet been deciphered, was found close by."

Whose was this skeleton? And what were these letters? As it turns out, they were not written in German, although the mistake was understandable, given the frequent occurrence of strange words such as "Meht," "Kniht," and "Eht." On further examination, it was discovered that they were in fact in *English*, only written backwards (that is, with the letters in backwards order, *not* mirror-backwards). Why this would have been done is a difficult question – for my part, I can only suppose that there was some desire to con-

Figure 5 Cape Herschel on King William Island, site where the "Peglar" body was found. Collection of the author.

ceal the contents of a sailor's letters from his shipmates, whose rudimentary literacy would have made transposing the letters a daunting task.

The ownership of the letters poses yet another question. Because among them was the seaman's certificate of one Harry Peglar, they have been dubbed the "Peglar Papers" for years, and the name has stuck. McClintock's description of the body, however, almost certainly rules Peglar out; on its being turned over, the uniform was found to be better preserved on the side that had faced the ground; his neckerchief was tied in the distinctive manner of a ship's steward – something Peglar, a senior seaman with the title of "Captain of the Foretop," would never have done. McClintock added that "in every particular the dress confirmed our conjectures as to his rank or office in the late expedition – the blue jacket with slashed sleeves and braided edging, and the pilot-cloth greatcoat with plain covered buttons." The assumption now is that this must have been a steward, likely a friend of Peglar's, carrying letters home for his since-deceased shipmate. An excellent candidate has been proposed in Thomas Armitage, who was the gun-room steward (servant of the junior officers) aboard HMS *Terror* and had served alongside Peglar on an earlier voyage aboard HMS *Gannett* from 1834 to 1838. More recent research by Glenn M. Stein has shown that, at least as of 1826, Armitage was illiterate, although since shipboard schools were a feature of Arctic voyages, he could have acquired or improved his literacy there. Stein suggests William Gibson, a subordinate officer's steward aboard the *Terror*, who had served with Peglar more recently aboard HMS *Wanderer*; both his and Armitage's height and hair colour (brown) are consistent with McClintock's description of the body.

Backwards writing, it turns out, is only one of many problems facing anyone who tackles these documents – the paper is blotched and foxed, and has heavy folds, along which in many places bits of the pages have broken off. At some point, an attempt to darken the ink with a re-agent damaged much of the writing on the seaman's certificate, perhaps irretrievably. Most frustratingly of all, where they can be made out, the papers consist mostly of a sailor's reminiscences of warmer climes, particularly in Cumana, Venezuela, a source no doubt of pleasure while trapped on board an ice-bound ship in the Arctic zone, but of little value in solving the Franklin mystery, and offering scant insight into the state of mind of Franklin's men. That the *Gannett*, with both Peglar and Armitage aboard, called at Cumana would seem to corroborate the body's identity.

Nevertheless, scattered about in these letters are passages that are highly suggestive of events on board the ships. Like many writers with limited literacy, Peglar (or Armitage, if some or all of the writings were his) added asides about current events in the midst of the old stories he was recounting. Thus we have phrases such as "brekfest to be short rations," "whose is this coffee," and "the Terror camp clear," which – if only we could know more of their context – would seem to have enormous potential significance. Mixed in with these, we have ample shares of doggerel verse, including a mildly obscene parody of the poet Barry Cornwall's well-known ditty "The Sea," accounts of tropical parties and turtle soup, and a paean to someone's dog.

The most intriguing passage of all is one identified early on by David Woodman and other researchers as possibly having some reference to life on the ships just prior to their abandonment: "We will have his new boots in the middel watch ... as we have got some very hard ground to heave a ... shall want some grog to wet houer wissel ... all my art Tom for I dont think for ... r now clozes should lay and furst mend 21st night a gread." The "new boots" are assumed to be boots such as those found by McClintock and other searchers, which had been modified onboard by the addition of nails or cleats – these were clearly meant for the sledge-haulers. "Hard ground to heave" may be a reference to hauling sledges – or perhaps to digging graves (one thinks of the sailor buried by Parry near Igloolik, in the clearing of whose grave six pickaxes were broken on the frozen gravel). The "21st night a gread" is most tempting of all; might this be 21 April 1848, four days before the amended record was left near Victory Point?

Richard Cyriax, the founding father of Franklin studies, spent considerable time studying these papers and wrote an article on them for the *Mariner's Mirror*, a draft transcript of which accompanies them in their archival box at the Caird Library of the National Maritime Museum in Greenwich. I myself have spent countless hours going over the original papers, which have been covered in archival gauze to preserve the fragile material, but have rarely been able to improve on Cyriax's readings; indeed, some of the text readable to him has since faded away. It may be possible someday, by use of ultraviolet light or computer-enhanced imagery, to recover something of what's now illegible, but even then, the enigmatic quality of these papers is likely to remain. Their writer never imagined that they would be among the very few written materials ever recovered from the expedition, and there are uncertainties in their contents that will probably never be resolved. Nevertheless, they add a further sense of wonder to the larger mystery of the final fate of Franklin's men.

Given all that, though, it's remarkable what we *can* learn. To begin with, it's worth noting that much – perhaps all – of the papers consist of real or apparently real correspondence. That many of the sheets were meant to be entrusted to the post can be inferred by their folding, by the remaining bits of red-sealing wax, and the presence of addresses on the outside corner or flap of several – although, since these too were written backwards, they would doubtless have caused some consternation had anyone tried to mail them. Still more puzzlingly, the documents themselves have none of the elements of a personal letter; there are no salutations, no signatures, nor any other such niceties. The assumption has been that papers – most of them light-hearted stories, songs, and reminiscences of travel – were writings the sender composed in his idle hours aboard ship and simply wished to forward to his friends or family. Whatever their purpose, the fact that there *are* addresses offers at least a glimmer of hope that learning something about their intended recipients might shed light on the larger mystery.

The most sensible, and – as it turns out – verifiable address is the notation "In care of Mr. Heaithfield, a Squier, no 10 Pelmell West, London" – Cyriax and Jones readily identified this from a London directory for 1845 as William Eames Heathfield, a chemist whose shop was at 10 Pall Mall; he thus has the honour of being the only definitely identified correspondent of Peglar or Armitage. And, as it happens, he turned out to be readily traceable; by using online resources unavailable in Cyriax's day such as Google Books, I've been able to find out a good deal more about Heathfield. He was mentioned in a lawsuit in 1851 against one Robert Nelson Collins, a bankrupt drug wholesaler; by this time his address had changed to "Princes Square, Wilson Street, Finsbury." The quality of his preparations having evidently been challenged, he was defended by several eminent colleagues in the pages of *The Chemist* in 1853, and in 1856 he was party to another bankruptcy suit listed in the London *Gazette*. More notably for our purposes, in 1863 he was elected a fellow of the Royal Geographical Society, a rather unusual honour for a chemist, at a meeting presided over by the eminent geologist Sir Roderick Murchison. This suggests that he must have had some knowledge of, or connection with, Arctic exploration, but there is nothing in these records that gives us anything more specific. For a person such as the author of these "Peglar Papers," Heathfield was certainly an unusually distinguished correspondent, although since the direction on the letter was "in care of," it may be that they were meant for someone he knew *through* him, rather than Heathfield himself.

Another seemingly valid address is "Mr John Cowper, No. 47 John St., Commercial Road, London," but here there is considerable ambiguity – according to Cyriax, there were no fewer than six John Streets in London's East End, as well as two Commercial Roads, and in any case no John Cowper is listed as residing in any of them. One alternative reading of the name – as "Cooper" – is attractive but yields far too many matches. Another address of which the ambiguities are difficult to resolve is also written backwards: "IM E.q Evarglleb Raauqs, Ocilmip, West." Here it's the name that is ambiguous; while "Bellgrave Squaar, Pimlico, West" is certainly valid, the other letters are far less clear. They might very well be someone's initials; the "M" might be a "W," "I" may be "F," and the whole phrase might or might not be backwards; one possible reading (if forwards) is "F.W., Esq." Cyriax tried out all of these, and apparently there was no match for any in the 1845 directory.

One further scrap of paper bears a legible address, which Cyriax reads as "Mr Heather sen ... City ... ation, Abberdeen, Lond ..." – the temptation is to link this to William Heather, a private in the Royal Marines who served on HMS *Terror*, the same ship as Peglar. By chance, the records of Heather's career are a bit more detailed than for the other Marines; we know that he was born in Battersea and served on HMS *Prince Regent* and HMS *Castor*, aboard which he participated in in the siege of Bilbao in 1835. And, although the address "Abberdeen, Lond" may seem contradictory, there was an Aberdeen Road in London in 1845, along with an Aberdeen Place, Aberdeen Mews, and Aberdeen Park. None of these addresses are near Battersea, and all are in relatively posh neighbourhoods, which makes them very unlikely ones indeed for Heather's family; the Marines were almost entirely drawn from the poorer and working classes, and since they were ineligible for the double-pay for Arctic service offered to seamen, they were in fact the lowest-paid men on the expedition.

We can be confident, at least, that these papers were written aboard one of Franklin's ships during the expedition that departed in May 1845. There are no written dates prior to that of the ships' departure, and the events in Venezuela and Trinidad are consistently described using the past tense, e.g. "a Party wot happened at Trinidad." Cyriax and Jones found that Peglar and his shipmate Armitage had been on vessels that called on Trinidad and at Cumana, Venezuela, and the recollections are doubtless those of one of these men. Some of the place names, such as "laying in asham Bay," don't seem to correspond with any known place, although since "asham" is also the name of a variety of corn flour used in Caribbean cuisine, "laying in asham" might simply be glossed as "taking on grain." There is also a reference to "Comfort Cove," which might be taken to refer to a graveyard on Ascension Island where sailors who had died while quarantined on the island for illness were buried; though that was its name in the 1830s and 1840s, it is now known as Comfortless Cove. Cyriax found that Peglar and Armitage had been on ships that had called at Ascension, so this name could be what was meant – but, importantly, the recollection of this place could have been the cause for a sailor's newly applying the name to a place in the Arctic, perhaps a graveyard adjacent to an onshore sick camp for Franklin's men (this possibility will be examined in a moment).

There are other lines that self-identify as having been written while on the expedition, such as the date "September 1846" or the inscription "Lines writ on the North" – though in both cases these are on the reverse side of pages containing other text, and thus have no contextual information and indeed could have been written before or after the text on the rest of the page. Similarly on its own is a small drawing of an eye with an eyelid, and the words "Lid Bay," which suggests a place encountered and named on the expedition on account its eye-like shape, though we have no way of being sure of this surmise. Lastly, there is the aforementioned reference to "new boots" and the need to wet one's "wissel" – which at first seems quite promising, since it's in the present tense and can be correlated with a known event. Oddly, though, the context of this passage is in the past tense and seems to describe very different events; prior to the "boots" passage there is a reference to someone of whom the writer says, "I think he navil officer," while the section immediately after carries on about another man who "made his appearence" and "wos a marine by the cut of his big ..." In both phrases, one has the sense of identifying a stranger by the cut of his clothes or outward appearance, something that would never have happened on the Franklin expedition on which crew members would have known each others' ship, rank, and branch of service quite well. My best explanation for this is that, as I've suggested above, a relatively naive and untutored writer might break into the midst of a past-tense recollection with some present-tense news, then "return" to his story without making any clear division.

But the most significant lines in the entire "Peglar" collection are surely those that begin with the couplet, "O Death wheare is thy Sting / the Grave at Comfort Cove." These lines are without question part of an account of, or eulogy for, someone who has died and has or is to be buried, since the first phrase is from the Service for the Burial of the Dead in the *Book of Common Prayer*, an official Church of England text with which every member of the ships' crews would have been familiar – and a personal copy of which each been supplied prior to the voyage. The mention of a "Grave" makes the meaning quite clear, as do other phrases on this leaf, such as "thy right hand" and the enigmatic but all-important line "[the] Dyer was and whare Traffalgar." Since Sir John Franklin, the commander of the expedition, had been at the Battle of Trafalgar, we have strong though circumstantial evidence that the burial described was his own.

But who is the "Dyer"? There was no one of this name among Franklin's men, though there *was* a William Dyer at the Battle of Trafalgar, aboard HMS *Temeraire* just astern of Nelson's *Victory*. The line remains enigmatic, since the definite article in "The Dyer" would seem odd if it refers to a specific individual; the following word could be either "saw" (if read forwards) or "was" (if backwards). Still more intriguing, a man of that same name – perhaps the same man – was responsible in 1849 for forwarding a packet of letters from Mrs John Peddie, whose husband was acting surgeon on HMS *Terror*, to James Clark Ross prior to his departure in search of Franklin's ships. In his "cover letter," Dyer expresses the hope that "you may very soon have the good fortune" to fall in with the *Erebus* and *Terror* and so deliver the letters – but adds no details as to its writer; it survives at the Scott Polar Research Institute (SPRI), but the SPRI has no biographical information on this William Dyer. Another suggestion – brilliant in its simplicity – is that the writer, with his limited education, user "dyer" to simply mean the man who had died, that is, the deceased.

The rest of this text comprises a series of riddles, each wrapped within its own enigma – I give here my best transcription of this leaf, in its entirety, with a few new readings, suggested by William Battersby, which I have put in italics to distinguish them from my own; as I will throughout this essay, I've also underlined any words *not* spelled backwards.

> O Death wheare is thy sting
> The Grave at comfort cove
> For who has any douat how
> *Nelson* [?] <u>look</u>
> The Dyer was and whare Traffalegar
> as … s … Of him
> and … to … frends a. Laitor. a. <u>Cors.</u> [?]
> <u>Best</u>
> and w … … *addam and eve*
> a Nother
> Death … *right hands*
> … <u>new</u> [?] grave
> I … ham … to [?] will be a veray
> signed … me yes and a splended
> And
> <u>That</u> [m]akes trade Florrish
> <u>That</u> way the world
> … round
> *Florrish*

The conjectural reading "Nelson," offered by Battersby, is certainly an exciting possibility and if correct amplifies the mention of "Trafalgar" in the following line, which already links the text to that event. Sir John Franklin himself was the only veteran of the Battle of Trafalgar on the Franklin expedition, and a Nelson memorial ring preserved at the National Maritime Museum is his.

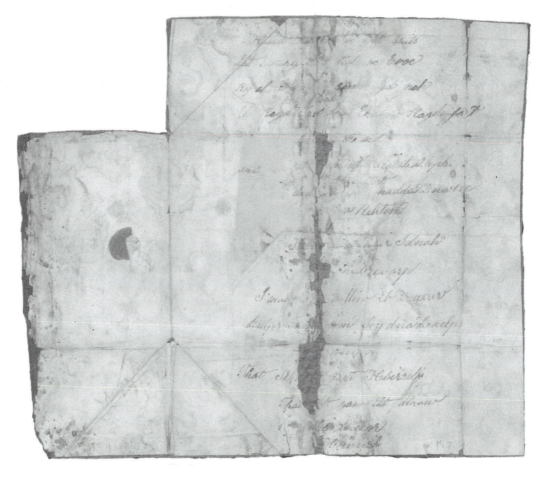

Figure 6 Leaf from the "Peglar Papers" describing a possible funeral service. © National Maritime Museum, Greenwich, London.

The reference to Adam and Eve may also point to these words being part of, or notes on, some eulogy or homily given at a memorial service – they were often mentioned in the context of man's fall from grace – as does the reappearance of "Death" – and although the reference to Christ sitting "at God's right hand" would also fit such a source, there is definitely another letter, which seems to give "right hands" a far less specific reference; "rigid hands" is also a possible reading and would make sense in this context. Just after this, the mention of a "new grave" seems promising, but again we are defeated by a series of vague lines with references to something "signed," something "splended," and the phrase "That makes trade [or trad.] Florrish," which seems out of keeping with a memorial service; Battersby has suggested that it refers to how the Royal Navy made trade flourish, but again the tone is wrong. The final few lines, "That the way the world ... round," suggests an absent "goes" and the repetition of "Flor-rish" suggests a "flourish" – perhaps the earlier phrase was meant to stand for "trad[itional] flourish," which could refer to a showing of swords or (less likely) the blowing of a trumpet or similar instrument in honour of the dead, though neither was a usual part of a naval funeral.

The sum of these lines, I feel, is that they do not constitute in their entirety any kind of funeral poem or oration, although they may have been rough notes taken upon the occasion of hearing such a eulogy; this could explain their fragmentary nature. Perhaps a witness to such a ceremony would have written down just the phrases he liked and added a few notes of his own (several of the words seem to have been added interlineally) as his time and inclination allowed. If that is the case, the funeral most likely was Franklin's own – there seems no other reason such a service would have mentioned Trafalgar, or Nelson if that reading is correct – but we are left with a view of this service which is very far from satisfactory. And yet, even when com-pared to the many enigmatic phrases in these curious notes, the roundel on the opposite side of the same leaf is still more confounding.

This, the crux of the papers as such, and the only mention of Peglar out-side of his seaman's certificate, was drawn, or written, over the fold – the paper seems to have been meant as a letter and bears a small fragment of red-sealing wax. A circle was evidently drawn, either by tracing or using a compass, and two texts were then added: the first round about the edge of this circle, and the second in straight lines within it; the circular texts seems to read "any W. bouat the harmonic he I ... ent wander money a night in" while within the roundel we find:

HMS Erebus
tell The ca ...
you are [or "and"] peglar
on bord onn hay
The Terror Camp
[is?] clear

Battersby reads this somewhat differently, suggesting "Oh Lord our God" in the place of "on bord onn hay" and "be clear" instead of "is clear" in the final line; he also fills out "Captain" from "ca ..." in the second line. The header, and the word "tell," strongly suggest that the roundel was a com-munication between the crews of the ships, from the *Terror* to the *Erebus*,

49

presumably after at least the former ship's crew was ashore and formed into a "camp." The exclamation "Oh Lord our God" suggests some horror, and yet the round writing seems a playful and enigmatic device, hardly appropriate for conveying bad news or the transcript of a funeral oration. The shift from "is" to "be" in the last line would seem to make it an example of the concessive or even imperative mood, which, as one period grammar notes, is "a sign of wishing and consequently occurs often in prayer"; so the meaning may be, "Let us hope that the Terror Camp is clear." This again is consistent with the earlier reference to God, if that's the reading one adopts.

The surrounding line, with its phrase "I wander many a night," seems almost like a snippet from a poem or elegy, and indeed this exact phrase occurs in a translation of Adam Oehlenschlaäger's Danish work *Axel and Valborg*: "Here shall I wander many a night alone, / And think upon my darling dream, and on / Thy coming home, and on our cruel fate. / Then shall my heart lift up itself to God / In prayer and holy song." Unfortunately, the correspondence is chimerical; although *Axel and Valborg* was published in 1810, this translation was not made until 1874. The other odd word is "harmonic," possibly part of the phrase "a bouat the harmonic." It's an unusual phrase and seems to suggest that the harmonic is what is being wandered (or perhaps wondered) about. The word has musical implications, and it's been suggested that it refers to the singing of hymns; it's also a phrase found in scientific treatises about vibrating bodies, though its use there seems far too technical for it to have been used in a note by a writer with student-level literacy. The capital "W" near "bouat" has also been suggested as an abbreviated form of "whale boat," and this, though promising at first, has no sensible relationship to any interpretation of the rest of the line. Battersby has suggested that the lines constituted a sort of word play or cryptic message between the ships' captains, and that's certainly possible, although if so its underlying significance remains unclear. One final, intriguing possibility: since Harry Peglar, William Gibson, and George Henry Hodgson had all served aboard HMS *Wanderer* in the years just before the expedition, could the "W" or the word "wander" refer to that vessel in some way? It remains at best an enigmatic possibility.

So in terms of what insight these texts give to events during the expedition, or to the state of mind of its writer or writers, we have at best some suggestive but inconclusive observations: that there was a bay dubbed "Lid Bay," that there was a camp on land where the crew of the *Terror* lived for some time, perhaps adjacent to a graveyard dubbed "Comfort Cove," that there was a burial, possibly Franklin's, at which it's possible that some of the crew spoke (or else wrote down what others spoke), and that there were "letters" sent from ship to ship. Cyriax also felt, as did McClintock when he first saw it, that the doggerel version of "The Sea," since it was on the same leaf that bore the date "April 21, 1847," meant that, at least as of that date, the mood on board the ships was good, and even jovial. Other playful and idle elements on other leaves seem to corroborate this sense; who, if dying of exposure, scurvy, or lead poisoning, would compose ditties about dogs and sea turtles, accounts of bygone parties, and idle references to land-bound matters such as "the grog shop opporsite"? They may well have been composed to fend off boredom in the long winter months, and preserved by the writer's shipmate as giving some account of the life lived by his deceased companion, long after these idle moments.

There are other aspects – the funeral text, the enigmatic roundel, the references to "new boots" and "hard ground to heave," which are suggestive of activities – either the abandonment of the ships or perhaps the departure of a burial detail – of a less pleasant nature. There's nothing, however, that directly speaks of sorrow, no last words to families and loved ones, indeed hardly anything personal at all, unless perhaps "All my art Tom" transcribes a dialect in which initial "h" is silent and can be read as "All my heart, Tom." Without salutations or signatures, and yet folded as letters and in several cases given London addresses – and even the memo "Paid" – these seem a very strange sort of letters indeed, ones that would no doubt have posed a problem to the Post Office, had they ever reached it. It's indeed possible that all, or nearly all, were written prior to the very last march of the doomed men, and thus can tell us very little about their state of mind when they realized that, despite their exertions, they were nearing the end of their journey, and their lives. It is to be hoped that, in the near future, the papers might be subjected to the kinds of multi-spectrum scans that have enabled, for instance, the reading of Livingstone's later journals, which were written crosswise in berry juice upon old newspapers and long defeated decipherment. But even if we had as perfect a transcript as possible, I very much doubt that it would clear up all the cruxes of the fragmentary, half-legible, and cryptic pages that have aptly been dubbed "the Dead Sea Scrolls of the North."

Figure 7 Tin of "Ox Cheek Soup" supplied to one of the Franklin search expeditions. Photograph by Jeff Dickie, used with permission.

4

Provisions

The whole plan for traversing the Northwest Passage depended on being able to sail through it. They didn't have a plan for getting away, except by sailing out. They didn't have, for example, lightweight sledges adapted to the terrain. All they had was what was on the ship, that lavish factory full of Victorian contrivances and "good ideas."
– Francis Spufford, *Arctic Passage*

The idea that Franklin's men carried the seeds of disaster with them on board their ships is a compelling one – it fits with our desire to see Victorian pride come before its fall, and makes a cautionary tale of their – and our – faith in technological advances. Yet, as Francis Spufford says, the whole idea of getting through the passage depended on their remaining aboard the ships – no plan or provision was made for extended travel on land, certainly not by the entire crew. In a way, that's understandable – the ships were seen as powerful, fortified, mobile homes of discovery; it's no coincidence that we have fallen into the habit of calling space vehicles "ships," or that the Star Trek franchise, filled with the jargon of Gene Roddenberry's Navy days, still uses words and phrases such as "aboard," "away team," "sick bay," and, for that matter, "captain." And, as has generally been the case with space travel, little provision has been made for completing – much less aborting and returning from – a space mission without a space ship. While it's true that, in one sense, Franklin's men's chance of survival was greatly decreased by their lack of preparation for, or even of familiarity with, the Arctic landscape and Inuit survival techniques, such ignorance was nothing new. After all, it's been estimated that fewer than one man in ten in the Royal Navy even knew how to swim.

It's often claimed that Franklin's ships were equipped with the "latest technology," but such statements are only partly true. Like nearly all the ships sent to the Arctic by Great Britain, they were ex-warships, heavily reinforced for the discovery service, but nearly everything that was done to them had been done before: iron sheathing of the bow, internal strengthening for their frames, and canvas tenting for "housing-in" the decks in winter. Each ship was also outfitted with a Sylvester Patent Stove – these had been used successfully as far back as Parry's second Arctic expedition in 1821–23, and had in fact been installed in both the *Erebus* and *Terror* six years earlier. Designed by Sheffield inventor and chemist Charles Sylvester in 1819, these stoves used an innovative system for their day, employing a heat exchanger to warm the air, which was then directed via ducts into various parts of the ship. The Sylvester earned the praise of Ross and others for its advantage over earlier systems, which had done little to relieve the damp and cold below decks. Still, as with other improvements, though relatively new to ships, it was by that time already tried and trusted technology. Similarly, much was made of the fact that the ships had been equipped with ex-railway boilers and screw-propellers, but steam as a source of naval propulsion had been around for well over a decade; a side-wheel steam engine had been tried in the Arctic aboard the *Victory*, by Sir John and James Ross in 1829, but the elder Ross found the "execrable machinery" so prone to trouble that it had it removed and abandoned it on the shore; the place was known ever after to the Inuit as *Haviktalik* – the place of metal.

The provisions, as with the other equipment, were essentially identical to those furnished ships headed for the Arctic since 1818: 36,000 pounds of ship's biscuit, 136,000 pounds of flour, 25,000 pounds of sugar, 2,300 pounds of tea, 580 gallons of pickled vegetables, 32,000 pounds of salt pork, 200 gallons of "wine for the sick," and 9,300 pounds of lemon juice to ward off scurvy. Smaller quantities of oatmeal, scotch barley, pemmican, suet, and vinegar rounded off the stores, along with 3,600 gallons of over-proof Navy rum: this, with sugar and some water, was to be used for the daily ration of "grog" – one-eighth of a pint of rum mixed with two pints of water – issued to every sailor in the Royal Navy from 1740 to 1970. Private ownership or consumption of spirits was a flogging offence, and while the ships were anchored off Stromness, Fitzjames disciplined some men who came back drunk from shore leave; he ordered their surreptitious spirits poured overboard.

Tinned food, often mistakenly said to be new to this voyage, had been supplied as long ago as Parry's voyage of 1819. The only thing new about the tinned food was the manufacturer; in an effort to cut costs, the Navy had put the contract out to bid, and one Samuel Goldner was the low bidder. Goldner's tins have been a singular focus of attention, since the lead solder used to construct them has been blamed for lead poisoning among the men and (by one writer) suggested as a source of botulism. The ships' cook stoves had also been redesigned, with a view to improving the distillation of water both for drinking and for use in the boilers – and this innovation, too, may have been another, or even the primary, source of lead exposure in crew members. In short, while the Franklin expedition was frequently hailed as the most "advanced" of its time, most of its advances were minor.

The only true innovation brought on the voyage was a daguerreotype apparatus – the same, apparently, as that used to take portraits of many of the expedition's officers before the ships' departure in May 1845. The apparatus was supplied by Richard Beard, a photographic pioneer who at the time lay claim to one of only two licensed daguerreotype franchises in England, operating out of the Royal Polytechnic Institution on Regent Street. Photography was still a young science, and its inclusion may well have been due to Sir John Franklin's early interest in it – he apparently had seen some of Beard's earlier daguerreotypes which had been brought to Tasmania in 1843 by photographer-churchman Francis Russell Nixon – and the subject was discussed on several occasions at the Tasmanian Society (later the Royal Society of Tasmania), which Franklin founded. Not everyone was enamoured of these new "sun-painted" portraits – the Duke of Wellington famously complained that it made his nose look too big – and it may be significant that while all of Franklin's officers aboard HMS *Erebus* sat for portraits, only Captain Crozier of the *Terror* joined them.

It seems likely that charge of this apparatus would have been given to Harry Goodsir, the expedition's surgeon-naturalist, whose scientific-minded family had close connections with the brothers John and Robert Adamson, who were among the earliest practising photographers in Scotland. In fact, Goodsir was one of only two members of the officer corps to be sitting for what we know to have been a *second* photograph – his first was a talbotype taken in 1841–42 by Robert Adamson – and his familiarity with this technology would have made him a natural choice as expedition photographer. There was a great deal of interest at the time in the application of photography to natural-history specimens, especially in Scotland, and one may speculate that Goodsir, rather than employ this novel system for portraits, might have turned his lens in that direction; if any developed plates are ever found, there's at least a 50/50 chance that they'll be of mollusks rather than men.

++++

The ships' officers, unlike the rest of the crew, brought with them their own personal provisions along with a wide variety of equipment designed for specialized use. By a chance reference in a letter, we know that Crozier, captain of the *Terror* and second-in-command overall, was miffed one day when he discovered that tea and sugar he had arranged to have delivered had been misappropriated and directed to Fitzjames instead. A number of officers had placed orders with Fortnum and Mason – a luxury London victualler still in business today; Lieutenant James Fairholme in one of his letters home declared that "Fortnum and Mason have done their part well, and we find all of their stores of the best description." The officers' perks included better-quality tea, tobacco, spices, wine and spirits, and a selection of tinned delicacies. The junior officers' mess on each ship, known as the "gunroom," was supplied with its own steward or servant; there was also a servant for the senior officers, who typically dined with the captain; both Franklin and Crozier had their own personal servants. Life aboard ship for the officers, who drank fine black tea from porcelain cups, had their fill of tinned meat, and could enjoy a glass of wine with dinner, was thus quite different than that of regular seamen, who ate in a large, common mess and whose diet consisted mostly of salt pork, hardtack, and a small weekly apportionment of tinned food. Given the very different mortality rates between officers and men, it's possible that their different diets, or the way in which their food was prepared, could have played a role.

Fresh water – the phrase may be a sort of euphemism in this case – was to be supplied using the Fraser galley stove, which employed a large tank for both melt water and condensed steam from the cooking process; it's possible that the reuse of hot water, in which more lead could have been dissolved, might be one source of elevated lead levels. The tinned food is the more usual suspect, since surviving cans have shown large, sloppily applied beads of lead solder on their interior seals. Goldner, known for his cost-cutting ways, had gotten the contract so close to the ships' sailing date that he had been obliged to rush the order – one possible cause of problems. His canning process, carried out as described in his patent, has been shown to be safe by modern tests, but under the circumstances, it's possible that quality control was not what it should have been. A few years after the *Erebus* and *Terror* sailed, in 1852, tins of Goldner's meats were examined at the Clarence Victualling-yard, where Navy stores were gathered and distributed – some of the cans were found to be so putrid that the odour forced the examiners to flee the room; Goldner's contract was not renewed.

Such problems have led some, such as Scott Cookman (*Ice Blink*), to suppose that botulism from improperly canned foods was a cause of some of the expedition's deaths – but this scenario seems highly unlikely for a number of reasons. First, since the bacteria that produces the botulin toxin is anaerobic, it can thrive only in places where oxygen is absent; with the tins inspected in 1854, the putrescence was attributed to their being imperfectly sealed – that is, with *air* in them – which would make botulism impossible. Secondly, according to recent studies, the high salinity and nitrate content of the concentrated soups – Cookman's culprit – would have greatly inhibited the growth of botulism. Lastly, we know that the men aboard both ships tried the tinned food fairly soon after their departure, and as of their last letters home from Greenland some weeks later, all had pronounced them excellent and flavourful. The Inuit, indeed, found unopened tins many years later, opened them, and ate the contents without ill result; indeed, they found the meat quite to their liking, since it was packed with "much ooksook" (fat). Unlike lead poisoning, which was poorly understood and could produce only mild symptoms, botulism would have led to sudden and dramatic illness or deaths, which could hardly have escaped notice.

As they dined in company with their fellow officers, Franklin's senior men enjoyed one other luxury: most had brought with them their own plates and silver service from home, in many cases embossed with the officers' family crests. Franklin's cutlery, crafted by the London silversmith George Adams, bore his crest, a conger-eel's head between two branches; Crozier's featured a griffin or phoenix; Lieutenant Robert Sargent of the *Erebus* had a winged dolphin on his; Lieutenant George Henry Hodgson of the *Terror* had a dove with an olive branch; and Edward Couch of the *Erebus* lay claim to a lion *couchant* (seated) and a large letter "C." Most poignant of all, perhaps, was the silverware of Lieutenant Fairholme of the *Erebus*, which featured the motto "SPERO MELIORA" – "I hope for better things." Alongside these crests and mottoes, many of the forks and spoons bore other, even more telling marks: scratched into their undersides, crudely cut into the elegant silver, were the initials of ordinary seamen. The officers, at some point, had apparently decided to distribute their silverware to the crews.

++++

But it's the tinned food that's the star of the show when it comes to provisions. First featured in a woodcut in the *Illustrated London News* which showed the stack "piled high" on Beechey Island, they returned to centre stage when anthropologist Owen Beattie and his team exhumed the bodies buried nearby. These bodies, which had (as the Inuit might say) "the flesh on," had the potential to give researchers the greatest insight into the state of the Franklin men. True, these three had died during the first winter, which suggested that they may well have had health problems at the time of sailing – and such conditions, indeed, were found. And yet, as preserved exemplars of Franklin's sailors, they quite literally embodied everything that a typical seaman would have experienced, as well as the treatment accorded to those who were ill, or died, when the vessels were still strong and secure. Finally, since images of these men were first published in the 1980s, they've also served as one of our strongest human connections to Franklin and his men – after all, we've quite literally looked into their eyes.

John Torrington, whose body was the first exhumed, had been the leading stoker on HMS *Terror*. Since the engines were designed to be used only when the ships were becalmed or a contrary wind made following leads in the ice difficult, it's quite possible that he did little or no stoking – but, be that as it may, he was certainly in ill health for a man who was only nineteen when the ships sailed. He had suffered, in all likelihood, from earlier bouts with tuberculosis, followed by pneumonia, though whether these illnesses had killed him was unclear. The physical autopsy was inconclusive, with the pathologist stating "no specific cause of Torrington's death could be identified." The lab results, however, raised another issue: samples of his hair showed evidence of elevated lead intake, intake that peaked a week or so before his death, then dropped off. This suggested that lead poisoning could have been a factor, and the levels support a scenario in which sailors, once ill, were placed in the ship's sick bay, where they received additional rations of tinned food, along with wine, which was thought to fortify the blood. Once Torrington became too ill to take any food or liquid, the levels would have dropped.

Further studies even showed that the isotope ratio of the lead in the tins matched that in the bodies, which seemed to confirm the tins as its source. It was this finding that John Geiger, who accompanied Beattie at Beechey and chronicled their research, has called the "smoking gun." Certainly, widespread lead poisoning would have affected the judgment of the men and damaged their physical health as well – and so, for some time, it's been quite common to assume that this "explains" the expedition's failure.

Nevertheless, there have been doubts raised – there were few sources of lead in industrial England, and so almost any lead would have had a similar isotope ratio – and what's more, we know so little about the average exposure of a typical person in mid-nineteenth-century Britain that we lack a reliable baseline to which to compare the Beechey Island bodies. Since the original work by Beattie and Geiger, further studies, looking both at the Beechey Island remains and at bones recovered from King William Island, have shown a wide variety of levels of exposure, ranging from negligible to quite high. The lead content of the bones indicated that some individuals would have been suffering from acute lead toxicity – but that for others, lead would not even have been a factor. This was true, too, of the Beechey Island bodies – Torrington's levels were high (413–657 ppm) but Braine (145–280 ppm) and Hartnell (138–313) had much lower levels. Taken in context, this evidence suggests that the case is not quite as closed as it had first seemed; lead may well have been a factor for some, but the effect of this exposure on the expedition as a whole is unclear. If there was a pattern in terms of the officers as opposed to the men, it's difficult to measure, since none of the skeletal remains have yet been identified – it's impossible to say which bones were whose.

A further tactic has been tried. A few years ago, researchers at McMaster University decided to test a tin – one not from Franklin's ships but from a vessel that had searched for him – which came into their hands (Figure 7). They tested the can itself and its contents and found lead levels that were very high indeed – but, of course, since the soup inside this tin had been sitting there for fifty times as long as any eaten during the expedition, such a measurement might well be on the high side. To see whether this same tin, refilled with fresh contents, would show high levels of lead over a shorter period, they cooked up a fresh batch of "ox cheek soup" (well, almost – ox cheeks being scarce, they used the same parts from a cow) and sealed it inside the tin using Goldner's original process. As of the last report, after six months inside the tin, the contents haven't shown elevated levels of lead;

this at least would explain the lack of any ill result for those of Franklin's men who tried the tinned food prior to the last letters being mailed from Greenland. As to longer exposure to the interior of the tin, that will have to wait – it is, after all, a "real time" experiment.

✦✦✦✦

John Torrington, while he lived, certainly had one possible exposure that set him aside from the rest of the crew: coal. Even when not being burned, coal and coal dust can pose health hazards, and once burned, coal ash contains a variety of toxins including heavy metals. The engines supplied to the *Erebus* and *Terror* were both ex-railway ones, adapted for use in driving screw-propellers. In their previous employment, these engines, and those who stoked them, would have at least been in the open, with the forward velocity of the train refreshing the air they breathed; deep in the holds of wooden ships, seated in an area not designed for their use, the engines must have produced considerable noise and fumes. The smokestacks fitted to them had to be several times longer than in railway use, and as anyone with a wood stove and a tall chimney today knows, getting a good draft can be tricky. It's certainly possible that Torrington's higher lead levels may have had something to do with his employment, although we don't know whether, or how often, the boilers were used during the first leg of the voyage, before he fell ill and died.

We know less than perhaps we would like about these engines too – for some time, it was believed that HMS *Terror* had a Stephenson engine of the "Samson" type from the London and Birmingham railway ("Our engine once ran somewhat faster on the Birmingham line," jested Lieutenant Irving in one of his letters home), while the *Erebus* was thought to have a "Planet" type made by Marshalls of Wednesbury. More recent research, however, seems to show that both were more likely Croydon or Archimedes engines built by G&J Rennie in 1838 and 1839. These engines would have been slightly smaller, but not very much less ravenous when it came to coal and water. Coal, as noted by many of the officers, took up a large portion of otherwise usable space in the hold and was also stowed on deck and in every available nook and cranny, accounting for ninety tons between the two vessels. Water, since fresh rather than salt water was needed, would have had to be melted and dispensed in advance, and when running, the engines might well consume more of it than the men. With just twenty horsepower, the engines were expected to move the lumbering ships at perhaps three to four knots, barely a crawl, and Crozier, at least, thought them an ill-advised waste of space and resources: "How I do wish the engine was again on the Dover line & the Engineer sitting on top of it; he is a dead and alive wretch and is now quite dissatisfied because he has not the leading stoker to assist him in doing nothing." So much for the latest technology.

The engines may, however, have offered one last advantage. For many years, various searchers, including David Woodman, used sledge-hauled magnetometers to seek the ships, hoping that the metal of the engines would create a significant blip in the background magnetism. These hopes proved false, but now that at least one ship has been found, its engine may add considerably to our knowledge of the vessel. One might suppose that, having been underwater for more than a century and a half, it might be in too poor a condition to identify, but in fact there's ample precedent for its being in reasonably good shape: in 1857, while the Franklin search was still ongoing, the *Thomas*, a 700-ton barque, set sail for Nova Scotia with two Glasgow-built railway engines as its primary cargo. The ship foundered in the Hebrides, and although some efforts were made at the time to recover the engines, they weren't brought to the surface until 2002. The divers had expected them to be disassembled in kit form, but they found both engines – broad-gauge tenders that had been custom-built for a Canadian railway – fully assembled, with many of their parts still readily identifiable.

+++++

There was one last sort of provision that served not the appetites of the body, nor the cause of science, nor the demands of the infernal engines. On long Arctic voyages, with their many months of "wintering-over" in ice-bound harbours, ennui and "cabin fever" could be as much hazards as scurvy or other illnesses. Ever since Parry's wintering over in 1819–20 at Melville Island, materials had been brought for shipboard entertainments and distractions: scripts, costumes, and props for amateur theatricals, slates and chalk for shipboard schools, and books – by some accounts, well over a thousand of them. Of these last, we have at least some anecdotal evidence. Officers, of course, could bring their own volumes, and as a form of charity, each crew member was supplied with a copy of the *Book of Common Prayer*; the ships, too, quite likely each contained a complete "Seaman's Library" of devotional and didactic booklets. How, after all, would one keep count of the days without Turnbull's *Arithmetic Made Easy*, or expect civil discourse without Josiah Woodward's *A Kind Caution to Profane Swearers*? And we know that, at least aboard the *Erebus*, this floating library was carefully enumerated; as James Fitzjames wrote in a letter dated 18 June 1845, "to-day we set to work, and got a catalogue made of all our books, and find we have amongst us, a most splendid collection."

What books, then, were these? Like the proverbial books-on-a-desert-island question, the choice of volumes for such a long and rigorous undertaking was not made lightly. Press accounts of the day indicated that the ships, as one might expect, had copies of all previously printed narratives of Arctic discovery, for reference more than for idle reading. Leisure, however, was not to be neglected; among the books we know were brought were copies of Dickens's *Pickwick Papers*, Goldsmith's *The Vicar of Wakefield*, and several early volumes of *Punch* (which had just been founded in 1841). Fairholme, an officer of religious disposition, brought Whewell's *Indications of the Creator*, along with Chambers's *Vestiges of the Natural History of Creation*; Gore had along a copy of *Christian Melodies* inscribed to him by a friend. Lady Franklin's niece Sophia donated copies of Samuel Green's *Life of Mohammed* and Bernardin Saint-Pierre's *Paul and Virginia*. Along with these, we know of several bibles, at least one in French, as well as scattered leaves of other volumes and even a tattered clipping from *Lloyd's Newspaper*, which was found to contain the "Weekly Summary of Maritime Casualties" for 6 April 1845. On a more immediately practical level, each of the ships' engineers was provided with a copy of Charles Hutton Gregory's *Practical Rules for the Management of a Locomotive Engine*.

We know of these books, in part, because quite a few of them were recovered by McClintock from the boat he found on King William Island. Indeed, the boat's contents are often read as an indication of the sheer useless weight of Victorian bric-a-brac that Franklin's men, either blinded by delusions of imperial invincibility or in the final throes of lead poisoning, or both, hauled to their eventual exhaustion and death. Even McClintock, though he was cut as it were from much the same cloth, wondered at this array:

Seven or eight pairs of boots of various kinds – cloth winter boots, sea boots, heavy ankle boots, and strong shoes, silk handkerchiefs – black, white, and figured – towels, soap, sponge, tooth-brush, and hair-combs; a macintosh gun-cover, marked outside with paint #12, lined with black cloth. Besides these articles we found twine, nails, saws, files, bristles, wax-ends, sail-makers' palms, powder, bullets, shot, cartridges, wads, leather cartridge-cases, knives – clasp and dinner ones, needle and thread cases, slow-match, several bayonet scabbards cut down into knife-sheaths, two rolls of sheet-lead, and, in short, a quantity of articles of one description and another truly astonishing in variety, and such as, for the most part, modern sledge-travellers in these regions would consider a mere accumulation of dead weight, of little use, and very likely to break down the strength of the sledge-crews.

Of all these items, perhaps books were actually the most practical – religious books in particular seemed to be most precious, offering as they did some consolation in the worst of circumstances. Yet it's worth noting that none of the admonitions, abjurations, and advice in these books helped stave off disaster, proving of no more value in this regard than the copy of *Bickersteth's Scripture Help* that fell from Robert Hood's hands when he was shot by Michel Terrehaute on Franklin's second expedition twenty years previous. *Comforter, where, where is your comforting?* One of the most poignant of these printed materials was a single, stray page from a book known as the *Student's Manual*; by fortune or by fate it had been folded so as to highlight one passage:

My first convictions on the subject of religion were confirmed from observing that really religious persons had some solid happiness among them, which I had felt that the vanities of the world could not give. I shall never forget standing by the bed of my sick mother:

"Are you not afraid to die?"

"No."

"No! Why does the uncertainty of another state give you no concern?"

"Because God has said to me – *Fear not: when thou passest through the waters I will be with thee; and through the rivers, they shall not overflow thee.*"

5

Maps

Along with the best training and equipment available, the Franklin expedition took the latest maps, specially printed for the lords of the Admiralty by the firm of John Arrowsmith. "Arrowsmith's Charts" were the maps of the British Empire upon which the sun never set (especially in summer and north of 60 degrees latitude). Unfortunately, the latest surveys of the area Franklin would be exploring contained a number of significant errors which would help seal his fate; although the surveyors and naval explorers who had contributed to them over the years were all capable with sextants and chronometers, these seemingly objective charts in fact contained a number of conjectures and suppositions that Franklin's expedition was to prove – too late – to be wrong.

The first error was that of James Ross, who, in his trip to what he called "King William Land" in 1829–33, traversed land and water indifferently, frequently mistaking iced-over water for land. As a result, a navigable route that lay to the east of King William was regarded as a dead end and shown on the maps as "Poctes Bay." The name itself is now thought to be an error for "Poets' Bay," corresponding with "Artists' Bay" on the opposite coast – but what mattered more was that Ross's mistake lent credence to the belief that King William was an extension of Boothia, whereas in fact it was an entirely separate island. Both James and his uncle Sir John Ross persisted in the equally erroneous notion that the "Gulph of Boothia," named by them for their sponsor, Felix Booth (of Booth's Gin fame), opened broadly into the waters at the mouth of the Back River. Arrowsmith's map, shown here, reveals the extent of both errors.

Peter Warren Dease and Thomas Simpson, who had mapped the southern coast of what was then still called the "Polar Ocean," added their own errors to the charts; their latitudes were accurate enough, but their longitudes seemed to drift with the tides; they misaligned the coast of King

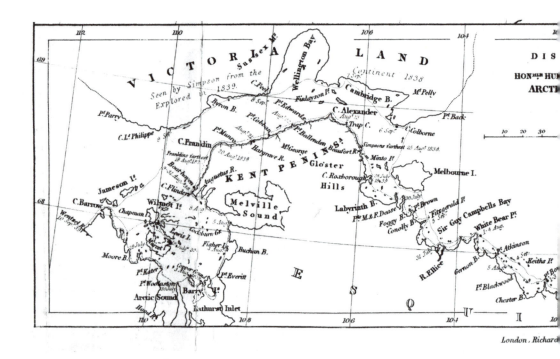

Figure 8 Dease and Simpson's survey, engraved by John Arrowsmith.
Collection of the author.

William Land with that of the mainland, and misstated the longitude of
their farthest point, just beyond the Castor and Pollux River – they gave
the river's longitude as 94°14′ W. whereas in fact it is 93° 53′, an error of
roughly nine miles too far west. Dr Rae, though he confirmed Dease and
Simpson's latitude, got a longitudinal reading of 93° 20′, which is fourteen
miles off. How could such practised hands make such significant errors, and
those errors not only go uncorrected but be compounded by new ones?

One answer lies in the difference between latitude, which can be readily
and accurately determined with a sextant, and longitude, which requires either a complex calculation using lunar altitudes and observations of fixed
stars or else a very accurate chronometer – one that's never allowed to run
down. The reason for this is that, while latitudes are fixed by the rotation
of the earth and the elevation of the sun, longitudes are relative – the official meridian of 0° was established, curiously enough, by then Astronomer
Royal Edmund Halley, as the very spot upon which he was then sitting at
his observatory in Greenwich. To know one's longitude relative to that
point, one had to know what time it was; knowing the precise difference
between the local time and Greenwich time enabled one to calculate one's

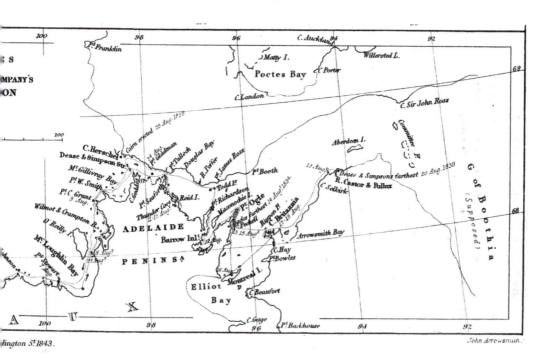

longitude with great accuracy. This was the reason that Harrison's chrono-meters – several of which are displayed at Greenwich today – won the prize for enabling ships at sea to accurately determine their location.

By the time of the making of the charts supplied to Franklin, a number of British firms manufactured marine chronometers – large ones, often supplied in a wooden case, for use on ships, and smaller ones that could be carried over land – and the Greenwich observatory became the natural home of all those used by the Royal Navy. The makers numbered their chronometers, and the Navy's Hydrographic Office made sure that they were precisely set before they assigned them to a ship. Most ships carried a number of them, both to guard against any rogue chronometers or outliers which might mislead them, and in case – horror of horrors – one of them ran down. On earth, if one could reach a point whose longitude was precisely known, one could reset one's chronometers, deducing time from location; but at sea – or on land without any such clearly fixed points – losing track of the time meant losing one's self, and quite possibly one's life as well.

One key consequence, then, of this use of chronometers, was that if they ran *fast*, the distance between one's position and the Greenwich meridian would be calculated to be too far, and the longitude recorded would be west of the actual location; if they ran too *slow*, the opposite problem occurred, and one would believe oneself to be farther east than one was. In addition, since the earth's orbit around the sun is elliptical rather than circular, the apparent "local noon" – the highest point of the sun in the sky, when longitudinal observations must be taken – is off by a small fraction, which requires a special table, given in the "Nautical Almanac." This problem of ascertaining local noon is especially difficult in the Arctic, of course, since, for a large portion of the year, the sun only barely creeps above the horizon line, and in the winter it vanishes for weeks or months. The severe refraction of the atmosphere can also compound errors, making the sun seem to rise before it has in fact risen, or seem to remain after it has in fact set. In the absence of the sun, the chronometer was useless, and the old, complex method of comparing the distance between the moon and certain fixed stars, and then consulting a table of "lunar altitudes," had to be used.

Given all this, it's little wonder that these northern charts – which, in some cases, were based on only a single survey – were distorted by longitudinal errors. In fact, we know that the longitude given for Beechey Island in the Victory Point record is off by several miles, as is that given for the landing site of the ships' crews; the difficulty in locating "Sir James Ross's pillar" may have been due to the same issues. This was despite the fact that Franklin's men, while on board their ships, had the advantage of using some of the best marine chronometers available. By tradition, the task of keeping them wound fell to the second lieutenants aboard each vessel; in winding, one had to take care neither to let the mainspring run too slack, nor wind it too tightly, and one had to observe and keep track of each timepiece in order to distinguish the reliable ones from the outliers.

We can see this in the curious history of just one such chronometer – known as Arnold 294 – which was found, intact and without any sign of having been exposed to the elements, by a senior horological specialist at the Royal Observatory, Jonathan Betts, in 2009. The find was a surprise, since this very timepiece appeared to have been issued to the *Erebus* and *Terror* in 1845 and should not have been in such fine condition – indeed it should not have been there at all. The chronometer had been converted to a "carriage clock" – which entailed its being built into a permanent wooden case, from which its back and works would not be visible; some effort had also been made to obliterate the maker's name on the faceplate. A case of theft, surely, at some point – but how could such a valuable piece of machinery have been stolen from under the noses of Franklin's officers, and the event go unremarked and unpunished as of the officers' last letters from Greenland, several months into the expedition?

The answer, as it turns out, lay in the records already at the Observatory, combined with some sleuthing-about using Google Books, a tool unavailable until recently, which – by enabling keyword searches across hundreds of thousands of scanned books and articles – has made locating needles in haystacks, or chronometers in books in this case, exponentially easier. The records at the Royal Observatory stated that, prior to Franklin's voyage, Arnold 294 was last given to HMS *Beagle* in 1837. Betts believed that the *Beagle* was then being used as a "packet" vessel, on short trips along the coast carrying mail and small goods – but in fact she departed that year for a new survey of Australia under the command of John Clements Wickham. Wickham fell ill on this voyage, and the command of the vessel was given to lieutenant John Lort Stokes. Stokes's narrative, online thanks to Google Books, indicated that fresh crew were taken on at this point, including, of all people, Graham Gore, who took up Stokes's position as acting second lieutenant, a position in which one of his duties would be to tend to the chronometers, Arnold 294 among them. In his narrative, Stokes singled out Gore for special praise and referred to the high hopes then entertained of the success of the Franklin expedition.

We know that familiarity with a timepiece was an asset – and that, indeed, some officers sought to bring along chronometers from previous voyages onto their next assignment; having at least one familiar timepiece would have been invaluable in calibrating and assessing the others. The *Erebus* and *Terror*, as it happens, were meant to have sailed with ten chronometers each, but when Betts double-checked the receipt for the *Erebus*, he found that there were only *nine*, and that Arnold 294 was not among them. Two other chronometers that *were* taken had also been on the *Beagle* with Gore, and so the implication is clear that he had made a point of bringing familiar ones with him. In all likelihood, he had meant to bring three, but some matter prevented him from including Arnold 294. It may, as was sometimes the case, have been sent to the manufacturer or some other specialist for adjustment and cleaning; such a practice was common, although there's no mention of it in the official records. Wherever it was sent, someone at some point absconded with it, altered the case, and scratched the maker's mark to conceal his crime, and from that point, as they say, the rest is history.

The fate of the rest of the expedition's chronometers was far less fortunate. Many were found on or near the bodies of Franklin's men by the Inuit and were returned in trade to Dr Rae and other searchers. Charles Francis Hall located a large wooden chronometer case marked with the Navy's "broad arrow," which was among the items he sent back to Greenwich. Given their absolutely essential value in navigation, these instruments, along with sextants – one of which was found by McClintock in the boat with the two skeletons – would have been among the men's most precious possessions, and the very last to be surrendered if they believed there were any hope of survival whatsoever. And this is where, although the men may indeed have had such hopes, the maps once more betrayed them. For Dease and Simpson indicated that the coast tended to the east as far as they could see (shown in figure 8 as a dotted line), whereas in reality it soon turns almost straight north. There was no wide passage there to the Gulf of Boothia, although, had Franklin's men made it so far, they might have stumbled upon the narrow cleft of Bellot Strait (which was not officially discovered until 1852).

With these charts as their guide, it's little wonder that Franklin's men, on their death march along the southern coast of King William Island, failed to cross Simpson's Strait at its narrowest point; they may well have planned to continue by land as far as the coast of the Gulf of Boothia. Perhaps they were setting out for Ross's old Victory harbour, or perhaps they hoped to launch their boats into the Gulf of Boothia and, like Ross, make their way to northern sea lanes. David Woodman, in his second book, *Strangers among Us*, chronicles accounts given to Hall of men seen on the Melville peninsula, thought by the Inuit to possibly be "Et-ker-lin" (*itqilit* – a word used for subarctic Indian tribes), who may have been a small group of Franklin survivors. The evidence is a bit sketchy, since the Inuit, concerned that the strangers might be hostile, did not approach them. This makes it difficult to tell whether these stories relate to some Franklin survivors or to John Rae's survey party, which passed through the same area a few years later. In any case, they seem to have left behind at least one red food tin (although that could have been scavenged), and the Inuit noticed that even their "ar-nuk" (*anaq*, feces) had a different appearance. We can only say for certain that this group, if indeed they were Franklin's men, died before reaching help.

✦✦✦✦

The maps that Franklin brought with him may have contributed to his demise – and yet, as Joseph Conrad noted, the maps made by those who searched for him gave accurate form to nearly all of the unexplored Arctic. The only thing missing from these maps was the human dimension: Where, after all, had Franklin's ships, and the scattered parties of his fleeing men, ended up?

Several searchers sought to amend this. Hall, in the course of charting the places he travelled, also solicited maps from the Inuit; the most significant of these, drawn by no less a figure than In-nook-poo-zhee-jook, was reproduced in his narrative. Schwatka also asked the Inuit to draw their own maps, as did Knud Rasmussen. One might expect that these maps, along with the testimony about the various places where bodies or ships had been seen, would greatly clarify and support the Inuit testimony, and make it easier to corroborate. Unfortunately, these maps – like the testimony itself – tend to be idiosyncratic, drawn from the experience and perspective of the mapmaker, and with an eye to memorable features rather than exact proportions. In the area on and around King William Island, hunting out on the ice shelf or its edge was the principal activity, and these maps thus tended to highlight coastal features while leaving inland areas where there was no hunting blank. And, although major landmasses had names common to most Inuit, smaller islands and other features were often given whimsical monikers based on their shape or events that happened there, names that might well have been used more than once by different bands at various times.

We can see this difference when we look at two maps – the one drawn by In-nook-poo-zhee-jook for Hall in 1869, and one drawn for Rasmussen in 1923 by Qaqortingneq. Both depict King William Island, but in shape and detail they almost look as though they could represent two different places. In-nook-poo-zhee-jook's map, showing both the island and the Adelaide peninsula to its south, obligingly highlights places important to Hall, such as #9 "Too-noo-nee" (the place where In-nook found the two boats, including the one with the stack of cannibalized bones) and #10 "Kee-u-na," where the last men of the party heading west along the island's southern shore perished. In-nook's island has no interior whatsoever – he did not fish or hunt there – whereas Qaqortingneq's has numerous details of inland rivers and lakes where he fished. His coastline, too, has many more landmarks, though none specifically connected to Franklin sites, such as #1 "malerualik," the place where one follows after caribou; #5 "kanilugjuak," the big headland; or #17 "saterteq," the place with many flat ones (stones). The north/south scale of the map is compressed, though this may be due to the dimensions and orientation of the paper he was given.

Identifying Franklin-related features on such maps as these can pose a considerable challenge – as an example, one might consider the rough map

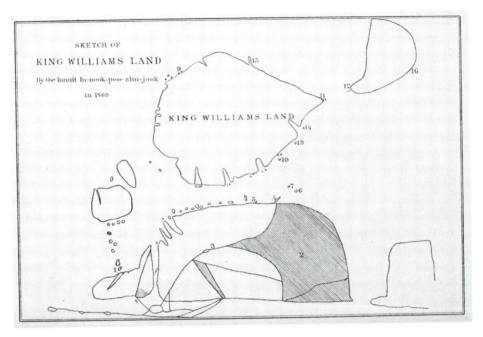

Figure 9 Sketch map of King William Island by In-nook-poo-zhee-jook.
From *Narrative of the Second Arctic Expedition Made by Charles F. Hall*,
Washington: 1879, facing 398.

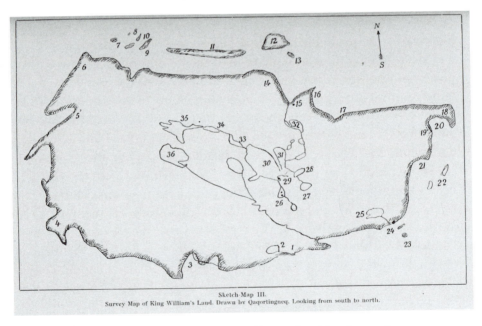

Figure 10 Sketch map of King William Island by Qaqortingneq.
From Knud Rasmussen, *Report of the Fifth Thule Expedition, 1921–24*, vol. 3,
nos. 1 and 2, Copenhagen: 1931, facing 100.

drawn by Godfred Hansen, who accompanied Rasmussen on part of the Fifth Thule Expedition, but with place names given by an Inuit informant named Qaqortingneq. This sort of map would seem to have greater potential value, since the Inuit – whatever the spatial vagaries of their own maps – instantly recognized the shape and arrangement of bays and islands and could give names to each – names that we can, with a much greater degree of accuracy, use to translate Inuit nomenclature into unambiguous locations. Most of the names given for the inlets and islands, like those on Qaqortingneq's map of King William, are descriptive, but in this case several of these refer – potentially – to episodes in the Franklin saga. Prominent among these is #28 *umiartalik*, "the place where there are umiaqs," near where In-nook and other witnesses placed the "Utjulik" wreck, and #56, identified as *qiunak*, "the place one can starve to death," which would seem identical to In-nuk's "Kee-u-na" (bearing in mind that Hall used his own odd orthography when transcribing Inuktitut words). As to *umiartalik*, this appears in shape, though not precise position, similar to modern "Hat Island."

Yet appearances can be deceiving. It turns out that the creatures who starved to death at *qiunak* were not Franklin's men but caribou, stranded on the island in an unexpectedly harsh season. And even *umiartalik* disappoints; an *umiaq*, often translated as "women's boat," was for the Inuit any large open boat that could carry multiple passengers; this island may have got its name from the fact that one of the whaleboats from Franklin's ships was found there. Such a find is consistent with one of his vessels being in the vicinity, of course, but it doesn't provide a definitive location for it. The whaleboats, which the Inuit could readily take to pieces and repurpose, were highly valued and worthy of being used as a name for a place. Rasmussen further complicated the matter by identifying this place as "Crenchel Island," which corresponds to no previously known name.

Thus, with Inuit maps as with Inuit testimony, we need to be extraordinarily careful to avoid reading our presuppositions into the evidence; we must bear in mind that the part of their long oral history and detailed geographical knowledge that specifically relates to Franklin is a small one. The arrival of these strangers in their land was a remarkable, memorable thing, but so were successful hunts, natural landmarks, and especially good fishing spots. The Qallunaat practice of filtering out anything that doesn't seem to relate to Franklin and his crews, and wanting only the parts of the stories that fit that one puzzle, is counter-productive. As we try to make sense of these complex sources, we need to be wary of our own biases and take care not to mistake conjectures – ours or those of others – for fact.

++++

One might despair entirely of making sense of all these maps of the Franklin search area were it not for the efforts of one man, cartographer and polymath Rupert Thomas Gould. Gould, who left a promising naval career after suffering a nervous breakdown in 1914, ended up at the Hydrographic Office, the same one responsible for keeping track of shipboard naval chronometers as well as updating nautical charts. There, he came upon several of the original Harrison chronometers – those that had earned him the Longitude Prize in 1765 – perhaps the most famous timepieces in history. They were, at the time, in a very poor state of repair, which stirred in Gould a passion for horology (the study of timepieces) that was both potent and persistent. The very day he first saw the Harrison chronometers, he joined the Royal Horological Society; soon after, he applied for and was granted permission to take the first of the Harrison instruments home, where – despite an almost complete lack of training in the subject – he set about cleaning and restoring them.

That Gould succeeded, not only in getting the Harrisons cleaned and repaired but in returning them to something quite close to their original working order, is a lasting testament to his genius; it's not for naught that his biographer, Jonathan Betts, dubbed him "the man who knew (almost) everything." He had, indeed, an appetite for difficulties, and when he heard through a friend of some of the mystery surrounding Franklin's lost ships, he too caught the fever. Before long, he was delivering a lecture at the Sette of Odd Volumes, an English bibliophile dining club, on the subject of "The Mystery of Sir John Franklin." His words were not idly received, for among his listeners were the Antarctic explorer Apsley Cherry-Garrard, W.G. Perrin, editor of *The Mariner's Mirror*, A.R. Hinks, the secretary of the Royal Geographical Society, and Major L.T. Burwash of the Canadian Department of the Interior.

Burwash, despite his professional interests in the geology and hydrology of the northern regions of Canada, might well be considered yet another obsessive Franklin amateur. Yet he had a few ideas of his own as to the fate of the *Erebus* and *Terror*. He was not the first to realize that a map showing all previous searches and finds was vital – the 1881 edition of McClintock's

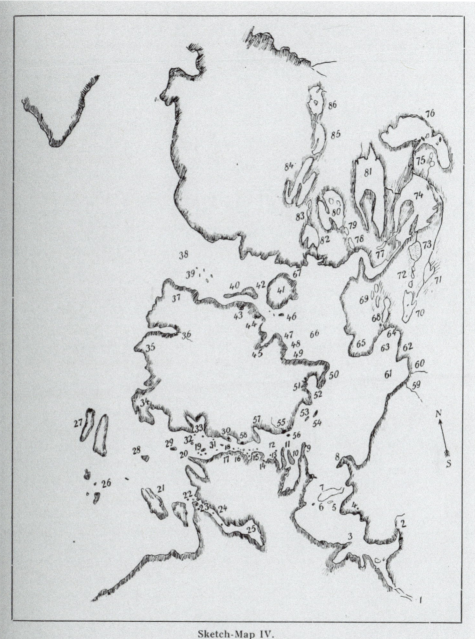

Sketch-Map IV.
Tracing of Godfred Hansen's map of King William's Land and environs; various details,
lakes, etc. and Eskimo place-names inserted by Qaqortingneq. Looking from south to north

Figure 11 Tracing of Godfred Hansen's map of King Williams Land and
environs. From Knud Rasmussen, *Report of the Fifth Thule Expedition,*
1921–24, vol. 3, nos. 1 and 2, Copenhagen: 1931, facing 102.

CHART SHOWING THE VICINITY OF
KING WILLIAM ISLAND
with the various positions in which relics of the Arctic Expedition under SIR JOHN FRANKLIN have been found.

Compiled by Lieut-Comm.^{dr} R.T. Gould. R.N.

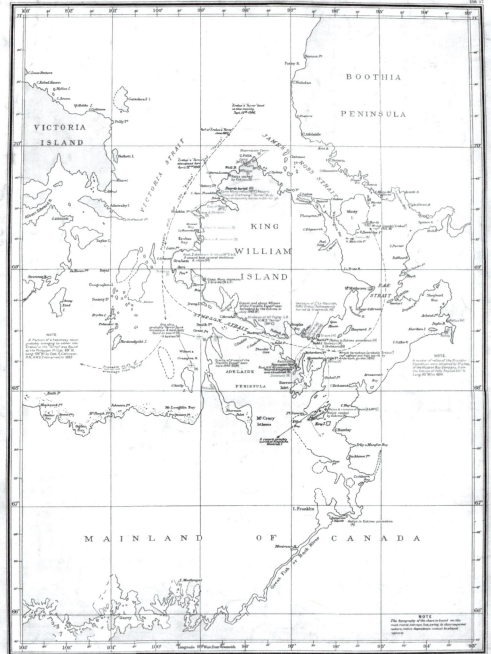

London. Published at the Admiralty, 11th May 1927. under the Superintendence of Rear Admiral H.P.Douglas, C.M.G. Hydrographer.

Printed by H.M.Stationery Office. Sold by J.D.Potter, Agent for the sale of the Admiralty Charts, 145 Minories.

5101

NOTE

The information shown in red is based upon the personal observations of various British and American explorers in this region.

The information shown in blue is based upon the various Eskimo reports obtained by these explorers, and probably is not altogether trustworthy.

In both cases the sources of information are indicated as follows: (A) Anderson 1855, (M^C) M^C Clintock 1859, (H) Hall 1866, (S) Schwatka 1879, (R) Rasmussen 1924, (N) Norberg 1926, (B) Burwash 1925

The dotted red line indicates the probable line of retreat, by sledge and boat, taken, after the abandonment of the 'Erebus' and 'Terror', by the Franklin Expedition.

* indicates positions where it is possible, although unlikely, that records of the Expedition may still (1927) be found.

account of his search had included one of "Franklin's Line of Retreat" so as to indicate Hall's and Schwatka's contributions – but he was the first to push the idea to a comprehensive level, including land and sea sites and Inuit as well as explorers' accounts (the former were given in blue, the latter in red, in original prints of the map). Burwash was particularly interested in the possibility of one of Franklin's ships having reached the eastern side of King William Island, via either the "Poctes Bay" or Simpson Strait routes, about which he had heard some Inuit stories; he also was the first to include the 1855 search by Anderson and Stewart, who approached by way of the Back River.

It appears to be primarily at Burwash's request that Gould prepared his map of the Franklin search area, formally known as Admiralty Chart #5101. The request may have come in response to Gould's talk on the history of the lost expedition; what Burwash had asked for, apparently, was a chart that would show all claims of traces of Franklin – skeletons, campsites, graves, boats, and the ships themselves – in all of the maps and reports compiled by previous search expeditions. According to his biographer, Gould had to rush the work to get it into Burwash's hands before the latter left for Canada; as a consequence, the cartographic elements were less precise than was usually expected. The professional cartographers at the Hydrographic Office protested Gould's receiving a credit for "drawn by" and insisted on the less respectable "compiled by," which after all is perhaps more accurate. The "Gould Map," as it's more commonly known, has been a landmark for amateur Franklin searchers ever since.

The books that were Gould's immediate sources for the map are given – McC for McClintock, S for Schwatka, H for Hall, and so forth. Precisely which maps or charts he consulted from these sources can only be inferred; in the case of Schwatka's expedition he did not have access to the commander's original narrative (which had gone missing and was not rediscovered until the early 1960s), only Gilder's published account, nor had he the stunning colour map prepared for Klutschak's narrative, which had appeared only in German. It does not seem that Gould used any Inuit maps as

Figure 12 *Opposite* "Gould" map (Admiralty Chart 5101), 1927.
Collection of Kenn Harper.

such, and indeed he deprecated their testimony by putting the findings of British or American searchers in red and those from Eskimo sources in blue, with a note in the key stating that "the information shown in blue is based upon the various Eskimo reports ... and probably is not altogether trustworthy." Despite this, as the first map to graphically depict all that had been discovered, or rumoured, up to that point, it's hard to overstate its importance – and yet, as with Dease and Simpson's survey, there are some errors and omissions on this map that need to be taken into account if it's to be used as a guide for searches.

First, the omissions. Most significant is that there is no "Hat Island" on this map – which seems odd, since Burwash himself, although he did not look for traces of Franklin there, wrote an account of its geography, included in his *Report of Exploration and Investigation along Canada's Arctic Coast Line from the Delta of the Mackenzie River to Hudson's Bay, 1925–26*. This early publication, prepared only in mimeograph form, describes the raised limestone bluffs of the island, using observations apparently made from a plane, illustrated with photographs. Hansen's map suggests it as a likely candidate for *umiartalik*, and later Inuit testimony collected from elders by Dorothy Eber describe it as a place where metal and wood from a white man's ship could be found. Given all this, its absence from the Gould map is disappointing, though perhaps simply an indicator of the haste with which it was prepared.

Secondly, while the drift lines given for the *Erebus* and *Terror* are reasonably plausible down through Victoria Strait, their divergence there is misleading. Gould shows one vessel, presumed to be the *Terror*, as already wrecked, with its debris carried to the east of the Royal Geographical Society Islands. That much is at least possible, but the sudden westward turn – made in order to account for the ship wreckage found by Rae and Richard Collinson on the shores of Victoria Island – is improbable in the extreme. Such wreckage as did not sink immediately would be carried atop the ice and follow its drift patterns; it's far more likely that the Victoria Island debris was carried along by part of the floe that drifted well to the west of the Royal Geographical Society Islands, then coming ashore when pressure from the floe pushed the ice up onto the land.

The third issue with the Gould map is that – by design – it shows not just one set of possibilities but many. On it, the *Erebus* sinks twice, once north of Ogle Point, where the hulk may have been seen but concealed by

Anderson's guides in 1855 (they were, it later came out, worried that such news would extend their hazardous journey still further), and again off Cape Hardy on Matty Island. The *Terror* sinks off the western coast of King William, its broken bits carried southwestward in the pack ice, but it also *doesn't* sink and becomes the ship found by the Inuit "in perfect order" – in Schwatka's version, a few miles west of Grant Point, as well as just off O'Reilly Island, the location deduced by Hall. Such doubleness is an asset, surely, to searchers, whose first task, as Sherlock Holmes might counsel, is be to consider all possible explanations – but it has led to confusion, since Gould's placement of this information lends a certain unwarranted solidity to speculations and conjectures. This is particularly the case with Burwash's Matty Island claim, which has the ship, supposed to be the *Erebus*, passing through Simpson Strait, a route that in fact would be extremely hazardous and difficult for a ship drawing as much water as she did. We now know that the *Erebus* was never in this area, but with the *Terror* still unlocated, the possibility can't be completely dismissed.

Gould, interestingly, was also the man behind another map, or set of maps, which are rightly famous in Franklin circles: the maps included as folding plates in R.J. Cyriax's magisterial 1939 book, *Sir John Franklin's Last Arctic Expedition*. In the mid-to-late 1930s Gould and Cyriax had developed a close friendship almost entirely through correspondence about Franklin matters, and so Gould was a natural choice to prepare the maps for this volume. Between them, they decided on a sort of "Before" and "After" set of views, the more dramatically to show how much of the undiscovered Arctic had been explored as the result of the search for Franklin; while not so much a map or chart in the conventional sense, they illustrate the degree to which the Franklin search mapped the un-mapped Arctic.

We live today in an age where nearly every person in the developed world has access to a computer or smartphone and can determine their location with a couple of clicks or swipes. Maps, to us, are dynamic entities on our screens, and static, crinkly, paper maps seem a thing of the past. Those seek-ing accurate maps or charts of the Canadian Arctic today can download them from a service known as GeoGratis, and a scalable version of Gould's Franklin map is available at Library and Archives Canada. Indeed, using services such as Google Earth, it's possible to peer down at any place on the

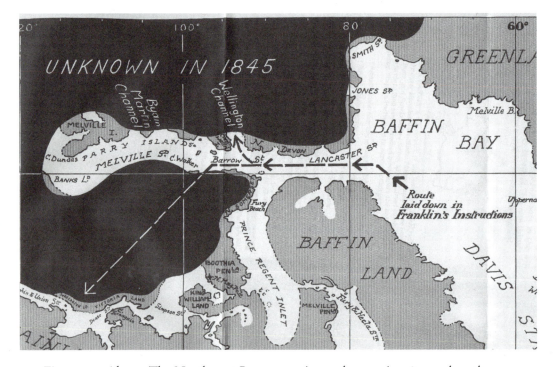

Figure 13 *Above*: The Northwest Passage region as known in 1845, when the Franklin expedition sailed. *Opposite*: The Northwest Passage region as known in 1859, after the return of Sir Leopold McClintock. Maps by R.T. Gould, source: Richard J. Cyriax, *Sir John Franklin's Last Arctic Expedition*, London: Arctic Press 2007 (original publication 1939).

planet, King William Island included, and see reasonably current satellite views, although, in thinly inhabited areas such as northern Canada, the resolution is set at a lower level than it is in denser, urban areas. One might think that, given such wonders of technology, the Franklin mystery might as easily be solved from an armchair as from a ship or a submarine – and yet, despite our new capabilities, our ability to reconstruct the final events of the expedition is still limited. Our maps remain incomplete.

We are in many ways still like our Victorian forebears, putting our confidence in our instruments, our computers, our remote sensing devices. We find it hard to fathom how more than a hundred men could wander the Arctic, slowly succumbing to exhaustion, scurvy, and starvation, even as the full force of the British Admiralty, with its excellent charts and clocks,

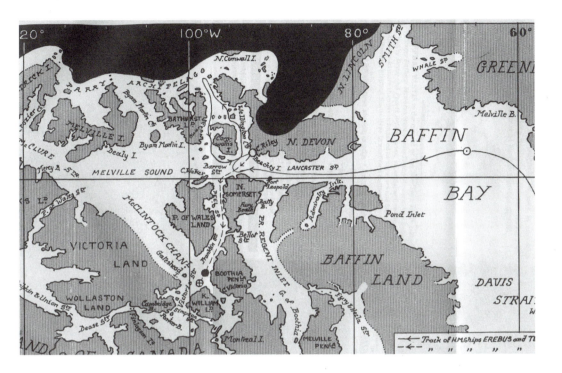

its dedicated and well-trained officers, its seaworthy ships and ample provisions, searched for them in vain. Once again, the late Canadian poet Gwendolyn MacEwen epitomized both kinds of hubris perfectly:

Crozier:

We scattered our instruments behind us
       and left them where they fell
       Like pieces of our bodies, like limbs
       We no longer had need for;
       We walked on and dropped them
       Compasses, tins, tools, all of them.
We came to the end of science.

DR. RAE.—(FROM A DAGUERRÉOTYPE BY BEARD.)

Figure 14 Dr John Rae, from a daguerreotype by Beard.
Collection of Kenn Harper.

6

Rae

The figure of Dr John Rae looms over the search for Franklin, troubling the waters of the heroic narrative of his accomplishments from the mid-1850s to the present. It wasn't just his having passed along Inuit testimony of cannibalism, disturbing though that was; nor was it his decision to hurry home to England with his news. The Royal Navy had searched for Franklin for six years, dispatching over a dozen ships and hundreds of men, with very little to show for it, and here was this buckskin-clad Scotsman who stole their fire. And, when compared with the privations suffered by Franklin's men in their final march, there was something still worse about Rae: his ability to succeed, even thrive in the same landscape in which Franklin's men marched to their deaths.

That Rae could journey by sledge for hundreds of miles, sustaining himself and his party and even giving extra meat to bands of Inuit he met along his route, while British sailors and officers stumbled, starving, unable to feed themselves or find their way, was extraordinarily galling. To top it all off, the fact that he received the £10,000 reward for ascertaining the fate of Franklin seemed to give official sanction to the stories he relayed, and undercut the valiant, albeit unsuccessful, British naval search. More recently, the claim, advanced by Canadian writer Ken McGoogan, that it was Rae, not Franklin, who should be credited with the discovery of the Northwest Passage itself, has rankled more than a few historians. In the wake of McGoogan's claim, Rae was the subject of a film by prominent Canadian filmmaker John Walker, as well as an extended public controversy about the desirability of placing a plaque honouring Rae in Westminster Abbey, where Franklin had long been memorialized.

To the middle-class English mindset of the mid-nineteenth century, Rae – a HBC employee whose principal work was as a surveyor – was of a distinctly different class and character than Franklin and his men. To begin with, he was a Scot, and although Scotland had long been the most common source of men for the northern fur trade, this was (so it was then assumed) because Scots were already, in a sense, closer to the wild, men who hunted not for sport but for sustenance and who thus quite naturally did well in a savage country. Never mind that the University of Edinburgh had long been the premiere school of medicine in Britain, or that it had its own department of literature a century before Oxford or Cambridge let go their belief that anything more recent than Horace was unworthy of academic study. Even the "Scottish doctor" was, in the popular mind, a type, a familiar character in the world of light comic fiction but hardly to be taken seriously when set beside a well-trained, uniformed English naval officer. Of course, quite a few Scots distinguished themselves in the Royal Navy, but somehow they never quite escaped the popular double standard, as with the pillorying of John Ross after his Arctic expedition of 1818, during which he had the nerve to be both cautious and successful.

Rae, too, possessed both those qualities. In his surveying trips, he travelled by dog-drawn sledge, Inuit-style, in the company of native guides and translators. A skilled hunter, he readily adapted to the Arctic, where fresh meat is the main, and often the only, source of food. And, unlike naval explorers, who tended to regard the Inuit as a dirty, uncivilized, and unreliable race, Rae came to respect and admire them, and counted many among them as his personal friends. His estimate of their character was not naive – he knew that, when a food cache was at stake, an Inuk might well be deceptive or, out of a sense of politeness, reluctant to pass along any news that he imagined might disappoint or anger the hearer. He knew, too, their generosity in times of plenty, and their willingness, in times of want, to do everything necessary to ensure the survival of the community, even at the sacrifice of the individual. His was, in short, not a romanticized view, but one borne of long and direct experience, the sort of which was rarely obtained by naval officers, who tended to remain in the fortresses of their oak-clad vessels.

All this might not have mattered had Rae not had the misfortune to be the bearer of bad news, even as his discoveries comprised the first substantial evidence of the fate of Franklin's men. He himself was deeply sympathetic to their plight and powerfully moved by the sadness and simplicity of the accounts he heard; it was not for him to judge. If we read his initial report, so vilified by many at the time, we can perhaps see what they did not: its directness, its simplicity, and its sense of compassion:

We were now joined by another one of the Natives who had been absent seal hunting yesterday, but being anxious to see us, visited our snow house early this morning, and then followed up our track. This man was very communicative, and on putting to him the usual questions as to having seen "white men" before, or any ships or boats – he replied in the negative; but said, that a party of "Kabloonas" had died of starvation, a long distance to the west of where we then were, and beyond a large River; – He stated that, he did not know the exact place; that he had never been there; and that he could not accompany us so far.

The substance of the information then and subsequently obtained from various sources, was the following effect: In the spring, four winters past [1850], whilst some Esquimaux families were killing Seals near the shore of a large Island named in Arrowsmith's Charts, King William's Land, about forty white men were seen traveling in company, traveling southward over the ice and dragging a boat and sledges with them ... None of the party could speak the Esquimaux language so well as to be understood, but by signs the Natives were led to believe that the Ship, or Ships, had been crushed by the ice, and that they were now going to where they expected to find deer to shoot. From the appearance of the Men (all of whom, with the exception of one officer, were hauling on the drag ropes of the sledge and were looking thin) – they were then supposed to be getting short of provisions, and they purchased a small Seal or piece of Seal from the natives. The Officer was described as being a tall, stout, middle-aged man; when their day's journey terminated, they pitched Tents to rest in.

At a later date the same season, but previous to the disruption of the ice, the bodies of some thirty persons and some Graves were discovered on the continent, and five dead bodies on an Island near it, about a long day's journey to the north-west of a large stream, which can be no other than Great Fish River (named by the Esquimaux Ool-koo-i-hi-ca-lik), as its description and that of the low shore in the neighbourhood of Point Ogle and Montreal Island agree exactly with that of Sir George Back. Some of the bodies had been buried (probably those of the first victims of famine); some were in a tent or tents;

others under the boat, which had been turned over to form a shelter, and several lay scattered about in different directions. Of those found on the Island one was supposed to have been an Officer, as he had a telescope strapped over his shoulders and his double-barrel gun lay beneath him.

From the mutilated state of many of the bodies and the contents of the kettles, it is evident that our wretched Countrymen had been driven to the last dread alternative – cannibalism – as a means of pro-longing existence. A few of the unfortunate Men must have survived until the arrival of wildfowl, (say, until the end of May), as shots were heard, and fresh bones and feathers of geese were noticed near the sad event.

Here we have one of the very earliest instances of published Inuit testi-mony, and in Rae's recounting it bears all the usual marks of such accounts: the speaker (In-nook-poo-zhee-jook) makes it clear that he himself was not a witness to the events described but only relaying stories he had heard (which speaks to his honesty, although Lady Franklin and others cast as-persions on his testimony as merely second-hand). Two encounters are de-scribed: one with a large party of living men, dragging sledges behind them and sleeping in tents, who looked to be emaciated and in poor health, and a second with the bodies of dead men scattered around a camp in this vicin-ity. The exact cause of their demise was unclear. While it appeared that they were amply provided with guns and ammunition, they had been unable to sustain themselves and so had turned to cannibalism.

From his informants, Rae collected the physical relics that attested to their accounts, and made it clear that these "Kabloonas" were indeed Franklin's men. Aside from the spoons and forks – which Rae, the first to receive such items, carefully catalogued – there was Sir John's own medal of knighthood, as well as a small silver oval plate engraved with his name, apparently taken from the butt of a pistol which had been given to him as a gift; other names were not engraved, but carved or scratched, such as the name on the handle of a knife (actually a modified surgeon's scalpel) carved by one (Cornelius) Hickey, a caulker's mate aboard HMS *Terror*. British industry – in the form of a steel blade manufactured by R. Timmons and Sons – had been flattened into an *ulu* or "woman's knife"; gun barrels had similarly been beaten down into spearheads and other implements. A gold hatband from an officer's cap had been worn as an ornament on In-nook-poo-zhee-jook's parka, and the dial plate of a naval chronometer, its mech-anism, case, and hands long gone, spoke mutely of the loss of time, and place, and utility.

In a perverse twist, even as Rae himself returned to England to endure at-tacks in the press and Dickensian diatribes, the relics he brought were revered as though they had been the last remains of a ship-full of saints. In-deed, they were universally referred to as "relics," and when put on display in the Painted Hall of the Royal Naval Hospital at Greenwich, they were vis-ited by long lines of the curious, seeking to find some sense of closure, some sense of truth, and (most of all) a physical sign of the terrible sacrifice made by Franklin and his men. Rae thus became the origin both of the fracturing of the Franklin myth and of the inevitable beatification of him and his men. And perhaps, in a way, both were ultimately versions of the same thing; to us today, cannibalism – though still disturbing – does not necessarily de-tract from the view of Franklin as hero. It may even amplify it. As recently as 1891, when these same relics were part of the iceberg-shaped Arctic pavil-ion at the Royal Naval Exhibition, they still exerted their magnetic force, and in illustrated plates and photographs they still do.

But what of Rae himself? He was accused of accepting second-hand ev-idence from a savage people, a race with "a domesticity of blood and blub-ber" (in Dickens's words). Beyond this, many faulted him for not going farther to try to reach the place described by the Inuit; ignoring Rae's ex-planation that the season was too advanced for such a long sledge journey, they blamed him for failing to corroborate the evidence he discovered. And, when it came to the £10,000 reward, he was blamed for claiming it; many suggested that it was the reason he had hurried back to England, instead of pressing on and searching for the site of Franklin's demise. Rae, as best he could, stood by his account and sought to duck the slings and arrows, but it proved to be a losing battle. His employers, the HBC, withheld his salary on the basis of the reward, deaf to letters in which he emphasized that he had indeed performed the expected work and that the pay due for his serv-ices was unrelated to any government bounty. The reward money itself seemed cursed; with some of it, Rae bought a small boat with which he hoped to continue his travels – but then the boat caught fire and sank at its mooring. Other "Arctic men" scorned his company, and he was left to piece together a living from the fragments of what had been, surveying routes for Arctic telegraph lines, in which capacity he once again briefly worked for his old employers, the HBC.

At his death in 1893, Rae was interred in the churchyard of St Magnus Cathedral in Kirkwall, and an elaborate full-length sculpted memorial was erected in the sanctuary. Many recalled his role in the Franklin search; in the *Journal of the American Geographical Society* his career was recounted with warm praise and his discovery of the fate of Franklin noted as a highlight of his career – but no mention was made of the "last resource." It concluded as follows: "His written contributions, though they testify to his thoroughness and accuracy and to his rare qualifications, bear no proportion to the magnitude and the solidity of his work. He wrote with simplicity and force, but he was more concerned to do things worthy of record than to record them. He had the gifts of the born explorer, the habit of exact observation, courage and fertility of resource, untiring energy, activity and strength; and with these a firmness and generosity of character that won the respect and the affection of men." His death inspired few such encomiums in Britain, where Rae's account had long previous been brushed off the coat of Franklin's heroic figure like an irksome bit of lint. His time, though, would come again.

✛✛✛✛

The first sign of Rae's rehabilitation came with Pierre Berton's landmark book *The Arctic Grail*, which was the starting point for many people's interest in the Franklin story, both in Canada and internationally. Berton was the first major historian to espouse the view, which has since become predominant, that Franklin failed in large part because of his ignorance of native Inuit skills for survival. Many since then have taken issue with this argument, but its main points are certainly worth recalling for they continue to play out in public reactions to the Parks Canada 2014 find. It's strange to see how many of the old stereotypes – the savage ("noble" or notorious), the explorer (noble, of course, but possibly a cultural ignoramus), the hubris of the British Empire (undeniable – but, of course, the hubris of the victor is quite different from that of the defeated) – have taken on new currency. Some now regard the struggle of Inuit today as that of a colonized people against the oppression and stereotypes of their former colonizers, a perspective that casts figures such as Franklin in an uncertain light. After all, he came not to conquer but to explore, and – at least until much later, in the latter half of the twentieth century – the sort of economic *exploitation* that usually followed acts of *exploration* in more temperate zones had been absent in the north.

Berton made several arguments in this regard. First, Franklin had failed by not recognizing the success of the Inuit way of living in a harsh environment, hunting both land and sea mammals in season, clothing themselves in furs whose insulating properties were vastly superior to European dress, and travelling by means of dog-drawn sledges (a method scorned by the British at least through the era of Scott). In this regard, though mistaken, Franklin was no more or less wrong than most of his day; his failure thus was not of a man but of a worldview. Then there was a second, closely related argument: because Franklin's men made no attempt to communicate with the Inuit, or seek their help, their own pride and cultural myopia made a bad situation worse. It's not entirely accurate – the expedition was in fact supplied with Inuit phrase books (albeit of a far more easterly dialect), and its sailing orders implored them to contact the "Esquimaux" whenever possible – but certainly the overall attitude toward the Inuit was not one of admiration but of condescension.

Seen through this lens, Rae suddenly seemed a far more admirable figure than Franklin himself: he was a friend to the Inuit, adopted their ways, and travelled in their company. There was, to be sure, the prickly detail that the Hudson's Bay *Company* existed to make a profit by trading in furs, unquestionably a capitalistic venture – but Rae's role as a surveyor kept him at arm's length from this side of the business. Rae passed the test of the postcolonial critique of European attitudes toward the Inuit; his having "gone native," though distasteful to middle-class Victorian values, was now his greatest asset. And it was then that Ken McGoogan, an aspiring young writer with a fellowship in post-colonial theory that took him to Cambridge University, decided that a book about Rae – originally meant to be a novel, but eventually evolving into a history – would be his next project. McGoogan's "eureka" moment, by his own account, was the realization that the "Rae Strait" to the east of King William Island was the route via which Amundsen finally sailed the Northwest Passage; the man who mapped this route, he reasoned, was its true discoverer.

In making this conclusion, however, McGoogan opened up the question of the discovery of the Passage to a number of other issues. What of the Victorian view that, since Franklin's men certainly reached Cape Walker, which connected their journey with Dease and Simpson's survey, they had "forged the last link with their lives"? What of the parliamentary view that Robert McClure, who traversed the Passage from west to east, albeit on two different ships and in part on foot, was entitled to be called the Passage's discoverer? Did a discovery only count if people lived to tell of it? Did the Passage have to be traversed in a ship? Did it have to be "navigable," and if so by what sort of ship? One thing was clear at the outset; had Franklin ignored his charts and ventured in the direction of the Rae Strait, his large vessels would almost certainly have run aground.

The problem was one of scale. The Admiralty reasoned that large ships, strongly fortified, and fully manned and equipped, would have the best chance at getting through the Passage. Yet such ships, which drew as much as fourteen feet of water and required considerable room to execute turns or other manoeuvres, were far from ideal when it came to the shallow, twisty, waters that connect to Rae Strait. The Strait itself is navigable, with care – but the route also involves the James Ross Strait and Simpson Strait, which are strewn with shoals and hazards, imperfectly charted even today. Indeed, in 1996, the *Hanseatic*, a ship with a draft only slightly greater than Franklin's, ran aground in the Simpson Strait and was stranded there for three weeks. Even Amundsen's own ship, the tiny fishing trawler *Gjøa*, which drew no more than ten feet when fully loaded, had to jettison a considerable amount of deck cargo to avoid running aground on this route.

Among today's Arctic navigators, Captain Patrick R.M. Toomey is one of the most experienced at piloting large ships through the Arctic. It's his view that Franklin's ships would have had enormous difficulty passing this way, and that even if Franklin had mapped the eastern route – which he believes he would have accomplished during his time there – he would have rejected it:

I would suggest that Franklin suspected there might be several routes to the north from Queen Maud Gulf – the south shore of which he had mapped – but that he was more interested in the wider channel to the west of King William Island, due north of his explorations along the coast east of Coppermine River. With two clumsy Royal Navy warships hardly capable of sailing to windward, with auxiliary steam power insufficient to make any progress in ice, for lack of power and sufficient coal to fuel the boilers, he would certainly have tried a wider channel to offer more sea-room. The full facts will never be known, of course, but I am sure that shore parties went out to King William Island while the ships were beset during the winter of 1846/7, to check out any channels to the east. I am equally sure that the report back would have been that such channels would not have been recommended, despite the lack of old ice, which is not usually found in those channels, because of the lack of sea-room to manoeuvre between the shoals, especially those of James Ross Strait. It was in James Ross Strait, I believe, that Amundsen had his problems, and he was in a tiny little vessel, of much less draft, and much more manoeuvrable when compared to *Erebus* and *Terror*.

This, of course, only establishes that Rae's route would probably not have been navigable for Franklin – a conclusion that not everyone may accept – but if we allow "navigable" to simply mean "navigable in theory by someone," then it might seem that the Rae Strait could be thought of as the fabled "last link."

But there's another, more fundamental problem: at the time when Rae surveyed the strait that bears his name, there still remained a substantial segment of that particular route which was yet uncharted and unsailed. As William Barr, one of the pre-eminent polar historians working today, puts it:

Maps showing the unexplored section of the Passage may be found in McGoogan (2001:256) and in Williams (2009:175). Rae himself was well aware that this section of the Passage was still unexplored in 1854. In a review of Captain Albert Markham's book "Sir John Franklin's life" in the *Journal of the American Geographical Society* Rae wrote: "Thus nearly 800 miles of the 1000 left unexplored in 1839 [i.e. following Dease and Simpson's explorations] ... were completed by me, but there still remained about 200 miles, between Bellot Strait and the Magnetic Pole on the west shore of Boothia, a blank on the charts, and these were explored by McClintock in his memorable journey [in 1859] ..." Although Rae has somewhat exaggerated the length of the unexplored section, this is irrefutable evidence of the fact that he was well aware that his discovery of Rae Strait did not represent the "final link" in the Northwest Passage.

McGoogan has not, however, altered his view. From his perspective, the fact that the Rae Strait represents the route that Franklin, at the moment of his great decision, *should* have taken but did not, still makes it the vital, final link. He thus attaches great importance to Franklin's sailing of the first part of the route, although he does not credit him with the later achievement of connecting with earlier surveys at Cape Walker (this on the argument that a discovery must be reported home in order to count). It's a tangled web, one that has since then ensnared quite a few people, and brought about perhaps one of the most curious episodes yet in the public regard for both Franklin and Rae. For, in Scotland, and in particular in Orkney, McGoogan's belief in Rae's accomplishment has fired up considerable feeling, leading the local MP, Alistair Carmichael, in 2009 to introduce a motion for Parliament to state formally that it "regrets that memorials to Sir John Franklin outside the Admiralty headquarters and inside Westminster Abbey still inaccurately describe Franklin as the first to discover the passage, and calls on the Ministry of Defence and the Abbey authorities to take the necessary steps to clarify the true position."

Some press reports from this time seemed to suggest that Carmichael actively wanted the Franklin memorial removed, though if that was his position, he eventually softened it to simply a request that a memorial to Rae be added near Franklin's. In 2013 he approached me to see whether I would write a letter to the dean of Westminster, the Very Reverend Dr John R. Hall, supporting his request for a memorial plaque, a request to which – once I had his assurances that Franklin's cenotaph would not be wheeled out a side door – I gladly agreed. The letter, with other supporting materials, apparently proved persuasive, and after winding its way through various committees, the proposal was approved in the summer of 2014. There was only one final question remaining, and – as with most that are left to the last minute, it was a thorny one – how exactly would the wording on the plaque read?

Carmichael almost certainly had wanted something which would credit Rae as the "true" discoverer of the Passage, and this much was realized when news of the plaque's approval first made the papers that summer. This alarmed a number of polar historians, Barr among them. He faced a great hurdle, though, in that he had no way to communicate directly with the dean, and his e-mails to the Abbey's general address had gone unanswered. He got in touch with the Arctic historian Glyn Williams, who in turn phoned Ann Savours, whose *The Search for the Northwest Passage* is a standard work in the field. Through her contacts, Savours was able to obtain a phone number for the dean, and she communicated her concerns to his secretary, following up with a copy of Barr's e-mail. The dean, who surely had not arrived at his position by being undiplomatic, quickly agreed to change the inscription to read simply "John Rae, Arctic Explorer." Interviewed by the BBC at the time of the stone's installation, he declined to make any comment on Rae's claim but spoke warmly of the monument as embodying "the spirit of reconciliation." For indeed, as Barr himself observed, Rae was now appropriately honoured, with "no false attempts at enhancing his already admirable reputation."

Such are the vagaries of Arctic fame. In the case of the Northwest Passage – or more properly, as I've said, "Passages" – there are any number of claimants, depending on how one defines the achievement. The way we value them says something about our times, as much as the mid-Victorian public's admiration for Franklin says about theirs. And perhaps nothing says more about the indeterminate nature of fame than John Walker's *Passage*, possibly the most curious film ever to tackle the theme of Arctic exploration. In part because of limited funds, in part to make the production of the film part of its own exposition, *Passage* intermingles drama and documentary, managing to champion Rae while at the same time painting a remarkably modern, compelling, and sympathetic portrait of Lady Franklin. And quite beyond the period scenes, which are sprinkled through the film like little glass windows into the past, we also glimpse a conflicted present, one in which such antipodal figures as Inuit politician Tagak Curley – who holds that Franklin deserves no credit for finding any passage – and naval historian Ernie Coleman, who clings to the Victorian belief that hostile natives, rather than cannibalistic comrades, were the cause of Franklin's demise, fight a quite literal war of words.

Walker's film opens with Rick Roberts, the gifted young actor who plays Rae, walking through London in the present day. In the background, we can see such cultural landmarks as St Paul's Cathedral and Trafalgar Square, along with London traffic and bustling pedestrians. Then, as Roberts enters the Admiralty building and goes to ascend its winding stair, we are in for a surprise: the moment he opens the door to the boardroom, he steps out of the present and into the perils and politics of 1854. Confronted by several of the members of the legendary "Arctic Council," Rae defends the Inuit testimony he has brought back eloquently enough that, for a time, it seems that he has acquitted himself fully. But, soon after, in an almost unbearably tense interview with Lady Franklin – memorably portrayed by Geraldine Alexander – he finds himself most severely dressed down. One can only imagine how either figure can carry on, and yet at just this moment we are jarred back to the present, with the actors – some in, some out of costume – are shown sitting around a table, discussing the historical background of the film and debating the reasons for the reaction against Rae.

The alternating structure, between beautifully sketched historical re-enactments and oddly awkward moments out of costume, continues throughout the film. At one point, a meeting – one that did not likely ever take place but is wonderfully imagined – between Lady Franklin, Charles Dickens, and Dr John Richardson, is shown. As introductions are made and tea is offered, we're shocked to realize that Richardson has never even *heard* of Dickens; Jane must explain that he's "internationally known"! Dickens, for his part, confesses himself "rather strong on voyages and cannibalism" (an almost direct quote from one of his letters), at which Richardson finds himself stunned. Hoping to rescue the meeting, Jane suggests "more tea, Mr Dickens?" – while Richardson, nodding over his cup, remarks "A writer! Is there a living to be made in that?" – to which Dickens (Guy Oliver-Watts in a brilliant turn) replies, "A precarious one." It's worth noting in passing that the *Dictionary of National Biography*, which always gives a person's "wealth at death," estimates Richardson's as less than £7,000 while Dickens's stood at £80,000 – precarious indeed.

Things begin to heat up, when, in one of the returns to the present, we meet Tagak Curley, a familiar figure in Nunavut. As one of the founders and the first president of the Inuit Tapirisat of Canada, he's sometimes referred to as a "founding father" of Nunavut; he's also an outspoken evangelical Christian whose campaign slogan at one time was "Jesus Is Lord over Nunavut." Taken by Walker to the Franklin memorial at Waterloo Place, Curley laughs at the claim that his men "forged the last link with their lives" – declaring that "dead men can't discover anything!" It's lost on Curley that the reason that those who find this claim credible do so because of Inuit testimony, but we soon realize that he's there not as a historian but rather as a sort of unofficial representative of all Inuit, as well as a ready supporter of McGoogan's claims about Franklin and Rae. Curley's unfamiliarity with modern London, and modern ways, is played up; it seems that's he's to be the good, simple Inuk elder, wandering the deceit-ridden modern city.

The situation reaches a boiling point when Curley reaches the Admiralty boardroom; after Walker explains how the rooftop weathervane displays the wind direction on a large dial over the mantelpiece, he's introduced to Ernie Coleman. Coleman, a navy veteran and amateur naval historian who's made several treks to King William Island, is one of the last individuals (perhaps the only one) to hold to the notion that Franklin's men were set upon by hostile Inuit. As Curley takes his seat, Coleman recites a lengthy diatribe in which he attributes the cut-marks – particularly those on the hands and fingers – to defensive wounds, and the breakage of skulls and long bones as post-mortem mutilation, citing an unspecified medieval battle in Yorkshire as showing similar cut-marks. He concludes by stating that "I believe that Franklin's people were attacked by the natives, and not only that, that they were mutilated afterwards ... so there's no evidence of cannibalism, but plenty of evidence that they were attacked."

Curley minces no words in his reply:

> I think it's shameful ... shameful, arrogant, to label people that you don't know as conspirators who murdered and conspired to take advantage of weak people. I think that's a very strong accusation. And I really truly believe you don't have any evidence, with what you're relying upon. You're relying on second-, third, and fourth-hand information. Charles Dickens didn't have any facts, he'd never been up to that part of the area. And yet he indicted the Inuit race. He created an animosity to people who were innocently standing by, waiting to help people that might be dying ... so for you to accuse my people, someone oughta apologize.

Walker allows the animosity to hang in the air, then cuts to the scene with Dickens, Richardson, and Lady Franklin, a shift made the odder since the actor Alistair Findlay, who plays Richardson, had just been sitting at the table, in full costume, next to Coleman. Such juxtapositions, whether intended or not, jangle our sense of time, giving the impression that we're still repeating the debates of 150 years ago. In reality, of course, only Coleman still believes in Dickens's account, but he's a straight-faced proxy for the past, and as such makes a perfect foil for Curley's own outrage. In a later segment, he even quotes a line about how explorers mustn't "avoid the hazards of the game by the vulgar subterfuge of going native," a remark that provokes astonishment around the table.

All this, though, turns out to be a sort of set-up for a further, and final, contemporary scene, one in which, wizard-like, Walker waves his hand and in walks Gerald Dickens, the author's great-grandson, with a more than passing resemblance to his famous ancestor. Unlike Coleman, he listens patiently to Tagak Curley plead his case, which he does at some length:

It's really important that I introduce myself to you; I'm one of those savages your grandfather wrote about ... I believe this was a time when this nation had to unite together; it had a national disaster at its hand ... instead everybody, including Jane, Lady Franklin, and your grandfather, were so out to destroy the character of a very important people, including my race, who are known, worldwide, as most innocent people of the whole earth. But that character assassination that your grandfather did, to call us murderers ... who would creep up upon the weakest of the white people and ambush them. He was so out to write an article that was cruel and false – and yet no one, no Englishman, has ever taken responsibility to say "I'm sorry" ... this still has an impact on my people, because no person in this room wants to take any sense of ownership and try to establish reconciliation. I really believe it is important, though. We could have helped you! Instead you destroyed any ability to work with you. Why do you think that happened?

And now Gerald Dickens finally addresses his Inuk accuser, with a remarkable degree of tact and directness:

I have absolutely no idea. I know it doesn't make any difference to history, but on behalf of my family, I certainly apologize for what Charles wrote, which was ... astounding in its vindictiveness. And the only thing I can think, because again it was very out of character ... and I just think it's very easy for him, in a London study, a London office, to take a pen and write, make these accusations, it ties in with public opinion, it's an easy way of selling magazines ... but to actually understand what effect it was going to have, on an entire race, an entire people, I don't think he could possibly have stopped to think about it; it would be completely out of character for him to do that, completely. I mean, he spent his entire career in England championing the causes of those that were fighting, those who were being downtrodden by the country, the government, by the ruling classes. And that's why I was so surprised when you first put me on to the *Household Words* article.

This electrifies the room, and the camera watches the expression on Curley's face intently, such that we can hardly bear to wait for his reply:

> Gerard [sic], you apologized to me and for my people about what your grandfather had written about us. This apology is very important, and I accept in on behalf of my people, for the people of Nunavut. It is more than I asked for when I came here … I was hoping something eventually would happen here, and so, on behalf of the Inuit people, particularly Netsilik people, who were impacted, as well as my tribe, Aivilik tribe, who were primarily John Rae's guides, I accept your apology and I want you to know you are a friend, and welcome to come to Nunavut any time.

The resultant applause, and the cutting of the tension around the table – from which, notably, Ernie Coleman is absent – has the effect of somehow seeming to ameliorate the original wound, to resolve the debate not just between Dickens and Rae but between Dickens and the Inuit. The extent to which great-grandsons can "represent" their ancestors, individually or collectively, is forgotten in the flourish of mutual relief and jocularity. In one sense, this does a sort of double justice to the wounds of past and present, but it's accomplished by subtle substitution worthy of an operator of any ball-and-cup or three-card monte game: now you see it, now you don't. None of this will really affect the people of Nunavut, nor does it seem likely that anyone present will take up Curley's invitation. Dickens's descendant, in the end, has it right: it *doesn't* make any difference to history but it does make an enormous difference in the modern drama in which Rae – now more than ever – has come to embody a powerful counter-narrative to the myth of the heroic Franklin.

TOOKOOLITO, CHARLES F. HALL, AND EBIERBING.

Figure 15 Tookoolito, Charles Francis Hall, and Ebierbing,
from *Harper's Monthly*. Collection of the author.

7

Hall

I've come to think of it as almost a kind of virus. The essential facts of the Franklin saga – his ships, his faithful wife, his "gallant" crew – meet up with the harsh malevolence of icy seas; the men are tested, again and again, and despite it all, they fall short. The paucity of physical evidence has an effect – and so the absence of the ships (until 2014), or of Franklin's grave, or any logbooks or records completes the process. It remains to be seen whether the discovery of HMS *Erebus* will make the infection more or less contagious – I suspect the former. In either case, once infected, it seems there is no cure. As with many seemingly small silences in history, the Franklin bug has been particularly catching among those whose interest is of an amateur nature, in the very best sense of that word – people who, though they lack archaeological training and perhaps have never been to the Arctic, have found the allure of the Franklin mystery impossible to resist. Although naval historians, archaeologists, and anthropologists have made their contributions to solving the Franklin mystery, a great deal of the most important research and fieldwork has been done by these dedicated, often almost obsessive, amateurs.

Charles Francis Hall was the first, and perhaps the unlikeliest, of these. His case shows no clear single cause of contagion. Unlike other Franklin searchers, he had never served in the navy or merchant marine of any nation, nor did he have any family or local connections with whaling, fishing, shipbuilding, or any other nautical trade. So far as we know, he had never travelled outside the eastern United States. Although he published a small newspaper in Cincinnati, it would be a bit of a stretch to call him a "journalist," and while for a time he had a business making engraved seals for business use, he himself was not a particularly skilled engraver. Never apparently much of a family man, he more or less abandoned his wife and children when he first set off for the Arctic, and they were rarely the subject of his letters and journals. Indeed, had it not been for the singular leap he made out of the ordinary course of commerce and middle-class life, he might very well have never made much of a mark in any of his endeavours. Hall's destiny was to do *one* thing, and to do it with faith and fury and a determination that bordered on the monomaniacal. In so doing, he revealed himself to be a deeply humane individual, unique in some ways and typical of his time in others.

Hall was born, by most accounts, in 1821 in Rochester, New Hampshire. The details of his early life may never be known, for his name does not appear in any surviving records until his arrival in Cincinnati in 1849. There, he established himself in business, eventually carving out a niche in the competitive trade in engraving seals and stamps. Like many men of his day, Hall was drawn to every new process and technology; he attempted to patent various improvements to his die and stamp products, and claimed to print his newspaper – the Cincinnati *Occasional* – on a press powered by a "Thermionic Engine," a machine that supposedly surpassed the laws of conservation of energy and thermodynamics by generating more energy than it used. Of course, it didn't, and couldn't have, but that fact did nothing to diminish its allure for Hall, and presumably the same was true of most of his subscribers.

At some point during his years in Cincinnati, Hall became deeply interested in the search for Sir John Franklin's expedition. It appears to have been the involvement of Dr Elisha Kent Kane, an American naval surgeon and adventurer, in the Franklin search that first piqued Hall's interest. A strong patriotic fervour was one of the marks of Hall's character, accompanied by an equally powerful religious feeling; to Hall, the sacrifices endured by Kane on his first and second expeditions showed both a "sacred" commitment to helping one's fellow man and the strength of American national character. When Kane, whose chronic heart condition was aggravated by the hardships of his Arctic ventures, died in Havana in 1857, the nation – and Hall with it – was swept into an outpouring of grief and national feeling unlike anything in living memory. Kane's funeral train was greeted at every town and city along its route – including Cincinnati – by legions of civic officials and local memorial societies, attired in mourning and wearing specially made armbands and badges recalling Kane's exploits. While there's no specific indication that Hall participated in these obsequies, his fascination with the Arctic in general, and the Franklin expedition in particular, was first noted around this time.

Hall began by undertaking an intensive course of reading the narratives of Arctic explorers; he also started keeping a series of journals and clipping books into which he copied all manner of advice about cold-weather gear, provisions, scientific instruments, and cases of survival in the north over long periods. Many of these notes were in turn used as the basis of items in his own newspaper, where he wrote of the efforts of Sir John Franklin's widow, the endlessly hopeful Jane, to send yet one more expedition in search of her long-lost husband. Some American explorers, among them Isaac I. Hayes, who had sailed with Kane, opined that there might still be hope that at least a few small groups of Franklin's men might yet be alive and living with the "Esquimaux." At some point, Hall decided that it was a matter of national and sacred duty that someone undertake a fresh search for Franklin's men – and that someone was *him*.

With his characteristic blend of bravado and naivety, Hall began his preparations by camping out in the October cold, erecting a tent on Avery Hill behind the Cincinnati Observatory. His attempt to simulate the cold conditions of his planned expedition came to an unruly end when he was accosted by a group of local Irish roughnecks; as one local paper described it:

ESQUIMAUX IN CINCINNATI. – Mr. C.F. Hall, of this city, has for many years been acquiring information in reference to the Arctic regions, and qualifying himself to visit the scenes made sacred by the sad fate of Sir John Franklin. Recent occurrences have caused him to make special preparations to join the expedition proposed to be made there next Spring. Latterly he has, to inure himself to fatigue, had a tent and equipage in simple style prepared, and with candle, books, and bottle of water, pitched his tent on Avery's Hill, in the rear of the Observatory. Last night he met with quite an adventure.

About eleven o'clock his tent was visited by two Irishmen, one of them, or both, perhaps, armed with a shot-gun, who demanded admission, and something to drink, and on refusal shot at the retiring enthusiast, who having donned his pants, in shirt-sleeves and bare feet made his escape in "Flora Temple" time to the city, not without the tent being often fired into. A man named Harrigan, driving his calves to market, was hailed by Hall, and the novitiate was brought home in his ludicrous condition. He returned at a late hour with a posse of police to review the scene of the hostilities.

We have not learned what is the result of their discoveries, but we are pretty sure Mr. Hall considers that he would not have been worse-served by the Esquimaux. Star-gazing is a novelty to our Milesian friends of the shot-gun. Mr. Hall must, by this time, have got over the hallucination of Hill-top midnight observations.

Such a farce might have proved an embarrassment (at least) or a defeat (at worst) for a lesser man; for Hall, it was merely a slight diversion from his unswerving purpose. The winter, ideal as it was for outdoor conditioning, was not a propitious time for sailing north, but perfect for heading east. Hall departed for New York in January 1860, hoping to manage a meeting with Henry Grinnell, the wealthy businessman who had funded both of the expeditions in which Kane had served.

In between Hall's outdoor fiasco and his departure, news had reached the world of the return of Leopold McClintock, who, with his lieutenant W.R. Hobson, had discovered the "last sad remains" of the main group of the Franklin expedition, among them skeletons, discarded instruments and provisions, and the "Victory Point" record which documented the increasing desperation of the commanders as they abandoned their ships in April 1848 – more than a decade before the note was to be recovered. Among most who had followed the Franklin drama, this was regarded as the final part of their story, and the idea that any might yet be alive so many years later was seen as a foolish and forlorn hope. A few dogged believers speculated that Franklin's men might have survived by living among the Esquimaux – an *idée fixe* to which Hall had long clung – but for nearly all the newspapers and public officials, this was a clear sign that any further searches would be both needless and foolhardy.

One might have expected that Grinnell, a thoughtful, eminently practical man, a friend of Lady Franklin's who knew all too well the import of McClintock's discoveries, would have sent Hall back home with a gentle remonstrance for such grandiose and belated plans, but beyond all expectations – even those of the pathologically optimistic Hall – Grinnell endorsed his idea, thus winning Hall's enduring loyalty as well as a sobriquet

– "*Friend* Grinnell" – which Hall in his journal reserved for his profoundest supporters. Grinnell was more modest, however, when it came to financial support, though he did introduce Hall to a number of his wealthy and influential friends, some of whom came forward with offers of funds or items for use on his expedition. Hall set about locating a ship suitable for his plans and at one point believed he had the commitments to secure one of his hero Kane's former ships – but here, his luck ran out. The purchase fell through, and he found himself both ship-less and nearly penniless as the season for departure drew near.

Yet, as things turned out, this disappointment became a saving grace. Sidney O. Budington, a whaling captain Hall had met through Grinnell, offered him passage north aboard his ship the *George Henry*. After all, Hall had most of the equipment he needed, and if there was no ship to be purchased, enough funds remained to fill out his personal Arctic kit. After further consultation with Grinnell convinced him that this far more modest plan was the most that could be hoped for, as well as that Budington was a worthy and reliable man, Hall took the one option remaining to him, sailing from New London aboard the *George Henry* on 20 May 1860 – quite nearly fifteen years to the day since Sir John Franklin had sailed from Greenhithe.

Once he arrived in the Arctic, the modest size and scope of Hall's mission soon proved to be a marked advantage. Without a ship to command – or a ship's crew to maintain – Hall could focus entirely on his mission: to find survivors of Franklin's expedition, primarily by seeking the truth where it had rarely been sought before, among the Inuit. Since the American whaling fleet had taken to deliberate wintering in order to prepare for whaling and returning their cargo south before fall freeze-up, and since they quite frequently employed Inuit as guides, harpooners, and even pilots, Hall was to be ideally situated for his first winter sojourn. The unpredictable ice, however, would first have its say; Budington was unable to steer the *George Henry* into the inland Arctic waters and so was obliged to winter in Cyrus Field Bay off the coast of Baffin Island. Barring a very long sledge journey, Hall would have to content himself with encountering the Inuit of Baffin Island, and learn what he could from them, before venturing to his final goal.

As it happened, the *George Henry*'s winter harbour was fortuitous: it brought Hall into contact with two Inuit, Tookoolito ("Hannah," as the whalers called her) and Ebierbing ("Joe") who were camped nearby that season. These two Inuit had, in fact, courtesy of the wine merchant John Bowlby, had already been to England, where they found themselves exhibited in Hull and London and even taken to Windsor to meet Queen Victoria. Tookoolito's talent for languages enabled her to learn English with a remarkable degree of fluency; later, what she had picked up in England she developed further in conversation with the whalers. Ebierbing, the quieter of the two, could get along tolerably in English but distinguished himself more as a guide and hunter. Hall was introduced to them aboard ship, and though he was quite taken by them both, it was Tookoolito who made the strongest impression; as he noted in his journal, "I could not help admiring the exceeding gracefulness and modesty of her demeanour. Simple and gentle in her way, there was a degree of calm intellectual power about her that more and more astonished me."

Throughout the next decade, Tookoolito and Ebierbing would be Hall's most faithful and trusted companions, accompanying him on numerous sledging expeditions, providing food and shelter, and translating and interpreting at hundreds of interviews with Inuit who had stories to tell about the Franklin expedition. Not only were they tireless and constant in their support for Hall's often very demanding Arctic plans, but they accompanied him on his lecture tours of the United States and permitted him to arrange for their exhibition in New York and Boston to raise funds for further missions. Still more astonishingly, they remained in Hall's service despite the deaths of two of their children while working for him, even though in each case the deaths were at least partly due to Hall's demands – in the first case, for exhibitions and lectures, and in the second, for a difficult sledge journey to King William Island (their second child, indeed, was named "King William" by Hall). Hall could be an imperious master, especially when his "sacred cause" of finding Franklin's men was at stake. Yet not once, during the entire time of their association, did Hannah or Joe waver in their service to this man who, without their assistance, would likely have never earned the title he most coveted – "Charles Hall, Arctic Explorer."

During his initial northern sojourn, Hall was unable to get anywhere near the Franklin sites; he consoled himself by practising his questions about white men and ships on local Inuit. And, as he did, he began to hear puzzling stories of men who had come on a ship and left some of their companions behind "a long time ago." The description of the ships – which carried heavy "stones" that the Inuit could barely lift – and of the small boat made by some men they left behind didn't seem to fit the Franklin expedition. How long, Hall wondered, was "a long time ago"? It turned out to have been a very long time ago indeed; what Hall had heard were stories of Sir Martin Frobisher's third voyage of 1578. The clarity and consistency of these Inuit stories, which matched perfectly with English accounts of Frobisher's time there, convinced Hall of one thing: if Inuit oral tradition could be that accurate over nearly three *centuries*, surely it would be even more so after a mere two decades.

Hall returned triumphant in 1863, touting the Frobisher stories along with a few relics of that expedition that he had brought back, including bricks and iron. Anxious to raise funds for a return north to pursue his Franklin quest, he rented out Tookoolito and Ebierbing to Barnum's Museum, then took them on a lecture tour of the eastern seaboard. Some funds were raised, but the exertion and travel took a toll on Hall's Inuit friends, who had brought their infant son, Tarralikitaq ("butterfly" in Inuktitut) with them. At the end of the tour, Tarralikitaq fell ill and died, and it was all that Hall and his friend Budington could do to prevent the grieving Tookoolito from taking her own life. Her slow recovery from grief further complicated Hall's plans, and the continuing news of the Civil War put any idea of funding another Franklin search quite out of people's minds. In the end, he returned to the Arctic the same way he had first gone there – as a passenger, along with Joe and the now-recovered Hannah.

Despite high hopes and much careful planning, Hall once again fell short of his initial goal; owing to an error by its captain, the whaling ship, the *Monticello,* dropped Hall and his supplies off forty miles south of the planned site, and it would be nearly two years before Hall, through a mixture of cajoling, bullying, and (less often) compromise, was finally able to reach his goal. In part, this was due to conflicts with the whalers and local Inuit, but there was also a further, unanticipated difficulty. Inuit camped in the area around Repulse Bay, among them some of the Inuit whose territory had apparently been nearest the site of Franklin's vessels, spoke in whispers of the threat of a hostile band of Inuit to the west, into whose territory they were most unwilling to travel. This group, possibly a subtribe of the Netsilik Inuit whose strength had been artificially enhanced by items obtained via trade or pilfering from Franklin's expedition, struck such fear into other bands that many had fled to the Repulse Bay area to escape them. Hall met with several members of the Utjulingmiut, whose hunting territory had been in Utjulik on the southeastern shores of Queen Maud Gulf. He was delighted to obtain from them first-hand accounts of what appeared to be encounters with Franklin's men, but the stories they told of the hostile Inuit soon spread throughout Hall's party and had a powerful effect on Joe and Hannah. As Joe, in his only surviving letter, put it: "2 years I stay Houdsons Bay try go King William Land then I give it up, meet 3 men from their tell me give it up make me afraid. Mr. Hall tease me all time. Make me go their never give it up. Next time I go like a soldier every body go so every body carry gun."

Hall, despite his incessant cajoling, was unable to convince Joe to proceed, and without him and Hannah, he was forced to postpone his plans indefinitely. The next season, complete with the guns mentioned by Joe, Hall did at last manage to reach King William Island and stand finally on those very shores where the last survivors of the Franklin expedition had made their final march. It was growing late, though, in the spring sledging season, and he was able to remain for only a few days; the snow hid most of the bodies and the best he could do was to locate a single skeleton. This, after some internal debate, he decided to take with him; the bones (as we've seen) were eventually shipped to Britain, where they were (mis)identified as those of Le Vesconte. His ten years' quest had, it seemed, yielded only this.

✦✦✦✦

He surely must have felt defeated at this point. But Hall's true legacy turned out to be not as an explorer but as a gatherer of tales; his collection of Inuit testimony is by far more extensive, and closer to the dates of the events described, than any other; it forms, indeed, the single most important body of evidence we have. It's true, of course, that as oral testimony, there are bound to be variations, omissions, and even contradictions in parts of this material, vast as it is. But that's no reason not to credit it; whenever it has been possible to compare this testimony with physical evidence, the Inuit accounts have been proven accurate in their essential elements. The most intriguing stories, to be sure, are those that can't yet be corroborated, although, with the discovery of the *Erebus*, there's a new opportunity to do so. There are few stories more compelling than those told about that very ship – which the Inuit visited at a place they called Utjulik – a ghostly vessel which, though it seems to have been manned on its arrival, had been abandoned by the time the Inuit visited it. Even more remarkably, there are even a few stories of visits to the ships prior to this time, and these are perhaps the most intriguing of all.

The most vivid of these tales was told by one Kok-lee-arng-nun, an elderly Inuk who Hall met at Pelly Bay (now Kugaaruk), home of the Arvilig-juarmiut, whose territory adjoined that of the Netsilik. His account deserves quoting in full:

The Pelly Bay men described the Esh-e-mut-ta [leader] as an old man with broad shoulders, thick and heavier set than Hall, with gray hair, full face, and bald head. He was always wearing something over his eyes (spectacles, as Too-koo-li-too interpreted it), was quite lame, and appeared sick when they last saw him. He was very kind to the In-nuits; – always wanting them to eat something. Ag-loo-ka (Crozier) and another man would go and do everything that Too-loo-ark told them, just like boys; he was a very cheerful man, always laughing; everybody liked him – all the kob-lu-nas and all the Innuits. Kok-lee-arng-nun showed how Too-loo-ark and Ag-loo-ka used to meet him. They would take hold of his hand, giving it a few warm and friendly shakes, and Too-loo-ark would say, "Ma-my-too-mig-tey-ma." Ag-loo-ka's hand-shaking was short and jerky, and he would only say, "Man-nig-too-me." After the first summer and first winter, they saw no more of Too-loo-ark; then Ag-loo-ka (Crozier) was the Esh-e-mut-ta. The old man and his wife agreed in saying that the ship on board of which they had often seen Too-loo-ark was overwhelmed with heavy ice in the spring of the year. While the ice was slowly crushing it, the men all worked for their lives in getting out provisions; but, before they could save much, the ice turned the vessel down on its side, crushing the masts and breaking a hole in her bottom and so over-whelming her that she sank at once, and had never been seen again. Several men at work in her could not get out in time, and were carried down with her and drowned … The other ship spoken of as seen near Ook-goo-lik was in complete order, having three masts and four boats hanging at the davits – whale-ship like. For a long time the In-nuits feared to go on board; but on the report by one of them that he had seen one man on the vessel alive, many of the natives visited it, but saw nothing of the man. They then rummaged everywhere, taking for themselves what they wanted, and throwing overboard guns, powder, ball, and shot.

It's hard to resist the urge to connect this story with the Franklin expedition: Sir John was indeed heavy-set, with a "full face" and a bald head. We know from the Victory Point record that the *Erebus* and *Terror* had been beset off King William since 12 September 1846 – this would have been the "first summer" – and that Sir John Franklin died on 11 June 1847, after the ships' first wintering-over in the area. The Inuit description matches all this perfectly. It's also significant that Franklin – an outgoing and friendly man – was so described by the Inuit. Kok-lee-arng-nun's mentioning that Too-loo-ark would say "Ma-my-too-mig-tey-ma" while Ag-loo-ka (Crozier) would say just "Man-nig-too-me" may also be significant. "Teyma" was a variant of universal greeting among northern peoples and European traders, and Franklin mentioned having used it himself on his earlier, land-based expeditions. "Man-nig-too-me," in contrast, is not a coherent utterance in Inuktitut, although it appears in a number of variant forms ("munnik-toome," "many-tu-me," and even "kammik-toome") in the narratives of other explorers. Still, both Crozier's more curt demeanour and his omission of a word known to have been used by Franklin would seem to support the view that he is the second-in-command in Kok-lee-arng-nun's tale.

Yet there's a problem with this neat fit: if indeed some of the Pelly Bay Inuit had visited both of Franklin's ships as early as 1846, and later seen one sink, how could they have missed finding the vast cache of abandoned materials where Crozier and his men landed in 1848? Not only did they not take any of this material, but the Inuit witnesses agreed they had first heard about it from McClintock and his interpreter Carl Peterson. On this basis, David Woodman has always argued that Kok-lee-arng-nun's must be a reminiscence of later events. One would then have to imagine that both ships were remanned after the 1848 abandonment, and that the two other people mentioned were the Ag-loo-ka and Too-loo-ark of this story. But, if we accept the premise, as Woodman does, that this refers to a later date, then we're faced with other problems: Crozier was not especially short or stout, though he was – to judge by contemporary portraits – bald. A quiet, sometimes brooding man, he seems hardly to merit the description of being friendly and liked by Kabloonas and Inuit alike. Since we know that Crozier was alive at the time of the 1848 abandonment, this then would push back Kok-lee-arng-nun's story to 1849 at least, at which point both the *Erebus* and *Terror* would have been some distance further south due to the slow movement of the pack ice. Ag-loo-ka would then presumably have to be Fitzjames, though everything we know about Fitzjames suggests that he was young, enthusiastic, and energetic, an unlikely candidate for the taciturn handshaker. Still, by the third winter, despair may well have set in, and the moods of the men and their commanders may well have darkened as well.

Another possible interpretation is that this story is a garbled account of the *Victory* expedition of Sir John and James Ross fifteen years before Franklin's. The possibility is supported by the fact that Kok-lee-arng-nun described himself as being a young man when he visited the ships of Too-loo-ark and Ag-loo-ka; by the time Hall met him, he was elderly and had an adult son – a bit on the old side if he was describing events of only twenty years previous. To add to the confusion, these same two names, Too-loo-ark and Ag-loo-ka, had been applied to the Rosses. Indeed, the Inuit used "Aglooka" for a number of explorers, including Dr John Rae; since it means roughly "one who takes long strides" – that is, a *tall* man – it could have described nearly any Kabloona, from the viewpoint of Inuit who typically stood a foot or more shorter than these strangers. As stories passed from one band of Inuit to another, the names sowed more confusion; one group swore that "Ag-loo-ka" was alive and well when last seen, while another declared that they had come upon his dead body at an earlier time.

There's one other piece of evidence that would seem nearly incontrovertible: before telling his story, Kok-lee-arng-nun showed Hall two spoons he had been given by the Ag-loo-ka of his story. One of the spoons bore Crozier's family crest and his initials, F.R.M.C., neither of which the old Inuk could possibly have distinguished from any other kind of markings. It might be argued that he obtained them from some site of abandoned materials or dead bodies – but then how, out of the dozens of utensils bearing all kinds of crests and initials that circulated among the Inuit, could he have managed to pick out one belonging to the very man from whom he claimed to have received it?

I've come to believe that this is simply what Inuit historian Louie Kamookak calls a "mixed" story – one in which elements of both the Ross and Franklin expeditions are commingled. Louie has recorded a number of such stories from elders still living in the 1970s and 1980s, and he tells me that they're not uncommon. The tendency to combine the two expeditions is understandable, since both became notable sources of wealth for nearby Inuit; the Netsilik, during their interactions with the Rosses' *Victory*, had acquired almost fantastical wealth in wood, and particularly metal, a source of these things that was still being talked about when Knud Rasmussen passed through this region nearly a century later. The Utjulik band, for their part, had acquired an equally enviable supply of such materials from the Franklin ship that came to rest near their hunting grounds, although this was cut short abruptly when that ship sank, and they subsequently lost much of their original range to the Netsilik.

This story takes on a different light now that we know this latter vessel was HMS *Erebus*. It lends support to Woodman's view that the Kok-lee-arng-nun tale must, to the extent that it describes the Franklin expedition, refer to events after the initial 1848 abandonment. The sinking of the first ship, the *Terror*, would then have taken place much farther down the western coast of King William Island, as would other events such as the death of Too-loo-ark – who would seem to have had to be Crozier or some other more junior officer on that vessel. The spoons, in this version, would have been given not as tokens of individual identity but as gifts made in the hope that some word would be got out of the situation of the ships, an act that makes even more sense if the event took place after some or all of the officers' silverware had been distributed to the crews.

And so the first part of this story, like some others in the Inuit testimony, turns out to be a piece that doesn't fit perfectly into our presuppositions. Yet its second part, in which Kok-lee-arng-nun told of a ship that had been abandoned to the south near "Oot-goo-lik," is one of the most widely distributed Inuit stories. Hall heard versions of this story from many witnesses, most dramatically from an Utjulik woman named Koo-nik:

> She says that Nuk-kee-the-uk & other Ook-joo-lik Innuits were out sealing when they saw a large ship – all very much afraid but Nuk-keeche-uk who went to the vessel while the others went to their Ig-loo. Nuk-kee-che-uk looked all around and saw nobody & finally *Lik-lee-poonik-kee-look-oo-loo* (stole a very little or few things) & then made for the Ig-loos. Then all the Innuits went to the ship & stole a good deal – broke into a place that was fastened up & there found a very large white man who was dead, very tall man. There was flesh about this dead man, that is, his remains quite perfect – it took 5 men to lift

him. The place smelt very bad. His clothes all on. Found dead on the floor – not in a sleeping place or birth [sic] ... The vessel covered over with see-loon, that is housed in with sails or that material, not boards.

Hall gave additional details of this account in a letter to Grinnell:

The party on getting aboard tried to find out if any one was there, and not seeing or hearing any one, began ransacking the ship. To get into the igloo (cabin), they knocked a hole through because it was locked. They found there a dead man, whose body was very large and heavy, his teeth very long. It took five men to lift this giant Kabloona. He was left where they found him. One place in the ship, where a great many things were found, was very dark; they had to find things there by feeling around. Guns were there and a great many very good buckets and boxes. On my asking if they saw anything to eat on board, the reply was there was meat and tood-noo in cans, the meat fat and like pemmican. The sails, rigging, and boats – everything about the ship – was in complete order.

Stories about this same vessel were told many times over the years and survived with remarkable consistency; a nearly identical account was given by Qaqortingneq, the son of one of the original witnesses, to Rasmussen in 1923:

Far out on the ice they saw something black, a large black mass that could be no animal. They looked more closely and found that it was a great ship. They ran home at once and told their fellow-villagers of it, and next day they all went out to it. They saw nobody, the ship was deserted, and so they made up their minds to plunder it of everything they could get hold of. But none of them had ever met white men, and they had no idea what all the things they saw could be used for ... At first they dared not go down into the ship itself, but soon they became bolder and even ventured into the houses that were under the deck. There they found many dead men lying in their beds. At last they also risked going down into the enormous room in the middle of the ship. It was dark there. But soon they found tools and would make a hole in order to let light in. And the foolish people, not understanding white man's things, hewed a hole just on the water-line so that the water poured in and the ship sank. And it went to the bottom with all the valuable things, of which they barely rescued any.

There are some differences in this version: now we have not one dead man on the ship, but many, and it's the white man's tools they use to cut the hole. Astonishingly, this same story was still being told by Inuit elders as late as the 1990s, a hundred and fifty years after the events described. Perhaps, considering the accuracy of the Baffin Islanders' Frobisher stories after three centuries, we shouldn't be too surprised. By this time, the tale has clearly begun to fade a bit, although the darkness of the ship's interior is vividly recalled. Michael Tiringaneak of Gjoa Haven gave this account, in which a living stranger is found aboard the ship, to Dorothy Eber in 1999:

> There was a man out hunting, who found a ship in the ice. He stayed outside it for a while and nobody seemed to be around. So he went back home and told people what he had found while out camping – a ship that was anchored and frozen in the ice. Three people decided to go over and see it next day … by the time they arrived, it had already gotten dark – so dark they could not see each other. But they decided they'd go inside although it was very dark, and decided that every time they touched each other they'd say "Uvunga" – "it's me!" They went inside and each time they grabbed one another they said "Uvunga" – "it's me! Then somebody grabbed somebody and that person didn't say "Uvunga!" He didn't say a word!

In Tiringaneak's tale, the Inuit try to grab the stranger, but he manages to escape and outrun them. Nevertheless, taken together, these stories of the Utjulik wreck form the single most consistent and enduring of all the Inuit accounts of Franklin's vessels. Some, even today, have criticized the Inuit testimony as unreliable, garbled, inconsistent, or fraught with potential inaccuracies due to hearsay or poor translation. Yet this story, told by eyewitnesses, as well as the descendants of eyewitnesses, has been consistent from the start: a white man's ship, found abandoned not far off an island in the Utjulik region (the northwestern coast of the Adelaide peninsula), with everything in "perfect order," which sank the next season in water shallow enough that the tops of its masts could still be seen. This, we now can say with certainty, is HMS *Erebus*, found exactly where the Inuit said it would be in 2014.

++++

Hall, ever restless, left his notes in no particular order before heading out on his next adventure, an expedition to the North Pole itself. His energy was consumed at first with lobbying the US Congress and President Ulysses Grant for funding, and then – once his expedition was approved – organizing it. Again, of course, Hannah and Joe would go with him, along with the daughter, Panik, whom they had adopted while on Hall's second expedition. This time, he would have no need to hitch a ride on a whaler; his own ship, the *Polaris*, was to be placed under his command, and his crew and supplies furnished by the government of the United States. There was only one slight hitch; although Hall had approached several young American scientists with a view to adding them to the expedition, the Smithsonian – which had been appointed by Congress to select the scientific staff – insisted on engaging German experts. While there was no doubt of their qualifications, the linguistic and cultural barriers between Hall and his shipboard scientists became a source of increasing tension almost the moment the expedition set sail.

Hall, though appointed "Captain," knew little about piloting such a vessel; his old friend Sidney O. Budington had been appointed the ship's master. This, too, was to prove problematic, since Budington was unused to being other than the absolute captain of a private ship; his proclivity for alcohol, which would surely have gone unnoticed on a whaling vessel, also became a contentious issue. All of this might have simply simmered had the ship made only modest progress the first season, or decided to turn back, but here Hall was cursed with good luck: ice conditions were such that he was able to sail easily hundreds of miles farther north than had Kane or Hayes, eventually reaching 82°29′ of latitude, an extraordinary record. The Germans, who had already shown their unwillingness to follow Hall's command and had had to be talked out of quitting by another officer, realized that, at this far northward point, there was no chance of their getting away for at least another season, if not several, with Hall in command.

And so it was that, just as Hall was returning from a successful reconnoiter by sledge, he was offered a cup of coffee, which immediately after drinking he fell ill with severe stomach pains. He, along with Joe and Hannah, believed he had been poisoned, but the ship's doctor, Emil Bessels – one of the Germans – discounted his fears. Hall was "treated" by Bessels for the remainder of his illness, during which he alternated between bouts of hallucinations and moments of lucidity, at one point scrawling "MURDER" on the wall of his cabin. He declared that the Germans had blue vapour coming out of their mouths, and that they were all trying to kill him. Bessels, brushing aside what he declared were groundless fears, continued to dose him with various medicines, and an injection as well, which almost certainly hastened his demise; scarcely two weeks later, he was dead.

Nearly a hundred years afterwards, at the instigation of Arctic historian Chauncey Loomis, Hall's body was exhumed from its simple grave at the place he had named "Thank God Harbour." Samples of hair and fingernails were collected, which under later analysis showed that he had been exposed to very high levels of arsenic during the last two weeks of his life. Although Loomis always hesitated to conclude that Hall was poisoned, there was one key piece of evidence he never knew: Bessels and Hall were both in love with the same woman. The object of their amours was one Vinnie Ream, a talented young artist lauded for her sculptures of Abraham Lincoln. Hall and Bessels had met her together, over dinner, in New York, and Bessels had written an impassioned letter, concluding, "I will never forget the happy hours, which kind fate allowed me to spend in your company before starting our perilous and uncertain voyage." Unbeknownst to Bessels, Hall, too, had fallen under Ream's spell, sending one of what would be his very last letters from aboard the *Polaris*; his passion was hard to miss: "Your notes, flags, & other valuables all quickly and safely received by the US Steamer 'Congress.' You should see my sweet little cabin. As you enter it our great noble-hearted President strikes the eye while beneath it hangs the photograph you gave me of the statue of Lincoln. Today I resume my voyage – the Smith Sound remarkably open – never known to be more so. You may expect that when again you hear from me and my company, that the North Pole has been discovered. How true is your faith that we are going to conquer."

At some point, the two men must have discovered each other's feelings. The evidence, I feel, is conclusive: Hall, the one man of his era who actually might have reached the pole, was murdered by Bessels, his own ship's doctor.

Ultimately, Hall became not only the explorer he had always sought to be but, like Franklin and his men, a martyr in the cause of Arctic exploration. He even managed to leave a final note, written on a printed form he had designed to look just like Franklin's, and rolled up inside a copper tube, in which it still lay when I examined the Hall papers in 2004. Like James

Fitzjames, he allowed his thoughts to spill into the margin of the form, detailing his successful sledge journey and his plans for an assault on the pole the next spring. He concluded by declaring that "up to the time I and my party left the ship all have been well, and continue with high hopes of accomplishing our great mission." Hall had, in the end, that gift for unintended irony reserved for the truest of true believers.

Figure 16 Frederick Schwatka, from the *Illustrated London News*. Collection of the author.

8

Schwatka

It would have been entirely understandable if, after Charles Francis Hall, no one ever headed north to search for Franklin again. After all, by 1870 it had been twenty-two years since the date on the Victory Point record; there could be no question that, whatever else might be discovered, no living men could possibly remain. Still, there was the galling absence of any further documents, the more frustrating since many Inuit had spoken to Hall of books and papers. In this early era of first contact, the Inuit had no idea of the value of the white man's paper; in at least one instance, a cairn was opened, a tin canister found, the papers inside removed and discarded, and the tin taken away. Some gave the papers to their children as playthings; some – as with the ship at Utjulik – just left the books behind, loading up on wood, metal, and other more useful things. That white men would pay dearly for these scraps of inky stuff was learned too late to retrieve any of it.

The Schwatka episode, curiously, did not begin with papers but rather with a spoon bearing Franklin's crest of a conger-eel between two branches. It had been offered in exchange by two Netsilik Inuit to one Captain Potter of the whaler *Glacier*, which was at the time wintering in Repulse Bay. The second mate from a neighbouring vessel, Thomas F. Barry – apparently a rather studious man – happened to be writing in his journal at the time of the exchange. Overhearing one of the Inuit remark that his book was much like the ones possessed by the white men who had been among them, Barry questioned them further, and this was the account they gave:

Many winters previous a party of white men came to where their tribe was then passing the winter, all of whom died of cold and hunger, the winter being very severe; that during that winter there was neither game nor seals, and they had themselves to subsist on the skins of seals and other animals; that one of the white men, whom the Esquimaux called a leader or father, was a stout man, who wore a coat with three stripes of some kind on the lower part of the sleeve, who gave directions to the others; that the white men died one after the other, those who remained burying those who died, wrapping up the body in a kepick or blanket with which the Esquimaux cover themselves while sleeping, laying it upon a rock near by, and covering it with stones to keep it from the wolves and bears, and that when the spring came all were dead; that after many had died the rest made a ketch (cairn or cache) and put under it something resembling the book in which Barry was writing.

That the winter was severe and the hunting poor at the time when the white men died is consistent with what the Inuit had told Dr Rae at the same place some years earlier; back then, when Rae inquired after several of his old acquaintances, the Inuit would not speak their names, a clear sign to him that many had died in this difficult time. The account of a stout man with three stripes, though, is puzzling; although the Franklin expedition was hardly short of stout men, there were no stripes on any of the naval uniforms the officers would have worn. It's possible that one of the sergeants of the Royal Marines on board might have worn such an outfit – but while on Arctic expeditions, the Marines seldom donned their brick-red dress uniforms, often gathering what they could from the ship's "slops" and tailoring it to their liking – and so this detail remains more frustrating than illuminating. Barry added that his Inuit informants, asked to point out the locations on a map, had indicated the vicinity of Cape Englefield on the Melville peninsula, as well as a "large island" (missing from the map he showed them) nearby. This location was a puzzling one, since it lay hundreds of miles east of other known Franklin sites.

Barry's account aroused great interest, and he was subsequently invited to a private meeting with Charles Patrick Daly, then president of the American Geographical Society (AGS). Captain Potter, apparently, was not available, since he was off on another voyage, but a few years earlier he had been only too happy to give *his* version of this story directly to the press, and one rather suspects that it grew in the telling. To a reporter from the New York *Herald*, he represented himself as having wintered "near" King William Island (he later admitted it was in fact two hundred miles distant); he also claimed that he had put Hall "through a whole winter," though by Hall's own account he had sheltered him for only a week. Potter happily displayed the utensils he had obtained in trade, seemingly unaware that some details didn't quite jibe: the "Franklin" spoon was described as having an "Indian with bow-and-arrow in hand" on its top – perhaps a misinterpretation of a well-worn eel? Still, the maker's stamp, G.A., was a match, indicating London silversmith George Adams, who was indeed the maker of Franklin's silver plate. As had been the case with earlier utensils, one of the spoons bore scratched initials on its underside, said to be "R.N.," which Captain Potter believed stood for "Royal Navy," though that would have been a departure from the others, in which men scratched their *own* initials. It may have been R.M., in which case the scratcher would have been Reuben Male of HMS *Terror*, the only man on the expedition whose name matched.

Potter continued his account to the reporter, saying that the spoons had been brought to him by a "very old man," who had come down from King William to trade but perished part-way through the attempt; he described him not only as a "friend" of Franklin's but as an eyewitness to the destruction of the vessels. Could this have been In-nook-poo-zhee-jook? It seems a bit of a stretch, since only a few years had passed since that well-travelled Inuk had last spoken with Hall, and he was not described as elderly then; as to Kok-lee-arng-nun, Hall's informant who claimed to have visited Franklin's ships, he had died shortly after his interview. In any case, the basic facts of this man's story seemed to be well known to Captain Potter, and this he briefly told: "Five men, all frozen to death, were found on the shore. From appearances, they had wandered around the bleak land surface, and finally, in despair and hunger, had lain down on the icy coast, turned a small sail boat over them bottom upwards, and thus, while taking an innocent snooze, unconsciously went into that immortal slumber which is the dread of all wicked and grasping humanity."

We know that groups of Franklin's men did drag boats on sledges, and that they may have used them for shelters, so the story is at least consistent with this. Yet oddly, the detail that most gripped the public – the claim that books or papers had been sealed up in a sort of vault – is missing from Potter's account. Could it have been fabricated by Barry with the intention of stirring renewed interest? Or had Barry, in his more recent interviews with the Repulse Bay Inuit, managed to get additional testimony that Potter had somehow missed? The answer to this question was vital, since it was to be the belief in these papers that would be decisive. The idea that documents, which could, at a stroke, solve the whole Franklin business, had been buried at a known location, was such that inaction seemed less defensible than action the only question remaining was whether to credit Barry's or Potter's claims, and how to reconcile their rather different accounts of where the search should be directed.

At the AGS, Daly, following his interview with Barry, wrote to the British Admiralty, which forwarded his query to both McClintock and Rae, seeking their expert opinion. In his reply, McClintock cast doubt on many of the details of Barry's story: "The white men are said to have been a large party; that several of them wore coloured stripes, and were supposed to be officers; and that their dead bodies were wrapped up in skins by the natives, although they were barely supporting their lives on scraps of skins. It is not usual to wear uniform in arctic expeditions, and it would be impossible to do so when out on land journeys." He also cautioned generally against putting too much stock in second-hand Eskimo evidence, suggesting that Barry had only a limited understanding of the language; Dr Rae echoed this view, adding one further and perhaps critical detail – yes, he agreed, there was indeed a cairn near the place described by Barry, about thirty miles south of Cape Englefield – but it was one that Rae himself had constructed. Some time later, the Inuit at Repulse Bay had told Rae of this cairn, unaware that he had built it; surely Barry's tale was but some echo of these. And, if that were not enough, Rae averred that the rugged coast in this vicinity was singularly inhospitable, "the last place that any one in distress would think of going to with the object of obtaining assistance and succour." Both men reiterated their belief that the various parties of Franklin survivors, in their poor condition, would not have been able to make it far from the shores of King William Island, certainly no farther than the Adelaide peninsula.

Despite these strong contrary indications, Daly persevered. He summoned Joe Ebierbing, then living in Groton, Connecticut, and asked for his opinion, both of the stories and of Barry's facility with Inuktitut. Joe was most emphatic in his views. After recounting his time with Hall, he continued: "I know Thomas F. Barry; speaks Repulse Bay Esquimaux. I have talked a good deal with him in Esquimaux. He speaks it pretty well; about as well as I speak English. I can always understand him and he always understands me. Several of the whaling captains speak Esquimaux very well ... Capt. Baker speaks it very well, Barry speaks it as well as he does. Those Netchelli whom Barry saw, as they had been living among the Repulse bay people, must speak the Repulse bay Esquimaux. Barry must have spoken to them in that language." He added his account of his visit with Hall to what may well have been the same cairn described by Barry, as well as other markers in the vicinity; in each case, they had dug down in an attempt to find any concealed records. He also confirmed the existence of a large island off the coast:

> I went in May and June with Captain Hall to Cape Englefield; we went in a sledge. We went along the north coast of Melville Peninsula, from Ooglik to Perry Bay. We saw a monument at Perry Bay, it was a small cairn, about three feet high, of stones. I dug it out. I think it was made by white men. We saw one of big stones, about two feet square, with a big flat stone on top, pointing north. Captain Hall had Dr. Rae's book with him and Captain McClintock's book. Every time that Captain Hall came to a monument he took it down. We saw another monument with a stone pointing to the low ground. We dug along the line where the stone pointed for about fifteen or twenty feet, but the snow was so deep and hard that we could not get to the surface of the ground, having no pick-ax, but only a knife and a shovel. I know there is a big island in 70° N. latitude and about 87° W. longitude. I saw it; but we could not get there, the ice was so very bad.

This, apparently, was good enough for Daly. Indeed, it seems to have been Joe's assurances, along with his undoubted familiarity with the places described in Barry's story, which tipped the balance in favour of a new search. Daly put out word that the AGS would sponsor an expedition to investigate the Barry story, and that they were seeking qualified men to undertake it.

It was then that Frederick Schwatka – a man of prodigious talents who had already earned degrees in medicine and law, as well as serving with distinction in the 3rd Cavalry during the latter stages of the Plains Indian wars – stepped forth. Schwatka had apparently long had an interest in Franklin, and as soon as he learned of the proposed search – by his account, in the pages of an Oregon newspaper – he volunteered, contingent on the permission of the Army. This being granted, he was appointed the commander of the expedition, and a small party was selected, prominent among them William H. Gilder, a journalist with the backing of the New York *Herald*'s powerful editor, James Gordon Bennett. Bennett had previously backed Stanley's successful African expedition in search of David Livingstone, and although there was in this case no chance of a "Sir John Franklin, I presume," he must have been confident that the search would make good copy.

Schwatka's expedition thus became the first Arctic venture sponsored by a newspaper in return for the commercial value of its coverage, an arrangement that would later feature in the fateful voyage of the *Jeanette* as well as Walter Wellman's efforts to reach the North Pole by dirigible. To accompany Schwatka and Gilder, the AGS selected Heinrich Klutschak and Frank Melms; Klutschak, a talented artist, had visited the Arctic at least once before, while Melms was described simply as an "experienced seaman."

And along with them the AGS sent Joe Ebierbing, who in a sense was the one indispensable man; only he had precise knowledge of Hall's journeys and could converse with other Inuit fluently. His had already been a storied career; along with his wife Tookoolito (Hannah), he had served Hall faithfully throughout all three of his expeditions over more than a decade, but in recent years his ties to the United States had come undone. After Hall's death and their narrow escape on the drifting ice, he and Hannah had tried to settle into an ordinary life in Groton with their adopted daughter Panik or "Punny"; as Joe noted proudly in his lone surviving letter, "Punny go to school every day." But it was not to be: Panik died at the tender age of nine, and a grieving Hannah followed her to the grave on New Year's Eve in 1876. Joe was ready to return to the Arctic; unlike other members of the expedition, for him this journey would be a sort of homecoming – albeit a bittersweet one.

++++

Schwatka's plan took advantage of the small size of his party, requiring only a modest amount of equipment beyond what could be obtained once they arrived; he planned to travel by dog-drawn sledge, Eskimo-style. This also meant that he, like Hall, required no vessel, taking passage on a whaling ship, in this case the *Eothen*, of which Barry was now appointed master. The party arrived at a point near Depot Island – roughly halfway between Cumberland Sound and Repulse Bay – in August 1878. Schwatka's first order of business, with Joe Ebierbing's help, was to locate the witnesses who had described this cache of papers to Barry and Potter, and so they set about interviewing every Inuk who came to their camp to trade, along with those hunting nearby.

Unfortunately, neither of the two original Netsilik witnesses could be found, and (according to Schwatka at least) none of the local Inuit knew anything about these men or their spoons. There were only two other Netsilik present: one was an aged paralytic known to the whalers as "Monkey," whose speech impediment rendered him scarcely intelligible even to other Inuit, and the other was "Natchilli Joe" (so called to distinguish him from Joe Ebierbing), who was far too young to have any personal recollection of Franklin encounters. Eventually, however, they met a third man, Nu-tar-ge-ark, about fifty years of age, who proved to be a fountain of information. And, although Schwatka neglects to mention it, he was – according to Gilder – the very man who had brought the spoon from King William Island, of which he gave a detailed account:

His father, many years ago, opened a cairn on the northern shore of Washington Bay, in King William Land, and took from it a tin box containing a piece of paper with some writing on it. Not far from this same spot were the ruins of a cairn which had been built by white men and torn down by Inuits. The cairn had been built upon a large flat stone, which had the appearance of having been dragged to its present location from a stony point near by. The cairn itself was found to be empty, but it was generally believed by the Inuits that there was something buried beneath this stone. It was very heavy, and as they had only been there in parties of two or three at a time, they had never been able to overturn the stone, though they had repeatedly tried. Nu-tar-ge-ark also said he had brought a spoon with him from King William Land, which corresponded in description with the one Barry took to the United States. He said it was given to him by some of his tribe, and that it had come from one of the boat places, or where skeletons had been found on King William Land or Adelaide Peninsula, he could not remember exactly where. He had not given the spoon to Captain Barry, but to the wife of Sinuksook, an Iwillik Esquimau, who afterward gave it to a Captain Potter. We saw Sinuksook's wife a little later, and she distinctly remembered having given the spoon to Captain Potter. It was necessary, therefore, to find this officer.

Following this intelligence, Gilder himself set out by sledge for Repulse Bay, where Captain Potter was said to be present aboard another whaler; the journey proved a difficult one, as Gilder several times fell through loose or rotten ice and had to wait at journey's end for the wind to close an open lead in the ice near where the ships were anchored. Once he reached them, and had exchanged his icy furs for dry "kodluna clothing," he asked Potter about the spoons. The latter expressed surprise, saying that he had known nothing of Barry's account until he read of it in the newspaper, adding that one of the three spoons he had received while on board the *Glacier* had subsequently gone missing. And it was this very spoon – identifiable from a crack in its bowl which had been mended with copper by the Inuit – that had been stolen, presumably by Barry. He cast further doubt, too, on Barry's understanding of Inuktitut:

> Captain Potter further said, that to one who had lived with the Esquimaux, and acquired the pigeon English they use in communicating with the whalers in Hudson's Bay, and contrasted it with the language they use in conversation with each other, the assertion of Captain Barry, that he overheard them talking about books and understood them, was supremely ridiculous. There is probably no white man in the Arctic, or who ever visited it, that would understand them under such circumstances unless it be one or two in Cumberland, who have lived with them for fifteen or twenty years. In this crucible of fact the famous spoon melted. So far as Captain Barry and his clews were concerned, we had come on a fool's errand.

The whole story is peculiar, though, and leaves substantial room for doubt: after Potter's denial, why didn't Gilder confront Barry, or Barry defend himself, since he was supposedly present nearby? And as to Potter's learning of Barry's claim only through reading the papers, that seems disingenuous, since he, as we've already seen, had given a lengthy account to the New York *Herald*, the very paper that employed Gilder. Potter himself had earlier vouched for his and Barry's ability to understand Inuktitut; why did he suddenly retreat on this claim? And why Schwatka, contradicting his second-in-command, would deny that the Inuit near Camp Daly had given him *any* information about the spoon is a further puzzle – indeed, in Schwatka's version, Gilder's sledge trip to Resolute Bay is described merely as a mission to obtain more dogs.

Whatever the answer to these – largely unanswerable – questions, it seems clear that there was considerable bad blood between Potter and Barry, and that both, though disparaging each other as publicity grabbers, were quite actively seeking public attention. Barry's own testimony to Daly, later published by the AGS, shows that he was indeed acquainted with Inuktitut, and proves that he, as had Hall, had carefully inquired about every aspect of

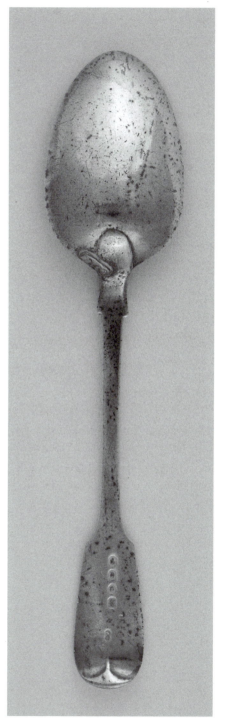

Figure 17 Franklin spoon.
Below: Collection of the author.
Left: Scott Polar Research Institute,
N980(b).

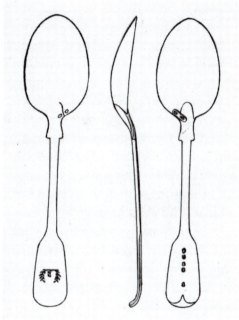

the stories he had been told. Twice, he asked different groups of Inuit to show on a map where they had seen white men; twice, they looked for a large island off the northwest coast of the Melville peninsula near Cape Englefield, and declared that even though it was not on the map, it was the place where they had seen the white men. Years later, as Joe Ebierbing had testified, he and Charles Francis Hall had sighted it, and for a time it was referred to as "Hall Island." The vagaries of Arctic mapping being what they were, though, it did not appear in its proper place on standard charts until 1922, when Peter Freuchen – unaware of its history – named it after Crown Prince Frederik of Denmark as he was passing through the area as part of the Fifth Thule Expedition. In the more than ninety years since then, it's never been searched for traces of Franklin's men.

Rae had discounted Inuit tales of Franklin survivors near Cape Englefield, describing the terrain as rough and foreboding – but Crown Prince Frederik Island, in contrast, is described by the United States Hydrographic Office as "mostly quite low, composed of sand and small stones." Might it have been a likely camp for some escaping party of Franklin's men? The Inuit who spoke with Barry averred that it was: "We gave them a chart, and pointed out the starting point upon it, from Repulse bay, and they traced the coast along Melville Peninsula northwards, as far as the projection of Cape Englefield. Then they looked for an island on the chart to the N.W., in the Gulf of Boothia, which they could not find, as it was not on the chart. They said that it was 'connie tuck-a-lu' (not far off, or close to that), and used the word kig-a-tunn, which is their word in Esquimaux for island. We asked them if they had ever seen any white men since; and they said no – none – until they had seen us." It's a compelling account, and it's not at all clear why Schwatka and his party regarded Captain Potter's word as fact, and Barry's as unreliable.

In all likelihood, the truth lay somewhere in between these two stories – one of a whaleboat on King William Island with men starving underneath it, and the other of a cairn and possible camp on the coast of the Melville peninsula. Schwatka, observing the impossibility of visiting both places, opted, perhaps wisely, for the one that everyone but Barry seemed to feel held the greatest promise – the familiar but long unsearched shores of King William. He and Gilder apparently never had a chance to compare notes, and for whatever reason, only Gilder's account was published, while Schwatka's languished in a steamer trunk until it was rediscovered in the

1960s. The expedition's artist – Heinrich Klutschak – also wrote his own account, published in German in Vienna in 1881; in it, he makes no mention of the spoon, simply stating that "the stories of Captain Thomas F. Barry ... revealed themselves to be total falsehoods." In the absence of any further accounts, we must content ourselves with the lack of certainty, but one clear fact comes through: even supposing that the Inuit told their stories as accurately as they could, the vagaries of the "Kabloonas" – with their rivalries, their distrust, and their presuppositions – were quite enough to garble things on their own.

✛✛✛✛

On 1 April 1879 Schwatka set out on what would be one of the longest sledge journeys ever undertaken, from Camp Daly to the northernmost tip of King William Island and back. He travelled with only minimal provisions, planning to depend almost entirely on hunting, in preparation for which he had brought along two Remington breech-loading muskets, two repeating Winchester rifles, a Sharp's Carbine, two sporting rifles, and two Smith and Wesson revolvers, along with a variety of older muzzle-loading muskets. The ammunition for these came to 700 rounds for the Remingtons, 700 for the Winchesters, 500 for the Sharp's, and 200 for the revolvers, not to mention 25 pounds each of powder and shot for the muskets. Unlike the Franklin expedition, or even those who searched for it – most of whom relied entirely on pemmican and other supplies they carried with them – Schwatka's party was to be self-sufficient.

That said, they were hardly alone in the wilderness – in fact, they travelled with a small village's worth of Inuit, thusly enumerated by Gilder: "'Esquimau Joe,' interpreter; Neepshark, his wife; Toolooah, dog driver and hunter; Toolooahelek, his wife, and one child; Equeesik (Natchillik Inuit), dog driver and hunter; Kutcheenuark, his wife, and one child; Ishmark, Karleko, his wife, Koomana, their son, aged about thirteen, and Mit-colelee and Owanork, Equeesik's brothers, aged respectively about twenty and thirteen."

This made thirteen Inuit, and seventeen in all, a fairly robust number when one considers that many of the party had to run alongside or behind the sleds, which – despite the plan to subsist on hunting – were loaded with hundreds of pounds of walrus meat and hides along with the guns, ammunition, cooking pots, clothes, and other necessaries.

Their route, ascending a branch of the Wager River, had been given a preliminary survey by Schwatka some months previous, but once they reached the headwaters of that stream, they were on their own. No white men had ever passed this way, unless it was Franklin survivors striving south, and if so, they had perished in the attempt. They made good time, stopping on several occasions to shoot caribou and musk-oxen, and by mid-May they were nearing their goal of the mouth of the Back River. Schwatka was delighted when, on 14 May, they encountered a camp of Utjulik Inuit, the very ones whose range included the coasts nearest where one of Franklin's ships was said to have sunk, but the delight of their meeting was tempered by the sad state of the natives. Schwatka, as he noted, could not hope for aid from them; indeed, he felt obliged to give of his stores. These Utjulingmiut were a poor and tattered band; their hunts had fallen short, and there was no seal oil in their lamps, so that their igloos were cold and cheerless. And yet, among their number, there was one old man whose testimony would prove to be of enormous value.

This was Puhtoorak, the band's senior man; he told Schwatka that he had seen white men only twice before in his life; once, as a young man, when he saw some in a boat on the Back River – this must have been George Back's expedition of 1834 – and then:

The next time he saw a white man was a dead one in a large ship about eight miles off Grant Point. The body was in a bunk inside the ship in the back part. The ship had four big sticks one pointing out and the other three standing up ... Puhtoorak told of how the Esquimaux, not understanding how to get into the ship, cut through one side. When summer came and the ice melted, the ship righted herself but the hole in her side being below the water line she sank as the water poured in. After the ship sank, they found a small boat on the mainland. When he went on board the ship he saw a pile of dirt on one side of the cabin door showing where white men had recently swept out the cabin. He found on board the ship four red tin cans filled with meat and many that had been opened. The meat was full of fat. The natives went all over the ship and found also many empty casks. They found iron chains and anchors on deck, and spoons, knives, forks, tin plates, china plates, etc. When the ship finally sank her masts stuck out of the water and many things floated on shore, which the natives picked up. He also saw books on board the ship but did not take them.

128

Here at last was an eyewitness to the ship about which Hall had heard only at second-hand. Every detail matched, although in Puhtoorak's version the body was not in a locked cabin but in a bunk. The tell-tale sweepings, said by others to be from the deck onto the ice, are here entirely within the ship; here, too, the presence of unopened tins shows that in this instance it was not starvation that wiped out the crew. And for once, the books were left untouched, although in this case that meant that they went down with the ship and were unlikely to be seen again – although it's certainly possible that, on a future dive, the Parks Canada divers may recover some of them.

Schwatka pressed on, skirting the coast of the Adelaide peninsula on his way to King William, and it was there that he had his second stroke of good fortune. It came in the form of an elderly Inuit woman, sent ahead of the rest of her band, who waited behind her in a line; perhaps they thought that, since she was old and expendable, she could, within minimal risk, test these strangers to see if they were hostile. Schwatka had his men fire their rifles into the air – a gesture he thought would be seen as indicating peaceful intentions! – but the old woman carried on, walking with slow, deliberate steps toward his party. She altered her stance only when she recognized among them Equeesik, one of her own Netsilik people whom she hadn't seen since he was a boy; this at once "broke the ice," and a proper welcome was forthcoming. The band knew little, they said, of Franklin's men, though one hunter boasted of having stolen a saw from McClintock, a claim that met with uproarious laughter, leading Schwatka to remark in his journal that the Netsilik were not nearly so trustworthy as were other bands.

Still, their meeting proved to be a fortuitous one, since the next day another group joined the first, and among their number was a woman, aged about fifty-five, named Ahlandnyuck. She described a meeting with ten men who were among the Franklin survivors at Washington Bay on King William Island:

When the white men were first seen, they were on the ice near the land. The Innuit women were afraid and only the men went forward. They remained with the white men four days on this spot. Half of the white men (five) stayed in the boat, and the other half in a small tent on the land. They did not have anything to eat. The Innuit men caught several seal which were divided with the white men, the latter giving her husband a small chopping knife. They started together eastward but the ice being very rotten the Innuits hurried on as they were afraid of not getting across on the mainland before it broke up. They did not get to Gladman's Point in time to cross and had to remain on King William Land during that summer, having first waited at Gladman's Point for the white men. When the latter did not arrive, the natives moved on towards Booth Point. This was the last she saw of the white men alive. They looked thin and worn out and their mouths were very dry, bleeding, and black. They were all wearing white mans clothing and had no sort of reindeer or other kind of fur dress. There were two white chiefs – Ahglookah and Tooloowug, as near as she could remember their names. The latter was the name of the head man who had given her husband the chopping knife. There was one man they called Doc-toor. Tooloowug was a little older than any of the other men and had a black beard mixed with gray, and was a big broad man. The other leader was younger and smaller with a reddish brown beard. "Doc-toor" was a corpulent man of low stature with a long red beard. These three officers with the boat had on spectacles (not snow goggles but were white the same as ice).

This story is quite similar to one told to Hall, but with a few curious differences: here we have Aglooka and Tooloah (though spelt differently), but both alive and both out on the land. This Tooloah, too, seems to have been a stout man, now with a grizzled beard; the story would fit with the conjecture that Kok-lee-arng-nun's story was about a later commander. As for Dok-toor, he, too, figures in a number of similar accounts; he could have been Alexander McDonald, assistant surgeon on the *Terror*, several of whose spoons and forks turned up among the Inuit, or possibly Stephen Samuel Stanley, surgeon aboard the *Erebus*, whose name was found on a plank at Montreal Island. The fact that the Inuit ended up stranded on King William Island but did not see the white men again suggests that this party must have crossed over to the Adelaide peninsula, either on a whaleboat or by using the inflatable gutta-percha "Halkett Boat" they were known to have brought with them.

Schwatka continued on, crossing over to King William Island itself, seeking items in barter with groups of natives he encountered along the way; among these was a complete sled, said to have come from Erebus Bay, where it had been found under one of the boats, as well as a board said to have been broken off from the interior of the ship found at Utjulik. This board, which had been painted black and covered with heavy black oilcloth, bore

an inscription of sorts spelled out in brass tacks, which seemed to read "I.F."
One could imagine that this, with the Latin usage of "I" for "J," could have
spelled out John Franklin's initials, or – and this is the solution suggested by
David Woodman – that the "F" was an imperfect "P," and the letters the last
two of a more general "R.I.P." Since the board seemed to have once been a
permanent part of the vessel, Schwatka was hopeful that it could be identified from the ships' plans, but if any attempt to do so was made, no record
seems to have survived, and this plank is not among the other Franklin relics
sent to Britain by Schwatka and now at the National Maritime Museum.

Schwatka soon reached Erebus Bay itself, following a trail of bones that
indicated he was retracing the retreat of at least one Franklin party. His was
the first summer search, and so it's not surprising that he found many remains and other articles missed by McClintock and previous searchers. His
first find was a large cairn, which – disappointingly – proved to have been
erected by Charles Francis Hall, with an inscription reading "MAY XII 1869
– ETERNAL GLORY TO THE DISCOVERERS OF THE NORTH WE ..." The
"ST PASSAGE" was on a portion of the stone that had broken off.

A bit farther on, they encountered another elderly eyewitness who dashed
their hopes. Yes, she said, there had been a central place where papers and
records had been deposited by the last survivors, but the Inuit had taken
them out and tossed them to the winds. She told also of several bodies, unburied, on Booth Point and the Todd Islets nearby. Worse still were her tales
of a camp on the mainland south of this point; here beside an overturned boat
the Inuit found many skeletons, along with a tin case that, when opened,
was found to be full of human bones which "looked fresh." There was one
body seen with the flesh on; this man was tall and had light brown hair, and
near his head they found a pair of gold spectacles. Many of the bones there,
she said, were sawed in two, confirming, along with the box of bones, that
cannibalism had taken place. Pressed about papers, she agreed that there
was a second tin case full of them, but the Inuit – valuing only the metal –
discarded the papers and took the case.

By this time, any hope that papers were likely to be recovered had faded,
but Schwatka was determined to reach the far corner of King William Island. He had no need, from this point, to rely on Inuit testimony as to bones;
he found plenty on his own. Near Erebus Bay, he came upon three skeletons
that had been buried in shallow graves but later disturbed by animals; these
he reburied near the spot. Farther up the coast, more skeletons, each of
which he similarly endeavoured to reinter with some semblance of dignity.

At last, as he drew near Victory Point, he became the first white man to visit the place since McClintock; here, much as he had feared, there was little but the rotted remains of the heaps of blankets, ropes, and other supplies left by the retreating crews. Or so it seemed at first: as they searched the area, Klutschak and Melms came upon a skull, and near it a more substantial grave, edged with large stones. In it were human remains; the body had clearly been wearing blue broadcloth and had thence been covered in a canvas shroud. And, on a stone at the grave's edge, having sat there so long that it had left a stain, they found small medallion.

Rubbing off the tarnish, they quickly distinguished the head of George III on the obverse of the medal; turning it over, they found it to be a Second Prize in Mathematics, awarded to midshipman John Irving in 1830 by the Royal Naval College. All his knowledge of math, it seemed, had done nothing to help poor Irving navigate his way from this desolate spot – yet that was odd indeed, since on the Victory Point record, deposited in 1848 in a cairn only a few miles away, he had been alive and well. What had become of him? Had he, who had been in the lead when the ships were first abandoned, been part of a group desperately seeking to return? In this one case, Schwatka made the decision to remove the remains, deciding – perhaps because Irving had been an officer, perhaps because this grave marked the final point of his journey – to return with them and send them back to Britain.

The Schwatka expedition thus, despite its many finds, did not do much to alter what's become the "classical" version of events following the 1848 abandonment: the men moved to shore and assembled into sledge parties; hauling boats on runners, they proceeded south as well as they could. At Erebus Bay, halfway down the coast, they remained a time, perhaps establishing a "hospital camp" to tend to those who, already on the southward march, were succumbing to scurvy or exhaustion. From there, some portion continued, meeting a group of Inuit near Washington Bay, where they traded a knife for some seal meat. Finally, their numbers diminishing as they trudged along the southern coast of King William Island, some of the party crossed over to the mainland, where they met their end, while others carried on as far as Booth Point, where their unburied bones testified that these were the very last men.

On his return trip, Schwatka managed to visit that spot on the mainland, where (by various accounts) at least ten and perhaps as many as thirty men had met their end. Unlike King William, the land here was marshy and – when not frozen – softly shrouded in coastal mud. At Schwatka's behest, Joe

Figure 18 Mathematics medal awarded to Lieutenant John Irving.
Frontispiece of *Lieutenant John Irving, R.N., of H.M.S. Terror in Sir John
Franklin's Last Expedition to the Arctic Regions, a Memorial Sketch with
Letters*, ed. Benjamin Bell, Edinburgh: 1881.

Ebeirbing searched as best he could, retrieving part of a sea boot, but little more. The Inuit who had guided them to the place supposed that the other remains had sunk into the soil or been washed away; the boat, of course, they had removed and repurposed. In his diary, Klutschak remarked "the view alone is sufficient to put the visitor into a mood which matches the historic significance of the site. Mother Nature could probably not produce a more desolate spot on this wide Earth than that where the last survivors of the Franklin expedition found their end." Schwatka dubbed it "Starvation Cove."

++++

News of the Schwatka expedition did indeed sell papers; accompanied by engravings based on Klutschak's sketches, it was featured in the New York *Herald* and serialized in the *Illustrated London News*. Gilder's narrative was later published as a book, which sold well, and Klutschak, returning to Germany, sustained himself on the lecture circuit, publishing a book of his own, *Als Eskimo unter den Eskimos* (As an Eskimo among the Eskimos). Schwatka's own journal, oddly, was not published as a book, although portions of it appeared in several magazines. Like Hall before him, Schwatka was a restless soul and was soon back out exploring, descending the Yukon River in a raft and reaching the Bering Sea in 1883. In the later 1880s, he led two further private expeditions in Alaska before retiring for a time to his home near Rock Island, Illinois; accounts differ but it appears that he had suffered either a stomach malady or some injury, and had become addicted to laudanum in its treatment.

From time to time, he took to the lecture circuit, where he was still able to command healthy fees. In 1891 he had been booked for a lecture in Mason City, Iowa, but had fallen down the stairs at his hotel and sustained internal injuries. Had he, under the influence of his sedative of choice, attempted the stairs when his faculties were impaired? Or had this man, who had set records for travel by sledge and by raft through the remotest regions of the frozen north, merely tripped on a bit of loose carpet, the victim simply of bad luck? His family had sought to hide his drug addiction, and the story of the fall was, if needed, a plausible one to cover a death by other causes. Yet, against expectations, he recovered, continuing to give public lectures for another year; it was on the night after one of these, in 1892 in

Portland, Oregon, that he apparently decided he could go on no longer. He was found dead in the street the next morning, still grasping an empty bottle of laudanum. Curiously, in the last years of his life, Schwatka had tried his hand as an inventor and designer. His very last design, as it happens, was for a *spoon* – a silver spoon with a stylized totem-pole of "grotesque figures" for its handle. It was granted US Patent #20,832 in June 1891.

Figure 19 Franklin expedition bones found at Douglas Bay in 1931 by William Gibson. Library and Archives Canada.

9

The Search Renewed

After Schwatka's search there was a long period in which there were no organized searches for Franklin of any kind. The Canadian Arctic had not yet become a region of national or international focus, and in the wake of Roald Amundsen's and Robert Peary's exploits, the impetus for exploration for exploration's sake waned. This is not to say that there were no notable figures of this era, but few of them went out of their way to seek for Franklin's footsteps. Rasmussen, on the Fifth Thule Expedition, visited several Franklin sites and collected testimony that strongly echoed that given to Hall and Schwatka, but the idea that anything new could be learned of men who had vanished more than half a century before seemed almost ludicrous; they were past all rescue, and whether they had met their end at one spot or another was a question for the gods of fate, not for the Inuit or the few white men who ventured so far.

Yet, though Franklin's men were long gone, their story did not perish with them. When, from the 1920s onward, various fur-trading concerns – Canalaska, Revillon Frères, and the venerable HBC itself – began establishing new permanent outposts in more remote areas, the men who managed those posts, along with those of the RCMP assigned to patrol the region, heard the Franklin story again, and some were motivated to use their time – the one resource of which the north was never short – and proximity to known Franklin sites to satisfy their curiosity. These men did not often communicate their visits to each other, much less to the outside world, but nevertheless their searches laid the foundation for the modern Franklin search era, and it's with them that a new kind of curiosity – one not driven by the hope of rescuing anyone or resolving anything, but a sort of restless poking at the edge of the known – took hold.

Lachlan Taylor Burwash was typical of this new generation of searchers. His fixation with Franklin came only after he took up a position in the north, working as an "exploratory engineer" for the Northwest Territories' Department of the Interior. This position gave him considerable freedom in his travels and provided the necessary support and supplies for extended journeys. Outwardly, his work was eminently practical: he surveyed geological formations, visited government and HBC posts and assessed their condition, and made sundry observations on the situation of the native Inuit peoples. Symbolically, at least, he participated in Canada's assertion of sovereignty in the north by demonstrating the territorial government's ability to send its representatives throughout the regions it administered (which at the time included the eastern Arctic, now a part of Nunavut). At the same time, as with the voyages of exploration before it, there was at least some justification for his mission from the scientific, geological, and ethnographic information to be gathered.

Burwash was nothing if not a methodical man, recording the findings of his journeys in lengthy typewritten reports, which he then reproduced mimeographically. He was also an avid photographer, making numerous images to document his travels; for his reports, he made prints of each, which were then individually pasted into the pages. These reports were originally produced in editions of only fifty copies, most of which were distributed to various government repositories; Burwash kept a few to give to friends. As a result, they're extremely hard to come by; I was fortunate in that Arctic historian John Bockstoce allowed me to use the copy in his collection. The bulk of Burwash's reports are consumed with methodical observations of geological formations, weather, and the conditions at local settlements and outposts – but gradually, starting in the late 1920s to the early 1930s, the Franklin story began to consume more and more of his attention. And, as we've seen in chapter 5, Burwash's obsession eventually brought him into contact with Rupert Thomas Gould, who prepared the maps that lent geographical substance to his Franklin theories.

Burwash first visited King William Island in 1925–26, at which time the outpost there could just barely be said to be "manned." A makeshift hut at the site had been destroyed in a storm, and the provisions delivered had to be stowed under tarps near the beach. Burwash carefully documented this situation in his report but also took time to visit Franklin-related sites nearby. When he came upon groups of Inuit, he – like Rae before him – always asked for artifacts, and was disappointed if they proved to be modern ones. Later, as the HBC schooner that was carrying him passed the Royal Geographical Society Islands in the Victoria Strait – quite near to where Franklin's ships had last been seen – he directed the pilot to Jenny Lind Island, where he surveyed its barren shores in search of clues. He also visited Hat Island, where Inuit testimony spoke of relics from Franklin's ships, but, finding none, he contented himself with describing its stratified limestone outcroppings. The ship's other duties prevented him lingering in the area, but it's clear from his report that he was beginning to catch "Franklin fever." As he wrote in an uncharacteristically rhapsodic introduction: "The unknown, with its eternal lure is ever beckoning the more adventurous, and throughout history; to those who answer the call must be credited much of the knowledge of today … no better exemplification of this can be advanced than the call of the great Northland, which has drawn so many, leading some to fame, some to death, but few to fortune. The names of Ross, Parry, Franklin, Back, Richardson Dease, Simpson and McClintock are prominent among those who have given the North their best years and efforts, even to the last great sacrifice."

On his return trips in 1928–29 and 1930, Burwash was at last able to fulfill his dream to make new discoveries about Franklin's lost expedition. The first and potentially most significant came about through his interviews with two elderly Inuit he met at Gjoa Haven on the first of these expeditions. These men, Enukshakak and Nowya, told a tale of an encounter from their youth with a cache of supplies found near Matty Island, on the opposite side of King William from where everyone had always assumed Franklin's vessels had remained. Their story is best told in their own words:

When they were both young men, possibly twenty years of age, they were hunting on the ice in the area immediately northeast of Matty Island. When crossing a low flat island they came across a cache of wooden cases, carefully piled near the center of the island, and about three hundred feet from the water. As described by them this cache covered an area twenty feet long and five feet broad and was taller than they were (more than five feet). The cache consisted of wooden cases which contained materials unknown to them, all of which were enclosed in tin canisters, some of which were painted red … They said that on the outside of the pile of the boxes the wood appeared old but the parts sheltered from the weather were still quite new.

All of the boxes were opened by the natives and the wooden cases divided for the manufacture of arrows. Enukshakak's share was eleven cases, Nowya's nine and their friend two, making twenty-two cases in all. After the wood had been divided they opened the tin containers but found them to contain materials of which they had no knowledge. In a number they found a white powder which they called "white man's snow" ... since learning more about the white man's supplies they have come to the conclusion that some of the cases contained flour, some ship's biscuits, and some preserved meats, probably pemmican.

They also secured at this time a number of planks which they described as being approximately ten inches wide and three inches thick and more than fifteen feet long. These they found washed up on the shore of the island upon which they had found the cache and on the shore of a larger island nearby. Before the time of the finding of the cache on the island the natives had frequently found wood (which from their description consisted of barrel staves) and thin iron (apparently barrel hoops) at various points along the coastlines in this area.

The wreck itself, which had long been known to the natives, lay beneath the water about three quarters of a mile off the coast of the island upon which the cache was found ... [Enukshakak and Nowya] gave it as their opinion that the boxes has been put on the island by white men who had come on the ship which lay on the reef offshore.

Burwash was fascinated by this account and certainly realized how fortunate he was – for this was a completely new story, placing one of Franklin's ships at a location no other testimony had described. He managed to reach the area himself in April 1929 but, owing to snow cover, was unable either to confirm or disprove the Inuit stories.

David Woodman has thoroughly analyzed this report, and his observations are worth recounting. He notes that one explanation of the cache could involve Amundsen, who ditched twenty-five packing cases from the decks of the *Gjøa* in 1903 to lessen her draft, which seems roughly consistent with the twenty-two found by the Nowya and Enukshakshak – but, as Woodman notes, the crates were thrown overboard and could hardly have stacked themselves. Nearly all of Amundsen's crates, moreover, contained pemmican, not the flour or ship's biscuit found when they were opened; the Inuit also described large pieces of wood that must have come from some other source. In addition, the timeframe poses a problem with the Amundsen angle;

if these witnesses were in fact old men in 1929, then they would have been in their twenties in the 1880s or 1890s, well before Amundsen's transit.

Yet, if the crates and wood were *not* from Amundsen, could they be from Franklin's ships? Burwash believed that either the *Erebus* or the *Terror* might have been piloted to Matty Island from the south – an implausible theory given the shallows and hazards of the route. But, what if the vessels had stopped there earlier, while still on their outward journey? It would have made sense to probe "Poctes Bay" and see whether a route might indeed be found there. If so, one or another vessel might easily have run aground and cached the supplies to help refloat the ship; perhaps the ice conditions were such that a hasty retreat was called for, and they were left behind. This explanation is consistent with what we know, but, without more concrete evidence, it is hard to test; despite the continuing interest in Franklin, few have visited the site since. Nevertheless, there exist reports from pilots flying over the area that they saw a sunken vessel in the water, and until Franklin's second ship – which we know now to be the *Terror* – is found, the possibility can't be entirely dismissed.

In 1930 Burwash made one final effort to recover evidence of the Franklin expedition, revisiting the northwestern shores of King William Island where Schwatka had searched more than fifty years earlier. On this trip, he was accompanied by Dick Finnie, whose father, O.S. Finnie, was at the time the chief executive officer (then known as the "director") of the Northwest Territories. The younger Finnie, like Burwash, had been appointed as a "special investigator" for the territorial government, and he enjoyed a similar freedom to travel in the region. They started by revisiting the Matty Island site but once more found it so choked with ice and snow that any investigation was impossible. From there, they were flown to the old site of the North Magnetic Pole on the Boothia peninsula, from which they proceeded over the ice to Cape Felix and thence south along the coast of King William, searching for any signs of the Franklin party.

Their first discovery was a cairn that Burwash believed was "not previously examined," but on taking it down, they found it to contain only a square of naval blue broadcloth. From the nearby camp they retrieved "the remains of a tent … part of a man harness for hauling sled, fragments of light cordage, and a small oak barrel stave." Also near this cairn they found a series of "quite regular" gravel mounds, one of which they examined but decided were natural features. Nearby they found more scraps of broadcloth,

Figure 20 L.T. Burwash with Franklin relics brought back from King William Island. Library and Archives Canada.

linen tent cloth, barrel staves, and some coal. They also visited the site on Terror Bay where Schwatka had surmised there was a "hospital camp," but they found only one grave, which "may have contained two or more

bodies" (this was quite likely the Schwatka reburial, later excavated by Stenton and Keenleyside).

In the end, Burwash and Finnie failed to discover any significant new evidence in the area. They took some photographs, and on their return Burwash posed with the relics – bits of sailcloth and rope, mostly – arranged atop a tasselled couch. It's an enigmatic image, seemingly one of a triumph, though Burwash himself looks more stoic than pleased – but, then, he does not seem to have been a man given to lively expressions. He returned south to his home near Cobourg, Ontario, and spent the remaining decade of his life writing and lecturing about his northern experiences. He had hoped to solve the Franklin mystery, but in the end his contribution was chiefly to remind those who later came to share that dream that not all the evidence supported the conventional reconstruction of the expedition's final fate.

The era of searches such as Burwash's – most of them conducted without archaeological permits, archaeologists, detailed surveys, or other modern niceties – had one other problem: the lack of easily accessible narratives. Many were privately published or (as with Burwash's) hidden in hard-to-find government reports, such that those who came after often ended up "discovering" the same things all over again. Take, for example, the Franklin camp just south of Cape Felix, located by Burwash and Finnie in 1930; in 1949 it was once again found by Henry Larsen, along with a fragment of a skull later shown to be that of a white man. Larsen left a note in a cairn there, and this cairn and note were rediscovered on at least three later occasions: by Canadian Forces staging "Project Franklin" in 1967, by Bob Pilot on the "Franklin Probe" search in 1971, and by Steven J. Trafton in 1989. And yet, despite these repeated searches, it was always possible that a keen eye, or luck, would reveal something missed by others. During his search, Trafton found a second cairn about a mile and a half farther north, and in that cairn was a green glass bottle which still contained a pencilled note left by Schwatka himself! After Trafton, the exact location of this Franklin camp once more became muddled, until it was relocated in 2013 by Tom Gross, using Gilder and Klutschak's accounts of the Schwatka search as his guide.

And so it goes. To be fair, of course, many of these visits were more like pilgrimages than efforts to gain new evidence of how and why Franklin's men died. When bones were found, they were typically reburied in some fashion – a practice that understandably caused considerable tearing out of hair among later archaeologists – but which made sense given the outlook of these early searchers. Despite the fact that they were, unlike Franklin, conversant with the traditional ways of living off the land, they felt a certain solidarity with him, a certain reverence for the bones of his men. Some even fired salutes over the reburied remains, even though there was no one there besides themselves to hear them. And, now and then, when a small artifact caught their eye – a brass grommet, a copper nail, or a bit of sailcloth – they pocketed it and took it home as a souvenir. Larger items were sent to the territorial archives, where many of them still remain to this day, imperfectly catalogued and rarely seen.

Quite a few of these pilgrimages were to cairns – at Victory Point, Crozier's Landing, Cape Felix, Cape Herschel – and other landmarks of indeterminate age. The difficulty in identifying any one cairn lay in the habit of searchers tearing them down to look for clues; the tradition was to build them up again afterwards – in the process of which, much of the key distinguishing evidence was reshuffled like an Arctic deck of cards. Yet, for the same reason, there was still something to be learned, since quite commonly the rebuilder left a new note and/or a copy of any note found there before. These old cairns were once again serving as the "post offices of the north" – only now for an entirely different group of travellers, whose gaze was directed not toward an imaginary future of Arctic glory but backward to the lost hopes of a would-be heroic past.

The cairn at Cape Herschel is an exemplary one. It stands at the end of the southern extent of Washington Bay, the very place where the party of Franklin survivors met with the Inuit hunters and traded a knife for seal meat. The fact that these men had made it so far was the underpinning of the "forging the last link with their lives" claim – for this cairn, erected by Peter Warren Dease and Thomas Simpson in 1839, marked the farthest extent of their coastal survey; to reach this place, for Franklin, was to connect one end of the passage with the other. The cairn was therefore a mark of great achievement and originally stood well over ten feet high, though, by the time Leopold McClintock visited it in 1859, it had been reduced to a few feet in height, many of its central stones scattered off to the side. McClintock searched it again, of course, certain that Franklin's crews would have left a record, but found none: "It was with a feeling of deep regret and much disappointment that I left this spot without finding some certain record of those martyrs to their country's fame. Perhaps in all the wide world there will be few spots so hallowed in the recollection of English seamen than this cairn at Cape Herschel." Seventy-four years later, in 1933, William "Paddy"

Gibson – then in charge of the trading post at Gjoa Haven – visited the cairn and offered this description: "In the dim and uncertain light, it was noticeable that it remains to-day much the same as McClintock found it in 1859. Owing to its elevated position it is comparatively free from snow-drifts. The north side stands about four feet high, while the south side is reduced to a mass of tumbled rock ... may we hope that one day a traveler on this highway of the North may have the opportunity to build again to its once stately height this simple monument to the adventurous and sedulous spirit of Thomas Simpson." The feeling with which Gibson spoke of this pillar is evidence of his own sense of the past and its importance, and his expression of hope for its rebuilding was partly ironic – as readers of his account in the September 1933 issue of the HBC journal *The Beaver* could readily see, there's a photo of the cairn rebuilt to its full stature, with a "pointing stone" on top, taken by Gibson himself four months after his initial visit.

From his station at Gjoa Haven, Gibson had ample means to visit the place, which was only a few days' journey by dogsled west from his post. Along this route, of course, he had the opportunity to traverse the same path followed by that last, dying group of Franklin's men, the group that left behind the skeleton in whose pocket the "Peglar Papers" were found, and that met its end near the Todd Islets, at the place named "Kee-u-na" by Hall's informant In-nook-poo-zhee-jook. This place, which contained the bones of several of Franklin's men whose unburied bodies marked the very end of their journey, was first visited by Gibson in 1931, and there, too, he was industrious, locating and reburying the remains of at least three individuals under a modest cairn of stones. On that same trip, he also located a second, larger group of unburied remains, including seven skulls, on a low island in the midst of Douglas Bay. The photograph of these skulls, now in the collections of Library and Archives Canada (figure 19), is one of the more frequently reproduced images of Franklin remains. These two sites are of tremendous significance to discovering the fate of Franklin, but, although they've been visited over the years by many other would-be Franklin searchers, neither has had a proper archaeological study.

The unofficial keeper of the Todd Islets site today is Louie Kamookak, Gibson's grandson. He knows it well, having been taken there often as a child, back in the days when he and his family still lived in the traditional manner, travelling over the land, camping in igloos in the winter and tupiks in the summer. Louie's a well-known figure in Gjoa Haven, and a visit with him is *de rigeur* for any modern-day Franklin searchers. Not that they necessarily listen to him – indeed, when the site gets reported in the news, it's often treated as though it were a brand-new discovery – but like most of the other key sites, it's been visited again, and again, and again. In the old days, no one seemed to have thought the idea of an archaeological study worthwhile, and nowadays the process of getting permits is so daunting that no one – yet – has mustered the resources.

One other searcher deserves special mention here. Even before he arrived on the shores of King William, he had already been awarded the Gold Medal of the Royal Geographical Society for being the first man to traverse the Northwest Passage from west to east, while in command of the RCMP vessel *St Roch* – a feat he repeated in the opposite direction a few years later. This was Henry Asbjørn Larsen; no other searcher before him came closer to standing in Franklin's own metaphorical shoes. Larsen's experience extended to many other northern patrols over two decades; he eventually rose to the rank of inspector, in charge of all RCMP detachments in the Canadian Arctic. Both the breadth of his experience and his keen eye for detail served him well; despite poor weather conditions and limited time, his search of the area between Cape Felix and Victory point produced what may be some of the most significant finds since those of Schwatka.

Larsen's search took place in the summer of 1949, just before his promotion to commanding officer of the force's "G" division. He took two RCMP men with him, Corporal Seaforth Burton and Constable John Biensch. He had hoped to squeeze in the mission between his other duties, but news of his trip was inadvertently leaked to the press; as a cover story, an announcement was made that the trip was merely to scout a location for a new RCMP post. Larsen's pilot, Harry Heacock, flew them over Lind Island and Victoria Strait; despite poor conditions, he was able to land briefly to establish a fuel depot at Terror Bay. Returning the following day, they were able to land and establish a base camp near Collinson Inlet. From there, they proceeded on foot, working their way up the coast to Cape Felix. At Cape Jane Franklin, they found wood chips and part of a shoe sole; joined there by Bill Cashin (who had served as Larsen's mechanic aboard the *St Roch*), they began a close search the area around Victory Point.

Here they had better luck, turning up two iron braces (almost certainly from a ship's boat of the kind used by Franklin's men), along with other small fragments of wood, nails, and wire. Continuing to Cape Felix, they made their most significant find: embedded between two mossy stones, they came upon a human skull. On their return, the artifacts were brought back to the National Museum (the precursor institution to both the Canadian Museum of Nature and the Canadian Museum of History). There, the bones were examined by Dr Douglas Leechman, one of Canada's pre-eminent archaeologists, who identified them as "definitely that of a white man, and a fairly young one at that." Larsen and his companions had found the most northerly grave of one of Franklin's men on King William Island.

Yet, as with earlier searchers, the vital documentary evidence of this discovery has been misplaced and scattered. Larsen's report, if indeed he submitted one, has gone missing, although R.J. Cyriax's article about the search in the *Geographical Journal* was clearly based on some sort of fairly detailed communication from Larsen. Cyriax thought very highly of Larsen's account, declaring it "much more detailed and precise than any of the published accounts with which the [present] writer is acquainted." No trace of the report has been found, and though the bones were retained, the artifacts themselves appear to have disappeared. The curators I've contacted have no record of them, and they were never entered into the archaeological databases of either the Northwest Territories or Nunavut. Had it not been for the assistance of Doreen Larsen Riedel, Larsen's daughter, I would never have learned the details of their discovery. They were, fortunately, photographed, and the images deposited in the Library and Archives Canada; unlike Burwash's collection of ropes and rags, these mossy bones glimmer with an eerie presence, frozen in the camera's eye even though they, too, have since vanished from our sight.

It was, to be fair, a quite different era. All the figures who made these early searches did so as part of their "day jobs" – Burwash was a territorial official, Larsen a policeman and ship's captain, Gibson a trading-post manager. George Porter, who arrived to run the Gjoa Haven outpost after Gibson's premature death in a plane crash, carried on this tradition, visiting the Franklin sites and hearing – and retelling – many tales of his men. Those whose employment gave them the luxury of proximity had no need to raise funds, and those who worked for the government had no need to apply for permits – and in a strange way, this gave them an opportunity that amateur Franklin buffs back home in southern Canada, the United States, or the United Kingdom could only dream of. And, at the time these men did their work, there was no simple, single national repository for the artifacts they recovered, and no pressing national interest in them.

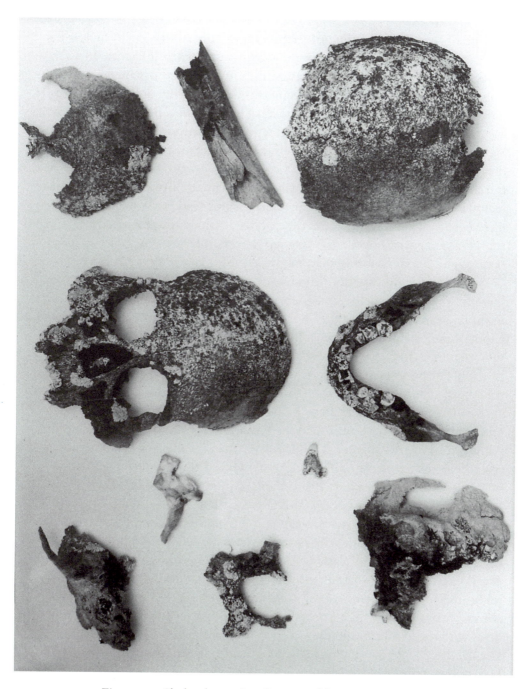

Figure 21 Skeletal remains discovered by Henry Larsen.
Courtesy of Doreen Larsen Riedel.

One of the last in this line of succession is Robert Pilot, who during his time as assistant commissioner of the Northwest Territories acquired a reputation as one of the first to organize a multi-member, organized expedition to the area. His personal obsession was not with finding Franklin's ships but with locating his grave, which he has always believed would be discovered on land. It might, he thought, be in the northwestern part of King William Island, where the ships were caught in the ice at the time of his death, or his men may have elected to give it some more prominent place of burial. The North Magnetic Pole was another possibility – what more perfect place of honour for such a man? Surely some significant memorial must have been made; after all, at the time of his death his ships carried a nearly full complement of men, including carpenters, blacksmiths, and as many diggers and builders as any plan might require.

Now in his eighties, Pilot thinks back warmly on his searching days, as he embarked on what he considered then, and still does today, the *true* Franklin search. His first foray was in 1971, when he and his friend Mike Moore hired a Cessna 172 with floats to take them up near Cape Felix. It was then that they located anew Franklin's camp, along with the cairn and the note left by Larsen, but poor weather conditions prevented them from tracing the coast as far as Jane Franklin Point, and they returned the way they came. The fire was lighted, though, for him and several of his associates, and in 1972 they established the Franklin Probe, a quasi-official entity with some powerful members. Pilot was by then the assistant commissioner of the Northwest Territories, and he convinced Stu Hodgson – the commissioner – to give the group his backing. Other members included Charles Lynch, Jake Ootes, Ray Creery, and Glen Warner.

In 1973 they followed up on the possibility that Franklin's body had been taken to the Boothia peninsula, near to where the North Magnetic Pole had been located by James Clark Ross in 1831. Proceeding inland eastward along the water route from Pattinson Harbour, they found a series of small lakes, the second of which they dubbed "Probe Lake." The basis of this search was said to be Inuit tales of a man's body carried to this place, a funeral with a gun salute, and the covering over of the grave with what looked like cement. This story, which can be traced to testimony given to one of Hall's men, is usually interpreted as having taken place on King William Island; David Woodman places it near Terror Bay – but in any case Pilot and his group found no remains of Franklin-era activity nearby.

In 1974 they organized an even more ambitious series of forays to various Franklin sites, revisiting Resolute Bay, Beechey Island, Starvation Cove, Dealy Island, and Fury Beach. At Resolute Bay, they found the grave of one of the unfortunate sailors from HMS *Resolute*, who had died while on a sledging excursion; about his grave were scattered broken rum bottles and ration tins, which Pilot considered to be "the remains of a roaring wake." At Dealy Island, they uncovered a roofless shed which still contained preserved stores intended for the relief of Franklin's men, while at Beechey they made a pilgrimage to the graves of Torrington, Hartnell, and Braine. On this trip, they brought a special guest – May Fluhmann, a gifted musician who was at work on a biography of Francis Crozier, *Second in Command*, published two years later by the Northwest Territories government. These trips, alas, yielded no fresh clues, though they were widely reported in the Canadian press and helped raise public awareness of the unresolved nature of Franklin's fate.

After the Franklin Probe era, visits to King William Island by Franklin searchers declined for a time, though in retrospect this period has the feel of a calm before a storm. The first searcher of the 1980s was Owen Beattie, several years before the exhumations on Beechey Island that would bring him fame and, for a time, make his name (and John Geiger's) synonymous with the Franklin mystery. As a professional anthropologist, Beattie brought a different and more practised eye to the human remains that still lay scattered about, conducting two searches on foot in 1981 and 1982 and recovering skeletal remains from seven to fifteen individuals, as well as more than eighty small objects. These were, in fact, the very first Franklin remains to be subjected to any kind of methodical study or analysis, and it was in the process of trying to make sense of them that Beattie decided it might be worthwhile to exhume the bodies on Beechey Island.

In 1981 Beattie began by tracing the southern coast; apparently unaware of Gibson's visit to the Todd Islets site, he proceeded west, locating a "partial skeleton" not far from the site where the "Le Vesconte" remains had been found by Hall. This was, in all likelihood, the same partial body, with an "unusually long femur," which Gibson had noticed and reburied in 1931. The remains showed the individual to have been male, and the skull fragments showed it had been "forcibly broken"; some of the longer bones showed scratches and cut-marks, but Beattie believed them consistent with animal gnawing. In 1982, near Erebus Bay, Beattie recovered a significantly larger number of bones, including a femur with cut-marks he thought might point to human cannibalism, though inconclusive. Here, too, the skulls showed "radiating stress fractures" indicating fractures due to "heavy blows," as well as evidence of periostitis – an inflammation of the bone surface that can be associated with scurvy, a disease from which doubtless a good portion of Franklin's men were suffering.

The fact that lemon juice, the sole effective anti-scorbutic supplied to the expedition, lost its potency over time, had still not yet dawned on the Admiralty, and nearly every Arctic expedition saw its outbreak not long after the first winter. The one other effective remedy – fresh meat – was probably out of reach of Franklin's men; they had not come prepared for hunting large land or sea mammals, and in any case it would have taken an enormous quantity of meat to sustain the more than one hundred survivors who left the boats in 1848. The only weapons they had – shotguns – were best suited to small game and birds; one thinks back to Rae's mention of "fresh bones and feathers of geese" as a sign that the last few survivors had at least made it to the spring.

Along with the bones, Beattie found all manner of small physical artifacts, testifying to the everyday life of the men as well as their final travails: a barrel stave, a wooden pipe bowl and stem, two leather fragments from a boot upper as well as a boot sole with makeshift cleats made from brass screws. And again, the findings correlate remarkably well with the available historical record: "We shall have his new boots by the middel watch," wrote some unknown Franklin sailor on one of the "Peglar Papers," recovered from a corpse found within a few miles of these objects recovered by Beattie. Some wooden fragments found nearby, one of them with a bit of green paint still adhering, suggested to Beattie that this must be the "boat place" described by McClintock, where some last desperate group of men were – apparently – trying to return to the comfort, however hemmed in with peril, of their ship.

Beattie recorded all his findings in meticulous detail, but the tale told by these broken bones and fragmentary objects wasn't yet the story that would soon electrify the world. Beattie may just have been hoping for some "soft tissue" – since, by themselves, the bones could offer only partial testimony as to the reason of the men's demise. But it was, of course, the sight of those bodies, of the faces – the eyes! – the clothing of those men whose death early in the expedition spared them the greater sufferings of their comrades who lived – that brought the Franklin story most vividly alive. It's a reminder that, whatever the value of the patient work of ground archaeology, the public at large craves a story – something that will, at least, make partial sense of the enduring mystery of the deaths of so many men, in such unimaginably horrible circumstances, in a landscape so bleak and vast that its very stones seem to mock all hope.

The story of the searchers who came after Beattie is a more complex one. Dedicated amateurs were at its core, but these were modern times: archaeological permits – and therefore, archaeologists – would have to be present. No one would – at least officially speaking – be picking up any souvenirs, and in order to ensure the safety of such parties, GPS transponders (then bulky and expensive), emergency beacons, and ample cold-weather gear would need to be brought in from outside. The expense of such an undertaking was no small thing – it's no coincidence that the next searcher, Steven Trafton, was a wealthy banker who could afford to fund his interests despite the cost – and in his wake, those who sought to pursue the trail of Franklin would need sponsors, patrons, and grants to make their passions possible. The essential element, though, was still the same as it had ever been: an obsessive interest, a refusal to let obstacles stand in one's way, and a certain intuitive ability to put one's self in the place of men who, a century and a half before, had arrived on these shores with only their hope and endurance to guide them. The stage was set for what would be the most active period of Franklin searches in more than a century.

Figure 22 Franklin expedition skull found near NgLj-3.
Photo by Andrew Gregg, used with permission.

10

Ranford

Barry Ranford was a photographer and high school art teacher in Palgrave, Ontario, about forty miles northwest of Toronto. He lived by himself in a converted gristmill far from town, where he had rigged up a turbine in the old mill-race so he could generate his own electricity. Like Charles Francis Hall before him, he had little background or prior history of Arctic interest, no training as an historian or archaeologist, and no knowledge of Inuit culture. Yet, to many, he became the most significant figure in the search for traces of Franklin since Dr Rae. It was his search, after all, that led to the recovery of the largest modern cache of Franklin remains and physical artifacts, including the bones that corroborated earlier findings of lead poisoning, and provided – most significantly – clear evidence that the final survivors had indeed turned to cannibalism. And, although his death by suicide a few years after his first discoveries ended his own career as a searcher, he influenced a generation of amateur Franklin detectives who continued to visit King William Island for nearly a decade afterwards.

It was, by some accounts, a book given to him by his son that started Ranford's Franklin obsession; no one seems to recall *which* book, but I like to imagine that it was McClintock's *Voyage of the 'Fox' in the Arctic Seas*. Whatever it was, Ranford was soon devouring every book about Franklin he could get his hands on, and when Woodman's account of the Inuit evidence was published in 1991, he read it with tremendous interest. He was particularly struck by the accounts of Franklin's men as they struggled southward down the coast of King William Island. How could the remains of so many have gone missing? Where was In-nook-poo-zhee-jook's second boat, the one filled with bones, or the skeletons reburied by Schwatka? And then there was the large tent full of bodies described in the Inuit testimony

– had it been a sort of field hospital for those too ill to carry on? Surely some trace of such a place must still remain.

And so, in the summer of 1992, Ranford, along with his former photography student Mike Yarasavich, flew up to King William. They brought their supplies with them in backpacks and a sort of modified garden cart with heavy-duty wheels, which they planned to haul down the entire western coast of the island, watching the ground beneath their feet, looking for any traces of Franklin's men. They found the going rougher than they had realized, and the plan almost went awry a week into their trek when Yarasavich came down with flu-like symptoms; for a time, Ranford had to haul *him* in the cart. Eventually, as they neared the area of Erebus Bay, where Schwatka had found the three skeletons, Ranford just let Yarasavich sleep at their camp and used the time to pace back and forth, his gaze unrelentingly directed at the ground. The surface there – broken limestone, gravel, and patches of thin soil that supported only moss and lichen – was monotonous in the extreme; everywhere one looked, it seemed the same. It was no wonder, Ranford realized, that so few had found any remains before.

It was on almost the last day, when the two men would have to leave in order to meet their plane at Gjoa Haven, that Ranford spotted it. In his own words: "Retracing a line for a second time, I saw from a distance what looked like a bleach bottle. A bleach bottle on the western side of King William Island made little sense, and as I moved forward, increasingly transfixed, the bottle resolved into a human skull bleached white by time. Then suddenly, I became aware of another skull close by. And then another. I was surrounded by bones. Femurs, a pelvis, two jawbones and part of a vertebra lay white on the rocky limestone, or half-buried, protruding through a carpet of dark green moss." Although he didn't realize it quite yet, what Ranford had stumbled upon was almost certainly In-nook-poo-zhee-jook's place of bones. Not being an anthropologist, though, he hesitated – these might be Inuit bones, after all – how could he be sure? And then something else caught his eye: "It was deeply embedded in moss, and it was warped and covered with a yellow lichen that almost camouflaged its true nature – a machine-stitched boot sole with a square, Victorian-style toe, the footwear of some unlucky sailor."

There could be little doubt that these, then, were Franklin-era remains. He stayed as long as he could searching the ground for some more absolute evidence, and spotted bits of rope, nails, grommets, and small fragments of wood. These, he realized, could well be the remains of a boat with a sail, its planks long ago carried off by Inuit. Further searching revealed a pattern: here, on a slightly elevated island surrounded by tidal mud, a boat had lain; there, up a slight slope, was a stretch of level ground that might have been a tent place. The more widely scattered bones seemed to be partway down the slope; perhaps these were individuals who had died when their comrades were still able to drag them outside. Another cluster of remains nearer to where the boat had been suggested that this site, too, had served as a shelter for a time.

Lastly, he stumbled on a tiny, gilt brass button, bearing an anchor, rope, and crown. This he took with him, and later brought to the National Maritime Museum in London, where it was authenticated as matching those of Franklin's officers; there could be no doubt now. The only problem was how to investigate the site further. Ranford knew that, under the law, he could not touch or remove these remains without a permit and an archaeologist present. Yet, were he to simply report his findings, it was unlikely that anyone would actually come to investigate them. Funding, and time, were limited in the north, and his report might well be classed as just another account of a miscellaneous Franklin site with nothing new to recommend it. And so he tried a different tactic: he called the Prince of Wales Northern Heritage Centre – the agency then responsible for the site, since it lay in the Northwest Territories – and made them an offer that was hard to refuse: either come and examine this spot or he would just go ahead and do it himself, permit or no permit. Ranford's gambit – some might call it blackmail – succeeded, and with assistance from the Polar Continental Shelf organization, an archaeological team was sent to the area the following summer.

Ranford was there to meet them; on this trip, he brought along his daughter Jennifer, as well as John Harrington, the vice-principal at his high school, who had both caught his Franklin fever. Yet, even when he took them to the exact spot, the archaeological team – Margaret Bertulli and Anne Keenleyside – had a hard time seeing the bones. Ranford explained: his trick was to put himself in the mind of a starving Franklin sailor, scouring the land for something to gnaw on. And then, just as had happened when he first found the bones, the others began to see them: one, two, and then many. In all, excluding bones of seals and other Arctic fauna, they would find more than four hundred. Quite a few of the large bones were broken, just as the Inuit had said, and there were visible cut-marks on many

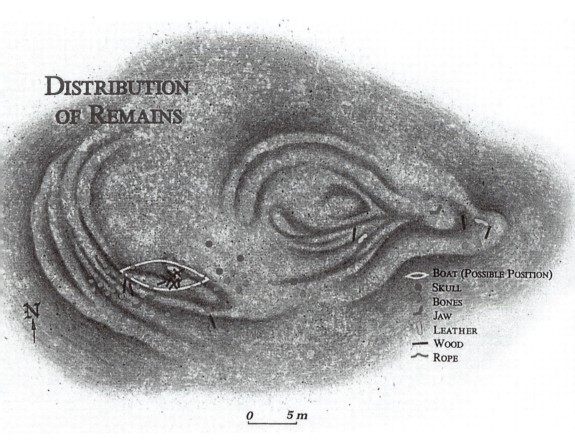

DISTRIBUTION OF REMAINS

BOAT (POSSIBLE POSITION)
SKULL
BONES
JAW
LEATHER
WOOD
ROPE

N

0   5 m

Figure 23 *Above*: Diagram of NgLj-2, *Equinox*, March/April 1994.
Opposite: Aerial view of NgLj-2, photo by Margaret Bertulli,
used with permission.

others. Later, using a scanning electron microscope, Keenleyside would confirm that these were deep, clear-edged cuts, made by a sharpened metal blade. They were located at points where the large muscles joined the bone, the very places where someone intent on defleshing a body would have cut.

Some people refuse to believe that cannibalism could have occurred. They point to the numerous cuts on the small bones of the hands, and suggest that these may be defensive wounds, made by men attempting to fend off

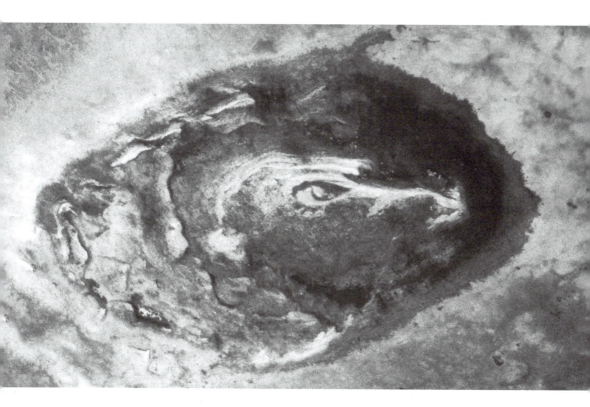

an attack. The location and number of these cuts, however, is inconsistent with such a scenario; according to Keenleyside, these show either an attempt to remove the hands altogether – something the Inuit testified to having seen elsewhere – or perhaps to amputate fingers that had been lost to frostbite. Despite this, there are still some who, like Ernie Coleman, argue as did Dickens that the Inuit set upon Franklin's innocent men. It suffices to me that, at the National Maritime Museum in Greenwich, whose shrine to Franklin includes the Victory Point record, Franklin's medal, spoons, and other relics, the caption is clear: "Several bones of Franklin's men have been found that have knife-scratches and marks on them that are usually associated with cannibalism. This is a normal resort of desperate humans, but the suggestion that the last of Franklin's men ate their dead companions was hotly rejected by Victorian society."

While at the spot, the searchers also identified, with Ranford's help, several nearby areas of human remains, including one that they designated NgLj-3, the site of three disturbed graves and at least two skulls; that site was not examined at the time, although more recently there's been some new interest in these remains. Back in 1993, even as the archaeologists did their work, though, Ranford wandered farther and farther afield; he told some of them he was looking for the "hospital site," where he believed that, at least for a time, those members of the expedition who were too weak to continue were cared for. They cautioned him not to touch or remove any remains he might find, then went back to their work. The season for such work is short in the Arctic, and neither they nor he felt that the opportunity should be wasted.

Ranford was so excited with the 1993 finds that he returned to England and personally researched the ages of crew members, looking for the elusive "cabin boy" whom most assumed must have been represented by the skull in which the state of the calcification of its third molars (one indicator of age) gave an age of between twelve and fifteen years old – which would have meant the individual in question was from nine to eleven years old at the time of sailing. The muster books, alas, seemed to show that all four "boys" (in British usage, more a term of duties than of age) had been eighteen as of 1845. Ranford kept searching, checking baptismal records in the parishes in which these "boys" had been born; he was able to confirm the age of three of them, but the fourth remains a mystery to this day. The early age would not have been all that unusual – Franklin himself joined the Navy at the age of twelve; John Ross was only nine – and in some ways, the namelessness of this young man only added to the fascination.

The next summer, Ranford was back, this time with filmmaker Andrew Gregg and the CBC's Carol Off, who together produced an influential television segment, *The Mysterious Franklin Disappearance*. Unlike the NOVA programs of 1985 or 2005, this show highlighted both Ranford's work and the relevance of the Franklin story to Canadian identity, featuring such luminaries as Pierre Berton, Margaret Atwood, Mordecai Richler, and Rudy Wiebe; for many, this was the cultural moment at which Franklin became relevant, not just as an historical figure but as someone you ought to know about if you were Canadian. In it, Berton, whose *Arctic Grail* had set the standard for northern history, declares Franklin "not much of a hero," a sentiment Rudy Wiebe echoes as he notes that Franklin suffered from the

British prejudice against Inuit knowledge and culture. Perhaps the most pre-
scient of the bunch, though, is Atwood, with both her wit (she refers to the
Beechey Island bodies as "fresh frozen") and insight – she emphasizes that
the Franklin myth is "one of the few that we can examine from every side";
the present story ("Franklin the dope") will likely change. Someday, she
speculates, we may even have "Franklin the mystic."

Throughout the program, Ranford serves as craggy anchor, taking the
CBC team on a tour of the ground, pointing out femurs, boot soles, and
skulls as he goes. Andrew Gregg's camera, tracing the broken stones with a
ground-level view, brings these remains into sudden focus and appearance,
much as did Ranford's own eye. He tells, once more, his story about how
he put himself in the men's mindset, insisting that "the psychological effect
of what happened up here ... had far more to do with their demise than
lead poisoning or scurvy." "They gave up." His arm in a sling, he nevertheless seems to be everywhere, sketching skulls, walking the perimeter, ar-
guing over the significance of bits of metal. It's *his* show, and he's relishing
it – until, as Gregg recalls, David Woodman's plane landed nearby. Since
Ranford's finds drew significantly on Woodman's accounts of Inuit testimony, one might think that he would have been delighted and honoured –
but according to Gregg, he was furious. "He just had this sense of ownership over the whole Franklin thing," Gregg recalled when I reached him by
phone in 2014. "He didn't want to share it with anyone else."

✦✦✦✦

Woodman was there, as it happened, to follow up on a piece of his own evidence – the story, told to Hall by one "Su-pun-ger," who had been among
the first Inuit to venture up to the area near Victory Point. As has been often
noted, the entire northwest region of King William Island was one seldom
visited by Inuit; game was scarce, there were no inland lakes good for fishing, and the ragged, ice-pounded coast was useless for sealing. After word
spread from McClintock that there were abandoned things there to be had,
Su-pun-ger, with his uncle, made haste to visit the area as soon as they could.
They went in the summer, when the absence of significant snow cover gave
them the best possible opportunity for scavenging, and they did well, returning with a sledge-load of precious wood and metal. Indeed, there was
such an abundance of the latter that many things were left behind, such as

several large oot-koo-seeks (kettles) and a heavy iron cook-stove, simply because they were too heavy. Su-pun-ger pointed out the place on the map as "above Back Bay, not far from Victory Point."

His story had a much more chilling aspect – he and his uncle had seen a large tent on the shore, collapsed, and near it, a grisly sight:

[They] came to a place where they found a skeleton of a Kob-lu-na (white man) some parts of it having clothing on while other parts were without any it having been torn off by wolves or foxes. Near this skeleton they saw a stick standing erect wh. had been broken off – the part broken off lying close by. From the appearance both he & his uncle thought the stick, or rather small pillar or post, had been broken off by a Ni-noo (polar bear). On taking hold of that part of the wooden pillar which was erect they found it firmly fixed – could not move it a bit. But what attracted their attention the most on arriving at this pillar was a stone – or rather several large flat stones lying flat on the sandy ground & tight to-gether. After much labour one of these stones was loosened from its carefully fixed position & by great exertions of both nephew & uncle the stone was lifted up a little at one edge just sufficient that they could see that another tier of large flat stones firmly & tightly fitted together was underneath.

Hearing of this "vault," so carefully and laboriously constructed with at least two layers of closely fitted stones, Hall and Tookoolito (who had come to share her employer's high enthusiasm for Franklin) pressed further; as he described it in his journal, "as soon as Su-pung-er had completed his description about the stones telling how carefully they had been placed so as to make it impossible for any water to get between them, Too-koo-li-too said to me with a joyful face, 'I guess I can tell just what that is for – for papers!' And, said I, I think so too." The great hope for papers, particularly logbooks or official records, was a persistent one; ever since McClintock, they had been even more keenly sought after than human remains, since they alone could solve the mystery at a stroke. Even Lady Franklin, once she learned of her husband's death, turned her attention to these; the very last expedition she dispatched, commanded by McClintock's erstwhile lieutenant Allen Young, was explicitly charged to seek such papers.

Whatever the contents of this particular vault, it was clear that those who built it must have spent an incredible amount of time and effort. And, to be sure that the site would be found, they had stuck the large pole in the ground at its side, a pole which to Hall immediately suggested a flagpole:

> The pillar of wood stood by one side of it – not at the end but on one side. The part of the stick or pillar standing was about 4 feet high as indicated by Su-pung-er on my person & the whole height on replacing the part broken off, about six feet from the ground. As nephew & uncle were in want of wood they spent a good deal of time in digging the part erect loose. It was deeply set in the sand. The shape of this stick or pillar was a peculiar one to these natives. The part in the ground was square. Next to the ground was a big ball & above this to within a foot or so of the top the stick was round. The top part was about 3 or 4 inches square. No part of it was painted – all natural wood colour.

The description matches that of a topgallant mast – both the *Erebus* and the *Terror* would have had spares of these – with its distinctive square foot and round top, although the ball was an unusual feature; it's possible that it could have been fashioned on board by one of the ships' carpenters. Su-pun-ger and his uncle were intent on obtaining the wood and so spent a considerable amount of time and effort getting out the part that was still in the ground. After finally prying it loose and tying it to their *qamutiik* (sled), they went back to examine the tent, then decided to return once more to the "vault":

> After a while they concluded to go & make other attempts to raise some of the stones where the pillar was found. At last they were successful in raising enough of the stones to see what they covered up. They found a hole of the depth from the feet up to the navel & of a length more than a man's height & wider than the width of a man's shoulders & this was all nicely walled with flat stones placed one above another, flatwise. In this vault they found a clasp knife, a skeleton bone of a man's leg & a human head (skull). There was much water, mud & sand at the bottom of the vault. The sand had been carried in by water, as they thought, running in at the hole that had been made by the wild animal on one side of the vault. Near this vault they saw parts of a human skeleton with fragments of clothing on the limbs. There was no head about these skeleton bones & Su-pung-er & his

uncle concluded that the same wild animal that had made the hole in the vault had taken these skeleton bones out of the vault & dragged them where he & his uncle saw them.

And so it turned out not to be a cache of papers after all but a grave. A grave that must have consumed hundreds of man-hours in the making, the more so if it had been done when the soil was still frozen – and, therefore, the grave of someone of considerable importance. Beside that grave, a flag-pole, on which doubtless a Union Jack or naval ensign had been flown, to mark the place for all to see. Yet, despite such considerable labour and pre-cautions, a polar bear – or bears – had violated the grave, chomped on the bones, and bitten the mast in two, the torn flag fluttering to the ground. What Su-pung-ger and his uncle had stumbled upon – or into – was a scene almost identical to Landseer's "Man proposes, God disposes." And so in-deed He *does* dispose, breaking open the hard-hewed shrines of men and scattering their bones to the winds.

✛✛✛✛

This was the story that had brought David Woodman to King William that summer, in an undertaking he called (using a simplified form of the name) "Project Supunger." He assumed, reasonably enough, that a vault in the ground four feet deep and larger than a man's body in height and width would be discoverable, even after nearly a century and a half. In the end, he was defeated by the relentless scree and broken rocks of the island; scoured by seasonal ice and rearranged by frost heaves and erosion, the land had swallowed up this man-made morsel without a hiccup, along with most of the other traces of Franklin's men. Woodman did do an extensive survey, using a GPS transponder (something of a bulky oddity in those pre-smart-phone days); he concluded that previous visitors had conflated Victory Point with the point on which Crozier came ashore (which he prefers to call "Crozier's Landing") some distance farther down the coast. Of the great heap of materials left there, they found only a few small pieces of canvas and a few rivets and nails; a skull found about a mile inland turned out to have been of Inuit origin. Time and tide – and scavenging – had done their work.

Ranford, back at Erebus Bay, alternated his energies between talking with the film crew and scouting for new sites. He had brought with him the requisite archaeologist – John MacDonald – but his habits drove the poor man to distraction. As Andrew Gregg recalls it, MacDonald was always trying to lay out a grid and mark any remains with little orange flags, while Ranford, heedless of protocol, leapt about from spot to spot, disturbing the ground, picking up what he could find, then putting it down as some other object caught his attention. His energy and enthusiasm were boundless, but so keen was he on making the next great find that it was impossible to find, or catalogue, the subtler story told by tiny fragments of bone and mossy scraps of cloth. Archaeology depends on data – set-points, grids, and careful mapping of scatter – for its patient discoveries; Ranford simply moved too fast for it – or John MacDonald – to ever quite catch up. As the season waned, frustrations grew; there had been no new find this year. No matter, Ranford told his friend John Harrington, who had also come up with him this time, there would be another chance next year; he'd be back, that much was for certain.

But it was not to be. A little more than a year after his last search at King William Island, Barry Ranford took his own life. This act, as far as anyone knows, had nothing to do with his northern travels or his Franklin fascination. Yet, in a strange way, it ended up adding a sad and curious codicil to the findings from the King William Island site – for, in his basement, his widow discovered a box of relics and bones, some of them apparently taken from the King William Island sites. None had been properly tagged, and without any provenance, it was difficult to say what sort of story they told, unless it was a tale of Ranford himself: a man who, in his quest to discover the fate of Franklin, would quite literally stop at nothing. Something in the story of those men had got under his skin, so much so that he had brought their bones home as macabre tokens of his esteem, a sign of some deeply felt affinity. After all, in his mind at least, he had walked among them, searching the ground for objects of significance, trying to imagine from the few, sad remnants of these men something of the final desperate days of the expedition.

✦✦✦✦

Ranford was gone, but his enthusiasm lived on after him. John Harrington took up the symbolic role of expedition leader and returned each summer for the next several years. Along with MacDonald, Ron Rust, and Doug

Stern, he carried on land searches in 1995, 1996, 1997, and 1998 (twice). Their finds were modest in scope – a bone here, a bit of sailcloth there – but they kept up a regular presence. They were also the first searchers to regularly share their discoveries via the Internet; through the "Franklin Trail" site run by Karis Burkowski back in Ontario, regular updates, called in daily via satellite phone, were posted to the web. And it was there, amidst the white spaces of early HTML pages, rather than the snows of the frozen north, that I came upon them. John's enthusiasm mirrored Barry's; in many ways, he was carrying on the flame. Because once bitten by the Franklin "bug," there's really no cure, other than to search where one can, as often as one can, and as carefully as one can.

The 1998 expedition had a special purpose – to revisit the site of Crozier's landing on the 150th anniversary of the abandonment of the ships in 1848. This required reaching the spot in April, a time when the land is still deeply frozen and the sun, though nearly constant, still lacks the power to penetrate the cold. Yet, despite the harsh conditions and remoteness of the place, Harrington and his team were startled to find, on arriving by plane at Victory Point, that a rival team was already camped nearby, plaque in hand, waiting to commemorate the same event! This group, led by rare-book collector and dealer Cameron Treleaven and Louie Kamookak, had travelled overland from Gjoa Haven a day earlier. Each group was irritated by the other's presence but ultimately decided to bury the proverbial hatchet; Treleaven and Kamookak even invited Harrington's party over to their tent for a dinner of freshly grilled Arctic char.

The next morning, once the plaque was placed, toasts were drunk, and a ceremonial moment of silence observed, Treleaven and Kamookak headed back to Gjoa Haven. Harrington, though, still had promises to keep; having arranged to place several satellite-phone calls to Franklin buffs around the world, he stayed behind at his own camp and hooked up the satellite transmitter. I was one of the recipients of these calls and experienced for the first time the weird, delayed dialogue of a signal that has to bounce into space and back again before it reaches land-bound lines. I couldn't help but imagine how different the fate of Franklin's men would have been had they had any such direct means to reach the world they had left behind. It was a moving moment for me, and very atmospheric; in the background I almost thought I could hear the howling of the winds.

It turned out that I could. Not long after placing the last of the planned calls, Harrington and his companions found themselves overwhelmed by a sudden blizzard, whose gale-force winds ripped away their tents and sent equipment flying. With help from their guides, they managed to quickly fashion two small emergency igloos, in which they hunkered down, waiting for the storm to cease. In those days, it was protocol to call in every twenty-four hours to the local authorities; if one failed to check in, a rescue crew would be sent – along with, once rescue was rendered, a hefty bill for its cost. As he tried the hailing frequency, Harrington realized that the expedition's battery was nearly spent; fuel for their stoves was also low. It wasn't until the third day, completely out of food and half-frozen, that the weather broke; there was just enough power in the battery to make the call, and their plane flew in to pick them up. Their journey hadn't been planned as a re-enactment of the Franklin disaster – but it came frighteningly close to being one.

They returned that following August, with a plan to travel the western shores of the Boothia peninsula, searching the area near where Ross had found the North Magnetic Pole and using a boat to carry their heavier gear. To assist them, they had hired two new guides, Abel Aqqaq and Tommy Totalik. As they looked over the charts, though, they realized that the boats would have a hard time getting near the rocky shore, with only perhaps one or two natural harbours available; nevertheless, they decided to press on. Along the way, they visited several hunting and fishing camps; their guides shot a seal on the coast, and another party bagged two caribou inland. It would have been enough food to feed the Franklin expedition for many days.

On their fourth day out, they reached their main goal, the area where Ross had surveyed the magnetic pole, but instead of just one cairn, they found several of various sizes. Like Crozier's party in 1848, finding "Sir James Ross's Pillar" turned out to be more difficult than they had imagined. They had his original observations but realized early on that Ross's longitude was in error and would have placed the pole twenty miles offshore; apparently his chronometers had been running a bit fast. After some effort, they finally located the right one, a cairn matching the latitude and description in Ross's journals from 1831:

> I made known to the party this gratifying result of all of our joint labours; and it was then, that amidst mutual congratulations, we fixed the British flag on the spot, and took possession of the North Magnetic Pole and its adjoining territory, in the name of Great Britain and King

William the Fourth. We had abundance of materials for building, in the fragments of limestone that covered the beach; and we therefore erected a cairn of some magnitude, under which we buried a canister, containing a record of the interesting fact: only regretting that we had not the means of constructing a pyramid of more importance, and of strength sufficient to withstand the assaults of the Esquimaux. Had it been a pyramid as large as that of Cheops, I am not quite sure that it would have done more than satisfy our ambition, under the feelings of that exciting day.

To celebrate the rediscovery of the spot, they opened a flask and shared 'round a tot of Scotch. In the midst of their mutual congratulations, a call came in via radio phone from a camp they had visited a few days previous. The people there had stumbled upon some graves and skulls, and not only that: a piece of wood or leather which seemed to have on it the date "1847." Immediately, of course, their plans were changed.

They reached this camp two days later and went at once to visit these graves. There, they were surprised to see a wooden casket protruding from the stones of one of them; it seemed old, but not perhaps so old as Ross's or Franklin's day. The nails were round rather than square-headed, suggesting machine manufacture. The ruins of an old trapper's cabin stood nearby, offering a possible explanation, but the idea of a piece of leather with "1847" on it seemed still to offer some promise. A skull was located, but not by the group that included MacDonald, so they couldn't say whether it was a white man's or an Inuk's. Continuing problems with the group's satellite phone and radio led to another several days of no news for those of us at home in our armchairs. What could be the problem? Surely the date must mean something.

And finally, three days later, came news: the item wasn't a piece of leather but of wood, and the date wasn't 1847 either but 1857; just before the date was a word that seemed to end with "NCE." The later date suggested to Harrington that it might be an artifact from one of the early Franklin search expeditions, so his excitement still ran high; a more exact identification would have to wait. Finally, back at Taloyoak, they cleaned the wood carefully and had a fresh look. That's when it became obvious to everyone that what they had found was in fact a broken-off bit of a crate that had once read "SINCE 1857," along with the last few letters of "store in a cool dry place" – instructions that identified it as a Borden's (founded in 1857) dairy crate, dating far more probably to the 1940s than to the 1850s. Everyone enjoyed a good laugh at their own expense.

The Franklin Trail crew were dedicated amateurs, to be sure. They had the money and resources to take trips, hire guides, and do a little scouring around on the ground, but with the exception of John MacDonald, they weren't archaeologists or professional historians. Their main contribution was that they kept Ranford's spirit alive, sharing their experiences and finds in a time when the idea of a sponsored expedition with real-time web postings was still so new that it didn't yet have a name; the word "blog" would not be coined until 1999. There was an easy camaraderie among these men, one that seemed to open up the world of Franklin searching to those who couldn't hope to venture there themselves, and for that we can be grateful. But it's with David Woodman, who, in addition to his two books led at least seven significant searches to the shores of King William Island and the Adelaide peninsula, that the modern Franklin search era really begins. Because, when you're looking for a needle in a frozen haystack, you can't afford to leave even one stone unturned.

Figure 24 Cape Felix, photo by David Woodman, used with permission.

11

Woodman

Every mind must know the whole lesson for itself, – must go over the whole
ground. What it does not see, what it does not live, it will not know.
– Ralph Waldo Emerson

One of the most daunting aspects of the region where Sir John Franklin and
his men disappeared is not its cold, its remoteness, or its seemingly feature-
less terrain – it is, simply put, its *size*. The possible routes of ships or men
cover an area of thousands of square miles, most of it freely accessible only
during a brief summer season of perhaps five to six weeks' duration. Just
getting to this area is expensive – the few commercial flights are far more
costly than in the populous south, and to reach the more remote sites one
has to charter a plane. Getting any sort of heavy equipment to these places
is more costly still, not to mention the technicians needed to operate it and
the support vessels or other personnel needed to keep it safe and supplied
while in use. For scientific fieldwork, there are a number of organizations,
Polar Continental Shelf chief among them, that have the resources to support such expeditions, but if one's goal is to search for long-dead sailors,
there's no space on a grant application for that.

From 1992 to 2004, though, David Woodman was a member or leader
of no fewer than nine expeditions to this area, pursuing his conviction that,
sooner or later, the Inuit testimony would lead him either to one of
Franklin's ships or to a site on land where relics and records could be found.
And, although it's true that Inuit evidence is sometimes less specific than
might be desired, its role in focusing the search in areas of higher probabil-
ity has been indispensable; without it, the sheer expense of searching so
large and area would have been prohibitive. Technology has been essential

to the task – and Woodman has tried everything from ground-penetrating radar to magnetometer scans and sonar booms lowered through the ice – but sheer, dogged perseverance has been the essential ingredient. By connecting the Inuit stories with each other, and with the recorded narratives of past searchers, Woodman's work laid the foundation of all modern searches; without it, Parks Canada's successful 2014 search for one of Franklin's ships would never have been possible.

As with those before him, his journey began with a book – in fact, the exact same book as theirs. As Woodman describes it, he was in his freshman year at the University of Toronto when, passing by a reshelving cart in the library, his eye chanced upon a reprint of McClintock's *Voyage of the 'Fox' in the Arctic Seas*. He picked it up, thinking it might prove to be a frothy sea tale of some sort, and was immediately swept away by the tide of its narrative. Seeing the latitude and longitude of the ships so plainly upon the Victory Point record, he decided then and there that he must find them. He had been scuba-diving since his teenage years and now indulged in the dream of diving on one of these vessels, planks wonderfully preserved by the cold water, peering into the rooms where once Franklin's men had lived, and died. He had all kinds of questions: Why hadn't the ships been found before? Were there no clues from previous searches that could help him narrow his? Over the next several years, whenever possible, he continued to pursue his quest, spending hours in historical archives, including those of the Scott Polar Research Institute at Cambridge and the National Maritime Museum. And, as he became increasingly familiar with much of the known evidence, he came to believe that the one most promising area of research, and one not fully taken advantage of by previous historians, was the vast body of testimony collected from the Inuit themselves.

The largest portion of this evidence, by far, was that collected by Hall. Everyone else had long assumed that most of it had been published by J.E. Nourse in his 1879 account of Hall's second expedition. Yet, as he corresponded with the archivists at the Smithsonian Institution, where Hall's papers were stored, he began to realize that a large proportion of this testimony had been omitted. In some cases, information from "field notebooks" has never been copied into the bound journals; in other cases, the journals, or Hall's letters to his patrons, contained additional details; in still other instances, Nourse had simply omitted material that he felt was redundant, or didn't fit neatly into the chronological scheme he used for the book. Woodman started writing to the Smithsonian, asking for copies, which they gladly made and mailed back – but before long he realized that getting these documents in such a piecemeal manner would take far too long; the only way to be sure he had everything was to search them himself.

He found the papers in general disarray – some dated, some not, with one sort of text jumbled with another; many of them were still stored in the old wooden drawers into which Nourse himself must have stuffed them. The Smithsonian gave him a small office to work out of; he was there each morning when the museum opened, staying until the janitorial staff kicked him out in the evening. It was then that he first read the full account of Su-pun-ger and the stone-lined vault, first saw Hall's sketches of the "tent place," and read the entirety of the original notes written during Hall's time on King William Island in the first three weeks of May 1869. He became accustomed to Hall's spiralling hand, his little asides, and he learned of how closely Tookoolito followed Hall's interests and joined in the excitement when stories of Franklin's men were told. He also learned of – and shared – Hall's frustration when one witness seemed to contradict another, or, when, just on the verge of finding some of the precious, long-sought papers, an Inuk witness would tell Hall that they had been thrown away. He realized at once that sifting through this evidence would be no easy matter.

Yet, as he read through these papers, Woodman could see that, throughout the body of Inuit testimony, Hall's informants were quite careful and specific as to what they had seen, or heard. Those who were not eyewitnesses would plainly say so; those who *were* would always name their comrades, so it was reasonably easy to separate hearsay from direct observation. Hall himself was often an ally, questioning his informants, constantly going over what they had told him, comparing it to similar accounts he had heard elsewhere. There were some problems. Hall, for instance, decided early on that the "Ag-loo-ka" he had heard about must be Crozier, and often simply wrote "Crozier" in his notes; he also tended to wax hot and cold, throwing out babies and bathwater together until – often just a few pages later – he would retrieve them. Throughout, Hall's spelling of Inuktitut names and words was highly idiosyncratic. The eagerness of Inuit to please their strange visitors, and Tookoolito's desire to bring Hall good news as to the possible survival of Franklin's men, also had to be taken into account.

It took several years, borrowing time from his ordinary duties and employment, but at last Woodman was able to assemble a coherent body of Inuit evidence, focusing on the most consistent and widely told stories, corroborated when possible by physical evidence and the accounts of white searchers. In doing so, he moved away from what he came to call the "standard reconstruction" – that of a single abandonment in April 1848, followed by a long, deadly journey over land in an attempt to reach the Back River and ascend it, ending with a final fatal camp on the mainland at the place Schwatka had dubbed "Starvation Cove." To his mind, the evidence was compelling: the Inuit almost never visited the far northwest corner of King William Island, off the coast of which Franklin's ships were trapped in the ice for at least two winters – and yet there were stories of them visiting those ships, and seeing one quickly and completely crushed in the ice. The ships, therefore, must have been remanned, and these stories must date from that time.

This was consistent with Inuit dating of many of these events – in their testimony to McClintock and Hall, it seemed clear that some of their encounters with Kabloonas had taken place in 1849 or even 1850. Significantly, the story of a ship at "Oot-goo-lik" (Utjulik) was widely known, and in almost every account signs of life were seen near or on board the vessel: deck-sweepings on the ice, a gangplank lowered, the footprints of white men nearby. That the second ship had been piloted, or perhaps drifted to this location with living men aboard, already extended the Franklin story beyond 1848. Secondly, Woodman found many additional accounts – not fully dealt with until the publication of his second book, *Strangers among Us* – which seemed to speak of white men, sometimes mistaken for subarctic tribesmen, making it far to the east on the Melville peninsula. The story the Inuit told made sense only if there were multiple abandonments and multiple groups seeking a way out by different directions at different times. This was corroborated when Woodman realized that the number of bodies actually seen at Starvation Cove by the Inuit was many fewer than others had assumed, probably only six men.

So where to begin? Woodman initially hoped only that his book might inspire others to seek to verify his theories, which it did – although in retrospect Ranford's efforts, though successful in one sense, only complicated them. Still, in the wake of the public attention to the Franklin story that followed, Woodman found support and sponsorship for expeditions of his own, which were always conducted with the proper permits and procedures. He focused on two sets of stories. The first were those of the Inuit who ventured to the north and west of King William, in search of wood and metal, and who were among the first to see many of the tents and camps of the white men. Their accounts told of cannibalism, yes, but also of many books, records, and papers, some possibly sealed up in a vault in the ground. The second set of stories told of the Utjulik ship, giving such detailed accounts of its location that Woodman was certain that the ship could be found. His expeditions focused both on land, particularly the sites near Victory Point and Crozier's Landing, and on water, using Inuit accounts to narrow the search area for giant umiaq last seen near Utjulik.

Woodman's land searches were conducted, as Ranford's had been, in the summer to ensure maximum visibility of artifacts on the ground. In 1993, and again in 1995, his "Project Supunger" scoured the northwest coast of King William Island, not only seeking the mysterious "vaults" but re-locating and surveying other landmarks associated with the initial abandonment of the ships. These searches, though they failed to find any new or significant artifacts, established the exact location of many of the key features along the coast near Victory Point. Among these, perhaps the most significant – and haunting – was the gravesite of Lieutenant John Irving, the man whose body was brought back by Schwatka and then sent to Scotland for burial with full military honours in Edinburgh's Dean Cemetery.

The intervening century had worn down the stones, but the outline was clear; just to be sure, Woodman tested it by lying down inside it – and found that, indeed, it could contain the length and breadth of a man. A later comparison of the arrangement of the stones, putting a photograph alongside Klutschak's original sketch, showed a clear correspondence, right down to the "pillow" stone at what appeared to have been the head of the grave.

Yet, if this *was* Irving's grave, it raises significant questions, questions that expose problems in the "classical" narrative. Its site, quite close to that of Ross's cairn at Victory Point, seemed wrong; since Irving was mentioned in the Victory Point note as having found Ross's cairn, we can safely presume he was fit enough to be sent on such a mission. And yet here, only a few hundred feet distant, lies his grave! Did Irving meet with some sudden end so soon after the Victory Point record that the main body of the expedition had not yet moved on? It's often surmised that Irving must have been sent back later to the ships, and that this explains the gap in time. Yet a gravesite such as his, with its heavy stones, would almost certainly have been beyond the means of a small party of men in the latter days of the expedition to construct; with scurvy and exhaustion rampant, the burials the later survivors managed to perform – when they managed the task at all –

Figure 25 *Left*: Probable site of "Irving" grave, photo by David C. Woodman, used with permission. *Right*: Sketch of Irving grave by Heinrich Klutschak.

consisted of laying out the body and covering it with a few shovels of gravel. The men who built this monument must have been fit, and the time ample, for such a substantial undertaking.

Woodman regards this as a key piece of evidence for his different reconstruction of events: "The fact that Irving was buried here is one of the main pillars of my contention that a return to the ships did occur in 1848 (otherwise they wouldn't have been manned in Erebus Bay in 1849 when the Inuit met them), but my assessment is that the 105 men didn't get very far and were back in the ships within a month after finding that they managed only three miles a day or so ... there would have been plenty of manpower available to build the grave that we found." That the ships may have been remanned isn't completely outside the traditional reconstruction – clearly, some men were aboard the ship that was piloted or drifted into Queen Maud Gulf – but the notion that the 1848 abandonment was itself abandoned early on is a far more radical revision. In addition to the presence of the Irving grave, Woodman notes that no Inuit came to search the northwest corner of King William Island until they learned – probably through McClintock's translator Johan Carl Christian Petersen – of the supplies abandoned there. It was a region seldom visited, since the heavy pack-ice that scoured its coasts made it unsuitable for hunting sea mammals, and the best lakes and streams for fishing were far to the south and west. If there were no Inuit present, there could have been no visit to the ships during Franklin's last year of command, and these stories must come from a later date. Woodman's version also has the advantage that it accounts for the significant time discrepancies in Inuit accounts, many of which date encounters with white men as late as 1850.

In extending the expedition's timeline to make it consistent with Inuit testimony, Woodman ultimately creates an entirely different picture of the expedition's demise. An initial abandonment in April 1848 goes badly, with most men returning to their ships; the ships make unexpected progress the next season, coming near to the vicinity of Erebus Bay. From there, regular traffic between the ships and land takes place, using the whaleboats when there's open water; it's there, then, that the Inuit visit the ships, there that they see one crushed in the ice, sinking so quickly that a good many supplies, and even some men, are lost. There, too, a funeral of a great captain is witnessed – in Woodman's version, this must be Crozier – and there, too, the "black men" appeared, men with "black faces," some of whom even appear "black all over," who, making noise and shouting, frighten an Inuk who ventures on board ship.

This last story, recorded by Hall, gives us another instance of just how ambiguous Inuit testimony can be. Here is its original version:

> Bye & bye he [the Inuit] went again to the ship all alone with his dogs & sledge. He went on deck, & a great many men – black men – came right up out of the hatch-way & the first thing he (the Innuit) knew, he couldn't get away. These men who were then all around him, had black faces, black hands, black clothes on – were black all over! They had little black noses, only so big: (the old lady here put her hand on the bridge of her nose showing that the noses were not more than half

the length & size of common ones) & this Innuit was very much alarmed because he could not get away from these black men but especially was he frightened when they made three great noises (three rounds of cheers as Too-koo-li-too thinks these great noises were). When three great noises were made, the Esh-e-mut-ta (Captain) came up out of the Cabin & put a stop to it, when all the black men went down the same way they had come up. This Innuit believed these men belonged down among the coals & that they lived there. Then the Captain took this Innuit down with him into his Cabin & made him many presents, for he (the Innuit) had been frightened so. Before the Captain took him down into his Cabin he told this Innuit to take a look over to the land, the Captain pointing out to him the exact spot where was a big Tupik (tent). The Captain asked him if he saw the tent, & the Innuit told him he did. Then the Captain told him that black men, such as he had just seen, lived there, & that neither he (this Innuit) nor any of his people must ever go there. After the Innuit had received the presents that the Captain made him, he left the ship & went home; & he would never go to the ship again because of the frightful looking black men that lived there down in the Coal hole.

This story was originally interpreted by Woodman as a cautionary tale; when he realized that his Inuit visitor had been frightened, the captain compensated him with gifts but also used the occasion to issue a warning against visiting the tent on shore. Could these be a band of mutineers or rogue crewmen who had resorted to cannibalism? Was the captain simply trying to keep the Inuit away from the hospital tent, or warn them about gunpowder cached on land (and there were incidents where Inuit, unaware of the explosive qualities of the black powder they found, injured themselves)? All these make sense yet beg the question: Who were the black men on the ship?

To this, it turns out, there's a fairly simple answer: the key is the "three great shouts" that Tookoolito interpreted as cheers. These are clearly huzzahs, sounds of celebration, not intended as a threat to the ship's unexpected visitor. And on what occasion would Franklin's men have blackened their faces and given three cheers? On Guy Fawkes Day, of course. There's even a description of a very similar observation of that holiday as it was celebrated on the *Fox*, by McClintock himself: "This evening a well-got-up procession sallied forth, marched round the ship with drum, gong, and discord, and then proceeded to burn the effigy of Guy Fawkes. Their blackened faces, extravagant costumes, flaring torches, and savage yells, frightened away all the dogs; nor was it until after the fireworks were set off and the traitor consumed that they crept back again." Just such celebrations doubtless took place aboard the *Erebus* and *Terror* on that holiday, and the story suggests that, at least at that point, there was still an ongoing effort to keep up morale and the spirits of the men were reasonably good. If this took place in 1849 at Erebus Bay, there must still have been hope then of some escape; the captain simply used some quick thinking to find a way to keep the Inuit away from the tent on shore.

Woodman's version of the expedition's demise suggests that, with the sinking of one of the ships, a camp was established on land, at least in the summer months, where the crew of that ship could escape the cramped quarters of the surviving vessel. And, since we know now that that vessel was HMS *Erebus*, this means that the *Terror* was the ship that sank. At some point, additional efforts were made to reach safety, but these were probably not abandonments either; their goal was more likely to contact others and send help, as well as perhaps to gather fish and game for the crews, whose three-year supply of foodstuffs must have been growing short, even with their diminished numbers.

Some, too ill for an overland march, doubtless stayed back at Terror Bay. Of those who set forth, Woodman's reconstruction suggests there were three primary groups:

- An organized group that set off to the east, aimed most likely at reaching Inuit settlements at Igloolik or shipping lanes in the Barrow Strait. This party got as far as some point partway up the Melville peninsula.
- A group who remained on the one ship, which then either drifted or was piloted to a point near a small island in Wilmot and Crampton Bay in Queen Maud Gulf. From this ship, a small party, perhaps as few as three or four in number, was traced on the land; they seemed to have a dog with them and successfully killed at least one caribou.
- A land party, perhaps a last and desperate effort, bringing at least one boat on a sledge, as well as the Halkett inflatable gutta-percha (rubber) raft. This party retreated along the southern coast of King William Island, with some men "falling down as they walked"; a small number – perhaps six to eight men – crossed over Simpson Strait and

ended their days at "Starvation Cove." The rest headed east, perhaps still believing that they could reach the Gulf of Boothia by land, and came to a final, fatal halt at Booth Point and the Todd Islets.

There are still some points of uncertainty: the small group of four men may have come from the ships or may have been a detachment from the third party. It's this group that Hall himself believed had lived on for a time, since he had heard second-hand tales of white men staying for a season with the hunter Too-shoo-art-thariu. When he actually tracked Too-shoo down himself, though, the man denied that he had hosted such men, telling a story that echoed previous ones of the Washington Bay encounter. In some versions of this story, two final survivors head south, avoiding (for some reason) the known Inuit camps near Repulse Bay and heading for Fort Churchill. Hall heard stories that they had come among the Kin-na-pa-too or Caribou Inuit, and that people there had said they were sure they were alive and had made it home. Later, he heard rumours that they had been killed, perhaps mistaken for a hostile band.

The one party unaccounted for is the one that marched east. Why they would have headed toward Cape Englefield is far from clear; they could have reached the Barrow Strait much more quickly by heading straight north. Fury Beach, too, would have seemed a sensible goal; after all, Crozier had actually been present when supplies from the wreck of the *Fury* were offloaded, and the Rosses had sheltered there for a season on their retreat, which ended in rescue from a passing whaler. One can only imagine that some very specific circumstance drove them to this choice; Crozier had wintered at Igloolik with Parry's second expedition, and – assuming he wasn't the captain whose funeral the Inuit witnessed, he might have sought that place for food and shelter in the winter, knowing that Inuit from all around would gather there. Woodman, in *Strangers*, documents numerous bits of tantalizing evidence – red-painted tins at campfires, men seen with rifles over their shoulders at a distance, and even strange "ar-nuk" (feces) that the Inuit knew were not from their own people. It's quite possible that the stories told to Barry about a camp on what we now know to be Crown Prince Frederik Island may also relate to this group.

Yet perhaps most enigmatic and haunting is the account of the final departure of the group of four (or, in some accounts, three) men. The story is the stuff of old chivalric romances: in gratitude for helping him and his companions survive the winter, an officer of the Franklin expedition presented

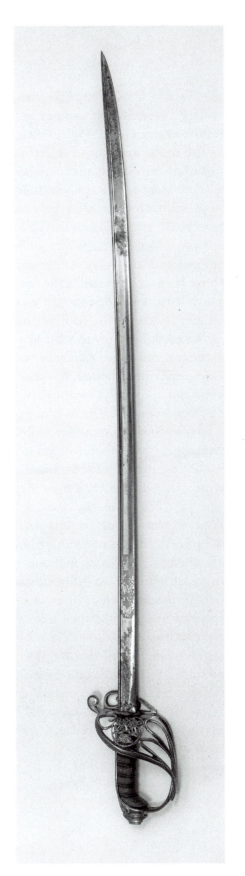

Figure 26 "The sword of a Great Officer."
© The Manitoba Museum, Winnipeg, MB.

an Inuk hunter with his most valuable possession – his sword. And then, years later, this same hunter, now grown elderly, presents this same sword to a trader at a HBC post, saying that it had been given to him by a "great officer." And then the kicker: this sword is still in the archives of the HBC, with the following catalogue record: "This ornate sword is documented as having been retrieved by Chief Factor Roderick MacFarlane from an Inuit man who claimed that the sword had been presented to him in 1857 by an officer of the Franklin expedition. The letters 'W IV' appearing on the blade and hilt refer to King William IV, 1830–1837. 'Moore, late, Bicknells & Moore, Old Street, London,' have been engraved on the brass ferrule and chape." The name of William IV ought to have been a clue – unlike the long reign of Queen Victoria, his brief time upon the throne (1830–37) gives a narrow window from which a candidate might be identified. Too narrow, as it turns out; Royal Navy officers were given their sword with their lieutenant's commission, and none of the officers on the expedition received their commission in this interval. On closer examination, though, this mystery is replaced by another: the open style of the basket on the sword's hilt shows it to be a British infantry blade, not a naval one at all. The only members of the Franklin expedition who would have borne such weapons would have been the Royal Marines, and yet here again we are frustrated: among the Marines, only commissioned officers would have carried swords, and the expedition's complement included no Marine with a higher rank than that of sergeant.

And yet, there the sword is. One possibility is that swords were stowed on board in case of necessity – after all, the primary duties of the Marines on board were military defence and security, and it might have been thought prudent to provide them. Another, still more intriguing, possibility exists: among the Marines was Solomon Tozer, one of the more senior in terms of service, having risen to the rank of corporal prior to Queen Victoria's coronation, at which time the Royal Marines were reorganized into a "New Establishment." Corporals could carry swords while in full dress and on parade, and it's conceivable that Tozer might have been issued one for such a purpose. There's one final, suggestive connection. As pointed out to me some years ago by Woodman, Tozer's name might, to Inuit ears, have sounded similar enough to Crozier's (which they usually rendered as "Crozhar") – he himself may have been the "great officer."

++++

Figure 27 Detail of Heinrich Klutschak's map. Collection of the author.

Woodman, though he too was fascinated by this story, chose in 1994 to focus his energies on the ship. After all, it was by far the most common and consistent part of the Inuit testimony: a ship anchored or stranded in shallow water, with signs of habitation; later, abandoned and visited by Inuit; and still later, sinking, but in water so shallow its masts were still visible. The location wasn't as precise as could be wished – Utjulik is a vicinity more than an address – but still, using the accounts given by various Inuit witnesses over time, it seemed possible to Woodman to establish a limited search area and probe there for the remains of the vessel. He collated all the evidence and looked at every available map – even the seldom-seen coloured lithographic map prepared by Henry Klutschak, on which the unknown vessel was indicated at "Schiff gesunken" (ship sunk).

This site, several miles off Grant Point in the direction of Kirkwall Island, was consistent with the most specific Inuit testimony, given by Puhtoorak, who had actually stood on the deck of the ship; he described it as three to five miles due west of Grant Point (known to the Inuit as the southernmost of the "two fingers" [*tikerqat*]). This also was consistent with Kirkwall Island, named by Rasmussen's informants as *umiartaliq* – the place of a boat or boats – although, as we've seen, it wasn't clear in those accounts whether the name derived from a whaleboat or the ship; any vessel made for many passengers was a umiaq to the Inuit. Woodman also gave some credit to stories that seemed to point to the area near the coast of O'Reilly Island, some miles to the south, where possible debris from the ships was reported; these were his original northern and southern search areas.

For "Project Utjulik" in 1998, Woodman's plan was much like that later adopted by Parks Canada; using the icebreaker *Sir Wilfrid Laurier* as a base, Woodman and his crews towed side-scan sonar booms back and forth across the sea floor, a process so methodical – and repetitive – that it's jokingly called "mowing the lawn" by wreck searchers. A helicopter on the icebreaker was also made available, so that small groups could quickly visit promising sites on the many islands in the vicinity. The search was hampered, not so much by bad weather as by the fact that the *Laurier* was pledged to many kinds of service – delivery of supplies, dropping off pilots, and assisting any vessel in need – all of these occurred, and forced the search to be switched to the O'Reilly area partway through. There, as at Kirkwall, the geography of the sea floor turned out to be far more varied than expected, which complicated the search. Nevertheless, on O'Reilly Island itself, a promising find was made: two sheets of copper, one with what seemed like tar on one side, a copper disk (later found to be part of a coffee pot), and an iron spike. And then, on a small island to the north of the search area, a skull, initially thought to be Inuit but later shown to be Caucasian. Lacking any other physical evidence, though, the significance of these items was unclear. Had they washed ashore from the wreck? Been carried hither atop the ice floes? Was the skull a remnant from some despoiled grave yet to be found? Once again, the Arctic had yielded up clues – and once again, they proved to be enigmatic ones.

In 2000 Woodman returned, this time aboard the *St Roch II*, a vessel renamed in honour of its mission to retrace Larsen's original voyage of the original *St Roch*, which had been only the second vessel to navigate the

Northwest Passage, after Amundsen's *Gjøa*, in 1940–42. The new vessel's shallow draft and catamaran design made it ideal for Woodman's purposes, and this mission proved the most successful in terms of the area mapped – about 240 square nautical miles in the Kirkwall Island area. The sea floor here was less varied, mostly a flat plain, but no trace of the ship was found. It's worth noting, though, that the *St Roch II* also called in Gjoa Haven on that voyage, and that – for neither the first time nor the last – Louie Kamookak led its crew to the gravesite of Franklin's men near the Todd Islets, the very one that had been originally discovered by his grandfather William "Paddy" Gibson. At the time, it was reported in the press as a great discovery, but neither then nor since has any archaeological survey of the site been made.

The two searches convinced Woodman – who now knew from ample first-hand experience how large the search area was, and how many seasons it would take to trawl with the "mowing the lawn" method – to change tack. He determined to find a way to reduce the area that needed to be searched, this time by using a magnetometer. Since both ships had been equipped with large ex-railway boilers, the hope was that such a large metallic object would show up as a magnetic anomaly. This plan also avoided the problem with the shortness of the open-water search season; the magnetometer would be drawn on a qamutiik behind a skidoo, and the search team would then return, again working atop the ice, drilling through and lowering a sonar boom only at those places where the survey indicated a promising target. Periodic depth soundings would also be taken, on the assumption that water too deep, or too shallow for Franklin's ships to have sunk with their masts still visible, could be eliminated from further searches. Given the hoped-for scope of the search, it was planned to take place over two seasons, in 2001 and 2002.

The plan went well enough, though there were the inevitable technical problems; one of the magnetometer's sensors was damaged, either by the buffeting of the qamutiik or by the cold, and some sections had to be re-done. Woodman and his volunteers adapted, covering the magnetometer in caribou fur to shield it, learning to pour vegetable oil into the holes drilled for the acoustic sounding head so that it wouldn't get stuck in the ice. The work was demanding, and no less repetitive; instead of trolling back and forth with a boat, they had to do their "lawnmowing" on the ice, back and forth, in tight parallel lines. The coverage they managed was impressive –

almost the entire southwestern corner of Wilmot and Crampton Bay – and they even managed to re-locate the skull on the small island, along with a glass prism and the outlines of several rectangular tents that were definitely not of Inuit make. Once the data from the survey was compiled and checked, they had a total of seven sites identified as the most promising targets for the return search.

Alas, every one of them turned out to be a natural feature. Some were in water that was too shallow, while others, though promising, turned out when scanned with the sonar to be but flat, lightly ridged plains, with "nothing suggestive of ship remains," as the report laconically phrases it. Yet, despite this, the various Utjulik searches proved invaluable, for they eliminated some areas completely (via depth soundings) and rendered others low priority for future searches (by the lack of any strong magnetic signals, or the negative sonar scans). As Woodman observed during the planning stages, it would have taken ten years, under ideal conditions, to search the entirety of both the Kirkwall and O'Reilly target areas, and even then there remained the possibility that the ship was outside these zones, just a little bit farther north, or south, or west. After the last of these searches, realizing that additional work would require not only enormous commitments of human and technological resources but at least one "friendly millionaire," Woodman chose to let others carry on the search for a time. And, just at that moment, Parks Canada was mounting the first of what was to be a series of annual searches, with – it was hoped – more substantial (and predictable) funding from the government.

The eventual result of those searches – the discovery of the wreck of HMS *Erebus* – is now well known. It's not often recalled, though, that in its first several years, the Parks Canada searches faced many of the same problems as Woodman; the commitment of resources was still relatively modest, and the mission of support vessels, once again primarily the *Laurier*, remained divided among many responsibilities. Under the leadership initially of Robert Grenier, and later Ryan Harris and Marc-André Bernier, the searchers returned year after year, missing only 2009, when resources were allocated elsewhere. Beginning in 2010, though, the support of the government increased substantially, and more and more of the "southern search area" near the Adelaide peninsula was covered, though still without result. The rediscovery of HMS *Investigator* in Mercy Bay that year re-energized the searchers, and by 2014 a small flotilla of vessels, both government and privately supported ones, was readied. That year, with the feeling that the southern area, largely covered, was becoming less likely to yield results, the expedition returned to Victoria Strait, near the initial site of the ships' abandonment. With the Utjulik wreck proving so elusive, the Victoria Strait Expedition, as it was now known, hoped for better results starting with the one point that at least they could be sure of. The ice, however, had plans of its own.

Figure 28 Captive iceberg, Resolute Bay, Nunavut.
Photo by the author.

12

Ice

The ice was here, the ice was there,
the ice was all around.
– S.T. Coleridge, *Rime of the Ancient Mariner*

The light was perfect. It was coming on 10 p.m., but the extended beams of
the never-quite setting sun gave golden highlights to the bluish ice of Resolute Bay in the Canadian Arctic. Standing in front of a "captive iceberg"
– one that had drifted into the bay the previous summer, and was now held
fast in the ice-sheet – was Roy Koerner, a glaciologist with Polar Continental Shelf, waiting for his moment on camera. As he stood there, he shifted
his weight from foot to foot, singing a little ditty, half under his breath, to
the tune of an improvised sea shanty:

> Come all ye Franklin experts, this warning take from me
> Be careful ere you speak or lose your cred-i-bi-li-ty ...

Koerner was speaking from experience – after all, it was his study, published
years ago, an analysis of ice cores dating to the mid-nineteenth century – that
had suggested that Sir John Franklin might have faced unusually cold winters. He had done his best to explain to the producers of the NOVA documentary that his paper was speculative and playful, not by any means
definitive – but they wanted something much more specific. Earlier, in Resolute, he had explained how ice cores reveal the climate record; in warmer
seasons, the ice melts, leaving a clear section in the core, while in colder years

the crystals retain their form. He pointed out to the producers that his study had a margin of error of plus or minus five years, but they were determined to pin him down and have him say that the ice in the winters of 1846–48 – the years Franklin's ships were ice-bound – had been unusually cold ones.

"Would the ice in those years have been unusually thick and dense?"

"Well yes, on average, it would, but there's not enough definition in those cores to specify which year, actually."

"CUT!"

"Let's try again. Would Franklin's ships have faced difficult ice conditions in the years they attempted the Passage?"

"Yes, certainly. But ships in those days didn't even have the capacity to get through *modest* ice … "

"CUT!"

"One more time. What kinds of conditions would ships such as Franklin's have faced in those years?"

"Well, it depends on the route they were taking. If it were an unusually cold year, the McClintock channel …"

"CUT!"

Roy went another few rounds with the producers, and they were on the last few feet of the last reel of film they had brought when they finally got him to say that the channels wouldn't have opened up, that they would still be "ice-infested" in a cold year – they could work with that – but Roy had had enough of working with them. He declined their offer of a ride back to Resolute on one of their skidoos: "I'd rather walk."

And so he did. Koerner – "Fritz" to his friends – was a man who had done more than his share of Arctic walking. Along with Alan Gill and Kenneth Hedges, he had been one of Sir Wally Herbert's companions on his legendary trek across the North Polar ice cap, a journey that – if, as do most historians, one discredits Peary's 1909 claim – was the first by foot and dogsled ever to reach the pole. It was, in a sense, the very last achievement of the old-school era of polar exploration, a fact underscored by the odd coincidence that, a few weeks after Fritz and Wally had completed their trek, the news of their achievement was lost in the excitement surrounding the announcement that Neil Armstrong had just set foot upon the moon. In many ways, the search for the Northwest Passage and the North Pole had, like space exploration, been framed by difficulty, demanding of tremendous investment by nations and individuals, and fraught with peril no matter the outcome. Herbert's may indeed have been "last great journey on earth."

Koerner had long since settled into his work as a glaciologist; indeed, by the time I met him in Resolute, he had been officially "retired" for some years – but he couldn't resist the lure of the ice. His routine – a flight to a remote glacier on one of the Twin Otters owned by Polar Continental Shelf, weeks or months on the ice drilling and retrieving cores, and then the off-season back in his laboratory analyzing them – had rarely varied. Like many men of his generation, he was inclined to admire Franklin, which was why he had thought to publish his paper years ago, despite the limited precision of the cores he had examined. The idea that it was unusually cold weather that doomed Franklin has gained currency in recent years, as has the parallel claim that it was harsh weather that had led to Robert Falcon Scott's Antarctic demise. But what sort of weather, after all, is *unusually* harsh? And wouldn't any polar traveller of those days prepare for the fact that, given a limited or non-existent ability to forecast the weather, the worst sort of weather was to be expected?

+ + + +

Ice comes in many varieties. Single-year ice, which forms in just one winter, tends to be smooth and thin; if the season has not been particularly cold, it's the first to go the following summer. Multi-year ice, which survives this melting and is added to by the following season, is thicker and harder to navigate; beyond that, the heaviest ice, accumulated in corners where the sun rarely manages to penetrate fully, is the worst of all. Even *that* ice, though, is less of a hazard than ice*bergs*, calved from glaciers whose weight has compressed ice and snow into an unyielding, dense conglomerate. Once set free, they drift at the whim of wind and currents, pushing away lesser ice in their wake, or bumping alongside other bergs in a dense and dangerous pack. When pressures within the ice build up, the thinner sheets crack and slide atop their neighbours; if the ice is too thick for that, pressure ridges – to the eternal bedevilment of those seeking to traverse them by sledge – form. And ships, of course, especially wooden ships such as Franklin's, tended to get caught at times – "nipped" is the word – by the ice, and when they did, the results could be disastrous. The Franklin search ship HMS *Breadalbane*, anchored off Beechey Island, was "taken by the nip" at 4:10 p.m. on 21

August 1853 – and by 4:30 her hull was completely stove in, and she disappeared beneath the ice.

The Royal Navy naturally did its best to fortify its vessels against this hazard. They nailed an additional layer of planks to the decks and hull, with iron sheathing at the bow; they put braces athwart the ship below decks; they devised systems whereby the rudder might be withdrawn from the ice and stowed to save it from being crushed. All these modifications, however, were really just additions to old warships that had never been designed to face the ice in such a manner; as Fridtjof Nansen demonstrated with his purpose-built *Fram*, it was a far better idea to design a ship so that it would be pushed up *atop* the ice, rather than one which depended on resisting such pressures from within. Even then, it was not in its destructive power that the ice posed its greatest threat, but in its ability to force the hand of navigators, rendering the chosen route – or indeed, *any* route – impassable. It could be fickle, too, opening wide one season only to snap shut the next; this, apparently, was what happened to Franklin.

He had sailed down Peel Sound – named after the late prime minister – without difficulty, only to encounter, on his planned route to the west of King William Island, the implacable floe of heavy multi-year ice that came down what was later named the McClintock Channel. If he had tried the passage to the east – which some suspect he may have considered – he would, as we've seen, faced other problems: the shallows in the James Ross Strait, and worse still in the Simpson Strait. These would have made it wellnigh impossible to steer his ex-Navy warships, with their draft of more than fourteen feet, through these channels without running aground, and thus the western route, with all its perils, was the one he chose.

We will, of course, never know exactly what went through Franklin's mind, but once the choice was made, he found himself in a bind – in fact, in several. Caught in the pack-ice, he would have been unable to steer his ships effectively or reach a protective harbour in the winter. Worse, he was condemned to move at the slow speed of the ice floe itself, which would have taken several years to carry his vessels through to Queen Maud Gulf. That his own ship – albeit after his death – made it so far is certainly a tribute to him and his men; that the other, which we know now to have been the *Terror*, did not, is no discredit to Crozier. The ice is often described as a *malevolent* force, but a better word would be *implacable*; that there were ships upon it, or men within them, mattered not to its churning calculations; indifferent to the fate of either, it but moved as it had always moved.

Figure 29 The *Breadalbane* nipped by the ice. Collection of the author.

Beyond all this, the belief that the season Franklin sailed in was an unusually cold and harsh one belies the fact that, even if it were, the effect on the ice would not necessarily be what one would imagine. A cold year often locks up multi-year ice and slows the calving of new bergs, leading to a reduction in sea ice; concomitantly, a warm year can free up greater quantities of ice, which, blown or carried along straits and passages, can make them far more hazardous. In parts of the Northwest Passage – the Victoria Strait among them – the flow of the ice and the flow of the current do not always agree, a fact demonstrated most dramatically when one Franklin search ship, HMS *Resolute*, having been abandoned in what seemed an unbreakable tomb of ice, freed herself and drifted, unpiloted, all the way out of the Passage and into the Davis Strait.

And it turns out that ice can even freeze time itself, as in the case of the *Resolute*. James W. Buddington – a nephew of Hall's friend Sidney who spelled his surname differently – first sighted the ship, apparently adrift and leaning badly to port, and dispatched a small party in a whaleboat to board and investigate. Their report makes for uncanny reading:

The ship was found not to have sustained any very material damage. The ropes, indeed, were hard, and inflexible as chains; the rigging was stiff, and crackled at the touch; the tanks in the hold had burst, the iron work was rusted, the paint was discoloured with bilge water, and the topmast and topgallant mast were shattered, but the hull had escaped unscathed, and the ship was not hurt in any vital part. There were three or four feet of water in the hold, but she had not sprung a leak. The cordage was coiled in neat little circles on the deck, after the fashion of English seamen, and the sails were frozen to such stiffness as to resemble sheets of tin. Several thousand pounds of gunpowder were found on board, somewhat deteriorated in quality, yet good enough for such purposes as firing salutes. Some of the scientific instruments were injured by exposure and rust; but others were in excellent condition. For a year and four months no human foot had trod the deck of this phantom ship, yet, amid those savage solitudes, where man there was none, and might never be, the pilot's wheel made a stern proclamation, for around it were inscribed in letters of brass the immortal words, "England expects that every man will do his duty."

Buddington and his crew were able to pilot the vessel back to New London, and the ship was restored, at the expense of the US government, and returned to Great Britain as a token of mutual esteem. Under the command of veteran explorer Captain H.J. Hartstene, the *Resolute* was brought first to Portsmouth, then anchored near the Queen's summer residence at Osborne House, so that Her Majesty could make a personal visit. The sight of the ship produced a profound feeling of awe and admiration, even among those who had once served aboard her. Somehow, against all odds, this brave vessel had freed herself from her icy death trap, her timbers as persevering as the men who once steered them. And everyone, Her Majesty included, was amazed at the care and thoroughness of the restoration. As described in the *Illustrated London News*, the ship was almost a "floating Pompeii":

As regards the arrangement of the furniture and the situation of each particular article in the captain's cabin, they were put into the same state as that in which they were when the crew forsook the ship. In fact, the ship is – so to express it – a floating Pompeii, and everything

Figure 30 Presentation of HMS *Resolute* to Queen Victoria. George Zobel
after William Simpson, restoration by Adam Cuerden.
United States Library of Congress.

comes to light just as it was left. Captain Kellet's epaulets are lying in
a tin box on the table. Lieutenant Pim's musical box occupies its old
place on the top of a "what not." The "logs" of the various officers
are in their respective recesses on the bookshelves. The portmanteau
containing the officers' greatcoats is thrown heedlessly on a chair. On
the wall hangs the picture of a ballet girl pirouetting – still for ever
pirouetting on the tips of her toes –and, as if in mockery of domestic
comfort, a little kettle that should be singing songs "full of family
glee," does nothing of the kind, but sits upon a tireless stove as cold
as a stone and as silent.

That these objects were still present on board the *Resolute* when she was found would seem to indicate a typical state of affairs when an ice-bound vessel was abandoned in an orderly manner, down to the music boxes, epaulet cases, and pictures on the wall. It's particularly interesting to see that the officers' logs or journals were still on the shelves – one can only hope that the same was the case when the Franklin ship was abandoned, since there would then be every chance for them to still be retrieved in readable condition.

As is often told, when the *Resolute* was later scrapped in 1877, three desks were made from her timbers. The most ornate of these, a massive flat-topped "partner's desk," was sent as a gift to then-president Rutherford B. Hayes; although for some time on storage or displayed elsewhere, it's been the most commonly used desk in the Oval Office in recent decades, chosen by presidents Ronald Reagan, Bill Clinton, George W. Bush, and Barack Obama. The second, designed as a ladies' writing desk, was presented to the widow of Henry Grinnell, the American shipping magnate who had funded so many searches for Franklin, including that of Charles Francis Hall; it's now in the New Bedford Whaling Museum. The third, a small portable writing desk, was originally meant for the queen herself to use at Windsor; in recent years, it's been in storage at Portsmouth. The idea that the wood itself, somehow, contains and maintains the virtues of the ship, and its men, is as old as "Hearts of Oak," the official march of the Royal Navy.

But wood, even stoutest oak, still gives way to ice. Until the discovery of Franklin's ship in 2014, it's actually quite remarkable how little of either vessel had been found, given that the two ships together were rated at nearly 700 tons. One hundred and twenty-nine men (Franklin included) were lost with them, but bones and scattered bits of clothing and supplies on land were long more common than so much as a twig of either vessel. In the 1850s, just two fragments – one the hatch-cover found by Collinson aboard HMS *Enterprise*, the other the small beam and block of wood discovered by Dr John Rae – were the sum total. Two other small pieces, as it happens, were recovered just before the *Erebus* was located and seem to have pointed the way; one was an iron davit designed to support the wooden arms for lowering and raising whaleboats, the other a disc of wood described as a "deck hawse plug." The ship herself, though majestically resting upright upon the sea floor, has clearly been damaged by the ice, her stern partly ripped away, and much of her decking missing or having fallen into the ship's interior. The tell-tale signs of ice – the pressure of its grasp, and the collapse that follows its release – are both evident in these timbers.

The ice will have its way. One of the most harrowing stories of its power – though we now know that it has nothing to do with either the *Erebus* or the *Terror* – was that told by Edward Coward, master of the brig *Renovation*, about the eerie spectacle he and several of his crew and passengers beheld off the Grand Banks of Newfoundland on 5 May 1851:

> When near the east edge of the bank, in lat. 45° 30′ N., wind northeast, fresh breezes and clear weather, as much as I could carry fore-topmast studding-sail, I fell in with icebergs, one of which was very large, with field ice attached to it, in which there were two three-masted ships, having their masts struck and yards down, and all made snug; to all appearance they had passed the winter together in the ice. At about five o'clock in the morning, when within one mile of them, the mate called me to see the berg and ships; by the time I got up, and dressed, and on deck, my ship was abreast of them; I took spying-glass and carefully examined them, to see if there was any one on board, but could not see any one. At the time I did not think of Sir John Franklin's missing ships; anxiety to get ahead out of the danger while the weather was clear from fogs, and being too far past before I could make up my mind, caused me not to reduce sail and examine them more accurately. I am since of opinion they might possibly be the missing ships.

Coward's account stirred great interest in Britain, and numerous witnesses were called to confirm what he had seen. That an enormous berg – to which ships, sometimes, anchored for safety when caught in ice-filled seas – could have carried two abandoned vessels with it was certainly credible; the voyage of the *Resolute* had shown as much. That they were not Franklin's ships does not diminish the horror felt at this apparition; like a sighting of the "Flying Dutchman" or the mysterious and ancient vessel in Edgar Allan Poe's "MS. Found in a Bottle," to see a ship abandoned at sea, caught in the grip of the implacable ice, drifting at the whim of the elements, was a terrible spectacle indeed.

✛✛✛✛

And the ice continues to defy us. Each year, as the Franklin searches have continued, it has called the tune and decided, by its absence and sometimes its presence, where and when these searches would be carried out. The 2014 search, as noted, was originally planned to focus on the Victoria Strait. It was there, after all, that Franklin's ships recorded their final latitude and longitude; there that the Inuit testified to one ship having sunk; there that a number of whaleboats, evidently launched from the ships, were left on land. The frustrating lack of finds in the more southern search area, near Kirkwall and O'Reilly Islands, had at last led searchers to try an alternative strategy. True, the ship in the Victoria Strait might be the crushed one, but it still might have secrets to tell. The *Breadalbane*, after all, had been found by Joe MacInnis in the early 1980s; the speed with which she sank turned out to have been her preservative, for she was found upright, with masts still standing and sails still set. Might not the crushed Franklin ship be in as good condition? Long-time Franklin searcher John Geiger, now the CEO of the Royal Canadian Geographic Society, compared it to looking for one's car near where one had found one's keys.

The ice, though, would have none of it. Although the *Laurier*, again serving as the main platform for the search, might have managed the field of medium-to-multi-year ice that choked the Victoria Strait, the other vessels, including the *Investigator*, Parks Canada's main search ship, and the *Martin Bergmann*, a research vessel funded by BlackBerry co-founder Jim Balsillie (who might, had he arrived a tad earlier, have been the very "friendly millionaire" sought by Woodman), needed open water to operate. For a time, they decided to try and wait out the ice, but when, against all hopes, the Victoria Strait remained inaccessible, they chose to return to the southern search area to see if they could salvage something of a much-vaunted expedition. The ice, again, had gotten its way – and, as things turned out, it had *shown* the way as well, for it was only then that the golden shadow of HMS *Erebus* appeared on Ryan Harris's sonar screen.

He and Parks Canada had been searching for one of Franklin's vessels for six years, before which David Woodman had searched the same area for a decade, before which a cavalcade of Arctic luminaries, from Hall to Schwatka to Rasmussen, had passed these same seas and wondered as to the fate of the *Erebus* and *Terror*. We can say, even without knowing its precise location, that the Inuit testimony, which had consistently placed one of the ships in this area, in water shallow enough for the masts – before the ice tore them, too, away – to be visible above the surface. The stories are well enough known in Canada that they were the subject of a spoof on the CBC comedy show *This Hour Has 22 Minutes*, in which a white explorer credits "the latest, cutting-edge technology" with the find, while another guest, "Inuit storyteller Philip Ayarowaq," asked what native oral traditions have to say, drily notes that "the elders tell of a ship of white men that was stuck in the ice off Queen Maud Gulf, or as we call it, 'White Man's Sinking Spot.'"

And it *is* funny – although in all fairness, it should be emphasized that, despite the use of new technology loudly touted by the Canadian government, the Parks Canada team and all the searchers have always acknowledged that the Inuit evidence was the one most vital element in their discovery. We're talking, really, about two different kinds of knowledge, two different ways of thinking. To the Inuit, the arrival of these strangers, who knew so little about how to live outside their giant umiaqs, was a great puzzle; how and why would men so ill-prepared be journeying through their land, seeking something – a "passage" – that would bring them neither food nor shelter? And for Franklin and his men, sanguine in the security of their little world of shipboard life, for whom land counted as knowledge only once its location could be plotted by latitude and longitude, these fur-clad nomads were living in a manner outside the boundaries of what they conceived of as civilization. For the most part, so far as we can tell, the Inuit did what they could to help these people, and felt only sadness and pity when they came upon their remains – though, being used to making the most of limited resources, they were happy to find useful things scattered among them.

There's something in this tale that touches both the sublime – the eternal tale of humans versus the elements, the impassive power of the ice, the perseverance of doomed men – and the absurd, with these same men dragging sledges filled with heavy, largely useless things to their deaths, leaving behind their bones and their spoons, along with enough sundry detritus for generations of restless searchers to puzzle over obsessively – and inconclusively. And, to my mind, the element most frequently missing in most attempts to make sense of it all is the perspective of the Inuit – not simply those of the past but those of the present as well – in whose backyard all kinds of crazy Qallunaat persist in looking, year after year, for something that their ancestors lost long ago and that may never really be completely *found*.

Figure 31 Hunter with dog team, Gjoa Haven, Nunavut.
Photo by the author.

13

Inuit

Gjoa Haven, Nunavut, is the closest modern Inuit settlement to the place where the last of Franklin's men perished. Roald Amundsen, the first man to succeed in Franklin's goal of navigating the Northwest Passage, anchored there in 1903 aboard the *Gjøa* and stayed for nearly two years; he named the place after his ship. A tiny trading post eventually was established there, but as with most northern hamlets, it was not occupied permanently by the Inuit until the late 1950s or early 1960s, when native settlements became a policy of the Canadian government. Its current population is a little over 1,200, most of whom live in the same sort of prefabricated insulated housing common in all northern settlements. There's an airport, and just one hotel in town, operated by the Inuit-owned Inns North chain – appropriately enough, it's called the Amundsen.

I first visited Gjoa – the local pronunciation is more like "Joe" than Amundsen's "yoo-ah" – in 2004, as part of a documentary team shooting a film about Franklin and Amundsen. The film's producer/director, Louise Osmond, had been advised that the scenes in the far north would look best on film, and so they were to be shot on 16mm. Local Inuit had been recruited to play the part of their ancestors; anyone who could bring a complete caribou-skin outfit and speak credible Inuktitut was invited to come to the set and paid with a crisp $100 Canadian bill for each day. The crew had already been there a week, filming the actors who were playing Crozier and Fitzjames and the men of Franklin's ships; by the time I arrived these actors had left, though Kåre Conradi, who played a quite capable Amundsen, was still there for a couple of days. One of the producers told me that Kåre was hugely popular in Norway, and that his arrivals and departures there were packed with teenage fans seeking autographs – but here, in the north, he could have been just any other guy.

The day I arrived, I was invited down to the town "beach" – a euphemism in April when open water was months away – where a large igloo had been built for the use of the film crew. As with most of our brief trips around the area, this was made by snowmobile, towing a qamutiiq or sledge made of 2×4s and plywood. It took some getting used to; the locals stepped on to and off these things the way you would a skateboard, but, for the rest of us, riding on one over rough, icy terrain was like trying to stay on a bucking bronco. Reaching the igloo, we waited for our cue, as two Inuit in furs sipped coffee from the film crew's canteen. Here in the north, I soon learned, you're burning calories, and losing heat, by just standing around breathing – constant replenishment with hot cocoa, candy, and coffee is a must. It was springtime here in Nunavut – the night was already reduced to a period of a couple of hours of semi-darkness – but the thermometer still hovered around twenty below zero for most of our time there.

Near the igloo, there was a small shack with clapboard sides, which I later learned was Louie Kamookak's fishing "camp." He was away hunting during my time there, so I never got to meet him, but in Franklin circles he's something of a legend. It was his grandfather, the legendary trader William "Paddy" Gibson, who was the first modern searcher to find the bones of Franklin's men near the Todd Islets, less than an hour's snowmobile-ride away. These bones had been seen before; the Inuit told Hall that among the bodies was one of the men they called "Ag-loo-ka," although Hall was unsure whether this was Crozier or some other officer. When he reached the place, the snow obscured them, and the only body he was able to find was the one later identified as Le Vesconte, and later still as Goodsir. Gibson collected the bones and built a new stone cairn over them, passing on the knowledge of the site to his family. His grandson Louie knew it well; almost every time a film crew or a shipload of Franklin buffs passed through, he would take them to see it, but for whatever reason, no one had ever made a proper archaeological survey.

There's a strange sense of the Franklin legacy in town. Everyone has stories to tell, and sometimes it's hard to distinguish genuine oral tradition – which, as Dorothy Eber has shown, still retains some faded echoes of the earlier tales told to McClintock, Hall, and Schwatka – from garbled versions of written and printed sources. One afternoon, while I was in my room at the Amundsen, I got a knock on the door from young Danny Aaluk, a local artist. He had a pen-and-ink drawing of a polar bear doing a drum-dance that he wanted to sell me, and I told him I would be glad to buy it. The only trouble was that I didn't have any cash; like a typical southerner, I asked where I could find a cash machine, but Danny just laughed. He suggested I come with him to a place where I might be able to get some money with a charge card, and since I wasn't due on the set that day, I got on my wind-pants and parka and followed him out and across town. We arrived at a blue building that looked more or less like one of the larger settlement houses; Danny gave a special knock on the door. It was opened by another townsman, who gave me a suspicious glance before Danny explained, then let us in.

It turned out to be a sort of town speak-easy. Most of the north is supposed to be a "dry zone" – the only alcohol legally sold is the low-octane "near beer" at the HBC store. The locals had found a quiet way around this: the place had the look of a private club, with a pool hall at one end and a kind of small store at the other. It smelled powerfully of disinfectant, and the crowd was all young Inuit men; hip-hop music was blaring in another room, and the dress code here seemed to be leather jackets and knit caps. The guy behind the counter greeted Danny, who introduced me and explained the problem. "All I got here is loonies and toonies," the man declared (referring to Canada's $1 and $2 coins), but he said he would give it a try anyway. It turned out, though, that the machine wouldn't take my MasterCard – "Up here, we only use Visa," the proprietor told me. It sounded almost like a commercial.

And so he and I fell to talking, as one does in those parts; word had got around that we were in town to film something about Franklin, and the proprietor was a man who followed such news pretty closely. He said he had heard the story about two last survivors heading south along the western edge of Hudson Bay, and dying there – now *that* was a story he believed. I had read that same tale in Woodman, of course – and now here I was, on King William Island, a first-hand recipient of real live Inuit testimony! I could hardly contain my excitement. The man told me a few more stories, each one of them remarkably close to the versions I had read; I wished I had planned ahead and brought some kind of voice recorder. Maybe, I thought, I could borrow one from the film crew. And so I asked him: Where had he heard these stories? Could he take me to some of the elders who still remembered them? He shook his head, laughing, then reached behind the counter and pulled out a battered copy of Woodman's *Unravelling*. He thought it was the greatest joke in the world, and I found myself laughing with him – back home, I might fancy myself some sort of Franklin expert, but here I was just one more crazy Qallunaaq.

+ + + +

What drives these Franklin searchers to come up here? Asked this question, the local doctor, with whom I shared a cup of coffee at the hotel, refused to speculate – but he noted that at least it does something to help the local economy. Unemployment in Gjoa Haven hovers somewhere around 30 per cent, and any kind of money, any kind of work, is scarce. Most Inuit families live in whole or at least part on the dole, since decent jobs are few and require some degree of higher education or training. The better jobs go overwhelmingly to Qallunaat: teachers (who get a "northern bonus" for a three-year tour), town officials, RCMP officers, and the workers at the HBC store. When the territory of Nunavut broke off from Northwest Territories – perhaps somewhat portentously on April Fool's Day 1999 – many Inuit hoped that, by refusing the "reservation" model and simply instituting majority rule, they would avoid the troubles experienced for generations by more southerly tribes. But when you compare Gjoa Haven with, say, a town on the Rosebud Sioux reservation in South Dakota, the similarities are more noticeable than the differences.

The housing is in better shape – up here, it has to be – but the common threads are numerous: unemployment is endemic, and the population, which skews young, is drawn to alcohol and drugs; suicide is the number one cause of death among young people. The local doctor shakes his head; he tells me the thing that bothers him most about northern suicides is how often they succeed. "See those houses up there?" he asks, gesturing to the slight rise atop which most of Gjoa's boxy, prefabricated homes are perched. "Every single one of 'em has a gun. Hanging is popular, too." Besides the speak-easy I had stumbled upon, plenty of liquor is smuggled in by passengers arriving by plane – there's no baggage check, no airport security up here – and anyone who tosses a couple of bottles of Jim Beam into their duffel stands to make a handsome profit by it. The Qallunaat, of course, live by their own rules, since they have the money to afford liquor, along with typical western fare; in a place where a bunch of bananas runs $10 at the HBC store, such food is a luxury.

There are a few families who still hunt seasonally – you can hear their dogs howling on the edge of town – and traditional foods (called "country food" up here) such as seal meat, blubber, and *muktuk* are still enjoyed. But almost no one lives on the land in the old way, migrating seasonally with the food supply, camping in igloos in the winter and *tupiks* (skin tents) in the summer. Ever since the late 1950s and early 1960s, the Canadian government's settlement policy has made it increasingly difficult for anyone to get by unless they have some sort of permanent home; without that, government checks, health care, and other basic necessities are impossible to obtain. Originally, every Inuk was given a red tag with their "Eskimo number"; later on, the government launched "Project Surname" and insisted that everyone take a surname so that they could distinguish one Inuk with the same given name from another. By the early 1960s, nearly everyone had a name and an address, but the settlements, or "hamlets," that this policy created were too poor and too isolated to sustain themselves, which has led to a cycle of dependency at least as bad as that on any southern "Rez."

Inuit traditions lasted longer, though. Back when most of the southerly tribes were first confined to reservations in the United States and Canada in the 1870s, the Inuit were still living the traditional life of their ancestors, and they would continue to do so for almost another century. Their language, Inuktitut, is still alive and spoken, although the median age of its speakers is creeping upward, and its oral traditions – including those about Franklin and other explorers – endure. The stories have become a bit tattered, the loss of detail and confusion of events probably inevitable; as Dorothy Eber notes, the starving, cannibalistic men of the Franklin expedition survive now as a species of weird Arctic bogeymen – be well behaved, the elders tell their grandchildren, or they might come out and gobble you up! And in this young territory, the elders are increasingly isolated, unable to pass on their collective wisdom to a generation raised on satellite TV, video games, and action films.

This was dramatically evident in my ten days in Gjoa, during which the town hosted an annual drum-dance festival. One of the oldest and most treasured of Inuit traditions, the drum-dance involves large skin drums with handles, upon the rim of which each dancer beats with a small mallet or stick, all the while chanting to the beat. Some are boasting songs and could be thought of almost as kindred to hip-hop's "battles on the mic"; others are traditional songs, usually belonging to a single family or individual, that recall their histories, their achievements. On my second night in town, I went with one of the documentary's producers and a friend to the festival, held in the school gymnasium. There, the elders, in their traditional fur costumes, were dancing and swaying vigorously to these songs, with those not dancing joining them in the chorus. Up against the edges of the gym, running and playing, were the youngest children of the hamlet, there in the care of their grandparents or great-grandparents, oblivious for the most part to the old peoples' songs. But where were these children's parents? Their older siblings?

The answer, as I found out later that same night, was at the local hockey arena, where the Gjoa Haven team was taking on a regional rival. The arena was packed with young people, many of them sporting leather jackets, bleached or dyed hair, and various tattoos and body piercings. These young people, clearly, had a Western outlook; they wanted to emulate the tough street kids they saw on television. The sad thing was that the best they could muster was a sort of knock-off of that culture; like kids in the old Soviet Union who craved Levi's but ended up with cheap imitations, you could see that most of the "leather" jackets were plastic, and the T-shirts and jeans looked like something a southerner might pick up at the Goodwill or Salvation Army. Their energy, though, was completely authentic, bound together as they were by a force greater than either traditional Inuit culture or syndicated cop shows: hockey. As the sport in which Canadians have always excelled, and which promised the kind of fame that could turn an unknown Inuk kid into the next Wayne Gretzky, hockey felt like their ticket to the future. Yet, as with the African-American kids in *Hoop Dreams*, such a future wasn't a very likely one for anyone there that night.

+ + + +

So what was the future to be for Gjoa Haven? With severe social problems, little prospect of improved employment, and traditional culture in danger, what could possibly be done that could really improve matters? The hamlet's proximity to the shores on which Franklin's men slowly, inexorably, expired seemed to many to be its one hope for distinction. And, in the anticipation and planning for such hopes, there were rivalries. On the one hand, there was Wally Porter, a descendant of George Washington Porter, who for many years ran a CanAlaska trading post at Gjoa Haven; on the other, there was Louie Kamookak, whose grandfather William "Paddy" Gibson had re-located the remains of Franklin's men near the Todd Islets.

Both men and their families had a special claim upon the Franklin story, and both thought that they would be the logical people to convert the Qallunaat obsession with that late great explorer into something that would benefit their community. How deep did that rivalry go? Late in 2009, some five years after I had visited Gjoa, I was to find out.

It began with an e-mail from Wally Porter:

> What would you do if I told you that my grandfather George Washington Porter, years before he passed away said to one of his sons where he buried the Actual records of Sir John Franklin. If you look up George Washington Porter in the web, you'll know who he was. I am one of many grandchildren of George Washington Porter.
>
> My grandfather was a fur trader with Can-Alaska Post, around the 1920's. You ever wonder why no ones ever found Sir John franklins Documents, records or what they call, A Diary that he may have when he died in around King William Island. Want to find more information. Call me. I live in Gjoa Haven, Nunavut Canada on an Island that's famous for expeditions called King William Island.

I wrote back, of course, expressing interest – as well as a good deal of skepticism that records of the Franklin expedition could have somehow survived until the 1920s – and asking for more details. He wrote back, saying the matter was too important to trust to e-mail, and again giving me his phone number. And so – throwing caution and long-distance bills to the winds, I called. In a roundabout, rambling account, he recounted how these records, which his grandfather had in his keeping, caused concern in his family. They had a "bad feeling" about them and didn't know what to do, and so the grandfather decided to bury them. I imagined that he must have done so under a cairn or *inukshuk* at some remote spot, but according to his grandson, they had been buried right in town in Gjoa, underneath – of all things – a stone memorial to "Paddy" Gibson!

This memorial, as it happened, had been built atop an earlier one – a marble slab left by Roald Amundsen in 1905 – and it was this slab that turned out to be the key to the story. Porter was quite clear as to his family's tradition that Franklin records were buried there, and the association with Amundsen lent a certain plausibility to the story. Amundsen, after all, had held a reverent attitude toward Franklin; in his autobiography, he wrote that, as a boy, what had appealed to him most were the "sufferings" Franklin and his men endured, which inspired him to become an Arctic explorer and take up Franklin's quest. Along with the crew of the *Gjøa*, Amundsen spent nearly two years with the Inuit; having learned their ways and formed a strong connection with their community, perhaps he would have entrusted something of value to them. And, as it turned out, he *had* buried a metal box buried under the slab, a box whose contents had apparently not been seen in several generations – could Franklin's records really be there?

Porter was unwavering in his belief that they were; the only question he had was how to turn their discovery to the advantage of his family and community. We spoke several more times on the phone; from me, he wanted an estimate of the value of such records, should they be found, and how much interest there would be in them among historians. I quite honestly told him that their value would be immeasurable; to have an authoritative record in Franklin's hand would rewrite the entire history of his expedition. Porter stressed that he didn't want to sell the records, but he *did* want their value to be recognized; he told me that he would like to see a special museum built for them in Gjoa, one that would help bring tourists to town. The Gjoa community centre – a small room attached to the hotel – needed expanding too, and the townspeople needed better services and help with issues ranging from health care to youth counselling. Having seen the poverty and desperation that young people faced there, I could understand his hope to use this discovery to help them.

He didn't want anything to go public, though, at least not yet. He and his family had retained the services of a law firm to make sure that the Canadian government would come through with the funding and support he wanted before they considered parting with their valuable knowledge and documents. I was privy to some of the discussions the Porters had about their plans; after getting nowhere with their first lawyers, they fired them and hired another firm; there seemed to be considerable distrust on their part – understandably so – about the lack of respect shown to Inuit by white lawyers, archaeologists, and government bureaucrats. Eventually, they must have felt that they had got their ducks in a row, since Wally broke the story to the press in September 2010. Doug Stenton, the chief archaeologist for the Nunavut government, arrived in Gjoa a few weeks later, and, amidst considerable media fanfare, the monument was removed, and the box – just as described! – was carefully lifted out of the ground and flown to Ottawa for examination. The world waited with bated breath to see what it would contain.

In the meantime, I tried a little sleuthing of my own; I contacted my friend Kenn Harper, long-time Iqaluit resident and historian, and he made some inquiries among his old Arctic friends. He had heard something about this box before, and eventually he tracked down Eric Mitchell, a retired HBC post manager who had a story of his own to tell: he knew exactly what was in the box, since he and George Washington Porter had dug it up back in 1957!

Mitchell described the original box, a small iron one that had been left by Amundsen under the marble slab in 1905. In it, Amundsen had placed an inscribed photograph of Dr Georg V. Neumayer, the man who had taught him all he knew about terrestrial magnetism, along with a note asking that the box be left where it was. "Paddy" Gibson had dug it up back in 1927 when *he* was the post manager at Gjoa, and – after copying the note – had heeded Amundsen's request and reburied it under the slab, where it lay undisturbed for the next thirty years. In the meantime, Gibson himself had been killed in a plane crash in 1942, and some years later the HBC had decided that a memorial to him should be erected in Gjoa. A plaque had been duly made, and sent to the post, though without any concrete or other materials from which to construct a memorial on which to place it. By then, George Washington Porter was the post manager; he requested concrete, but it was some time before any could be requisitioned and delivered. Mitchell – then stationed at Spence Bay – volunteered to pick some up from the DEW-line station at Mount Matheson and drop it off in Gjoa. He and Porter considered Amundsen's slab as an ideal foundation for this new memorial, and resolved to dig up the box once more to check on its contents.

The original photograph and note were still intact, wrapped in some old newspapers from 1927. Still, the iron box had grown rusty, and Mitchell and Porter were concerned that the documents wouldn't last long unless they were protected from water. To keep them dry, they asked Porter's wife to sew them into some waterproof cloth; after replacing them inside the iron box, they put the box itself inside a second box – a wooden ammunition crate, of the sort commonly used in the north – which they then filled with tallow to make it watertight. It was April, though, too cold for concrete to set properly, so they decided that erecting the monument would have to wait for the summer. After directing Porter to rebury the box and build the monument over the slab, Mitchell headed back to Spence Bay; so far as he knew, his instructions had been followed and the box was still there.

Kenn and I were fairly confident, then, that the box would contain nothing more than the Neumayer photograph and note, wrapped in waterproof cloth, inside a metal box inside the tallow-filled crate. And despite this, when the crate was examined, it was found to be full of sand; although the archaeologists carefully removed the sand – a small amount at a time – when they got to the very bottom, there was nothing but sand inside. Oh, and a trace of tallow. Where had the box and the record gone? Of course, no one had bothered to ask Louie Kamookak, Gibson's grandson.

Louie knew about the contents of the box as well, and more: that it had been dug up on yet one further occasion, back in the 1980s. At that time, as he described it, they had decided that the records in the box were too fragile to rebury, and so instead they had sent them to the Prince of Wales Northern Heritage Centre in Yellowknife. There, they were duly catalogued as part of the historical collections of the Northwest Territories; when Nunavut split off in 1999, all the materials from sites in this new jurisdiction were set aside to form the "Nunavut collection," including these relics. Unfortunately, the young government of this new land either wasn't made aware of this or simply needed the resources elsewhere; no one had ever been sent to oversee this new archive, or check on its contents. I did a quick online search, though, and there they were: Amundsen's photograph, along with a chunk of the marble slab itself; the items had been given the new catalogue number N–1985–005. The description read: "This accession consists of one print of a portrait of George Neumeyer with the inscription, 'Best wishes for success in exploring the North Magnetic Pole to his friend Roald Amundsen, 1905.'" Included is a mostly illegible note from George Porter and E. Mitchell of the HBC regarding the site's excavation on 14 April 1957 (from Paddy Gibson's cairn near Gjoa Haven).

I never had a chance to speak with Wally Porter and get his reaction to this news. In his conversations with me, he had offered many details – even recalling his grandmother's use of waterproof cloth – but apparently, the family tradition had been imperfectly passed along. That the records of a great explorer had been buried under this monument in 1957 was true enough – it's just that they were the records of the wrong explorer.

++++

Technology has always come readily to the Inuit. They're problem solvers, careful watchers, and intuitive engineers, and readily think in three dimensions; Robert Flaherty, filming what would become *Nanook of the North* in 1921, was astonished when, after his camera slipped into the icy water, the men he was filming as "primitives" were able to take the entire apparatus apart, dry and clean it, and reassemble it into working order, a feat that he himself could never have managed. Distance has always been a factor in the north, and the Inuit were quick to learn and employ Qallunaat technology such as radio, using it as a link between their now more-isolated settlements. The CBC's northern broadcasting service in Inuktitut began in 1960, and much of the content (along with a good deal of the announcing, engineering, and music) was provided by the Inuit themselves. And so it was to no one's surprise that Inuit also embraced the Internet, despite the fact that, as with radio, the connections from one point to another were at times slowed or blocked by clouds or bad weather.

In the early days of the Internet, many communities had only one or two computers, usually located in a community centre or other public area. But that number soon grew, to the point where Nunavut boasted more computers per capita than any other state or province. The service to connect them, though, was much slower in coming; as complaints about poor service mounted, the Nunanet company, which for a time was almost the region's only provider, collapsed. New companies sprang up in its wake, however, and service has rebounded since then. Satellite-based Internet is now a part of daily life throughout Nunavut. *The Nunatsiaq News*, the territory's paper of record, made the transition to the Net early on and is now primarily accessed online; nearly every house in every northern settlement has a satellite dish (though, to be fair, they have one other use: watching hockey games).

There's something, too, about the way the Internet works which makes it a particularly good match for Inuit culture. In the old days of the shamans, magic was worked through *tupilait*, helping spirits that would travel outside the shaman's body, diving to the sea bed to see where fish or sea mammals might be found, visiting sick relatives, or even voyaging to the moon. When, in the early 1940s Peter Freuchen told one shaman about the war against Hitler, the shaman replied that he would take care of the problem; after all, his *tupilaq* was a particularly powerful one – he had no doubt he could kill this man and bring the war to an end! Indeed, one early (pre-Google) search engine, popular on Nunanet, was called "Tupilak," while a later, similar page was dubbed *Nanivara* ("I have found it!"). The idea of a powerful spirit, conveyed invisibly over the air, travelling great distances to bring back information, fit perfectly with traditional Inuit mythology.

When I first started researching the Franklin story in the mid-1990s, it was enormously difficult to contact anyone in the far north; the main choices were satellite telephone (enormously expensive) or Canada Post (much less expensive but enormously slow and unreliable). By the later 1990s, I was able to contact Inuit and other northerners by e-mail, although I had to allow a few extra days in case of outages or technical issues. When I was in Gjoa Haven in 2004, I was able to post text and small images to a class website I had set up for my students, although it often took a whole morning to do it. And yet today the Net is instantaneous and ubiquitous; every day, Louie Kamookak calls out *Ublaakut!* ("good morning") to his Facebook family and friends, and every morning, within a few minutes, we say it back. Still, there are some limits; when news broke of the finding of Franklin's *Erebus*, reporters anxious to reach Kamookak (who has no land line, though he has a cell) called his employer instead. "They've been calling the school non-stop," he told a reporter for *Canadian Geographic*. "I've had to apologize to everyone there for it. I'm the only Louie Kamookak in the world ... just one, in the whole world. So people can find me. This might be easier if my name was Andrew Stewart. I'm just lucky that they can't find my cell number."

This same technology that's connected Louie and his community into the world of modern media has, at the same time, connected Franklin scholars, from those who actually search the ground each year to those – far more numerous – who work from their proverbial "armchairs." I started my own Franklin e-mail list in 1996; in 2001 I converted it into an automated LIST-SERV, and in 2009 into a blog, "Visions of the North." More recently, a "Remembering the Franklin Expedition" page on Facebook has emerged, where now hundreds of members around the world exchange Franklin news and theories. The vaunted documents, from the Victory Point record to the infamous "Peglar Papers," are now getting a fresh set of eyeballs – several hundred of them – and work that once took place in the pencil-scratching silence of an archive now flashes back and forth across continents and time zones, solving century-old cruxes as quickly as Alexander the Great cut the Gordian Knot. Some mysteries, though, will never be solved, and that's as it should be.

✦✦✦✦

Figure 32 Jacob Tirttaq and Jermaine Porter, Gjoa Haven, 2004.
Photo by the author.

Yet, for all the continuing interest in the "southern" world, it's to the Inuit that the future of the Franklin search will – and should – ultimately belong.

When I was in Gjoa in 1994, waiting in the community room at the Amundsen Hotel for my next camera call, two young Inuit boys – they were, I would guess, between eight and ten years old – came in and shyly asked where I was from. To show them, I opened the atlas program on my Mac and made Gjoa Haven and Providence, Rhode Island, blip on the globe. Then they wanted to see more pictures, so I opened up my iPhoto library and showed them all the ones I had taken around town. They especially liked the photos I had taken at the drum-dance festival. "I can drum-dance!" said one. "Me too!" said the other. "Do you use a small drum or a big drum?" I asked. "A *big* drum!" they both answered in unison. They wanted to know if I had brought my camera so that I could take their picture. Of course I could, I told them. They immediately went over and sat for a portrait with their arms around each other, then laughed as they saw the image on the back of the camera. "Can you put *that* picture in your computer?"

they asked. I loaded it into iPhoto and showed it to them, not noticing at first the red-eye effect from the flash. "We're monsters!" they shouted – but then I showed them how you could take it away, and they were delighted with the results. I asked them their names, and they told me "Jacob and Jermaine." They must be about twenty by now, if they've made it so far. In their community, unemployment is still bleak, and Iqaluit – the young capital of the young territory of Nunavut – never seems able to get the resources it needs from the Canadian federal government. It's nice to send search ships – great to be in the spotlight! – and (according to some) this will all help Canadian sovereignty somehow. But it would be a lot more meaningful if it could contribute something to the fragile northern economy, to Jacob and Jermaine, and their generation of young Inuit across the territory. Our histories, after all, are tangled up together.

EPILOGUE

Last Man Searching

The announcement of the discovery of Franklin's flagship, HMS *Erebus*, on 9 September 2014 was surely the most extraordinary news in the entire history of the search for Franklin. At a stroke, the Parks Canada team accomplished something that no one, in the nearly 170 years since Franklin was last seen, had managed: they had found his ship, in whose captain's cabin he had died, and brought to the surface the ship's bell, dated 1845, the very one that had tolled the mournful news of his demise. There's no question that work on this discovery is just beginning; given the short window of time each year for diving, the care needed in exploring a wreck that has not yet been fully mapped or assessed for structural stability, and the care with which any artifacts obtained will have to be treated – both on their discovery and in the slow process of conservation – will surely be the work of many years. In that process, some of the history told in this book will inevitably be rewritten – and yet, at the same time, these new histories will still be incomplete. The story of what happened to the men after they left the ships is still only partly understood, and the work of those who have laboured to understand *all* the pieces of the puzzle is also ongoing.

To begin with, there are some larger questions that have never been properly investigated at all. Might there be some trace of a Franklin party on the Melville peninsula, say at a camp on Crown Prince Frederik Island? No one, so far, has looked. The human remains at the Todd Islets, which Louie Kamookak has shown to dozens of different historians and adventurers over the years, have still never had a proper archaeological study. Neither has the supposed site of "Starvation Cove," where, precisely because of the mud and silt, it's possible that organic matter might still be found, even human remains (one thinks of the bog bodies, such as Tollund Man, almost perfectly preserved by the low oxygen content of the bog and the acidity and tannin-rich water).

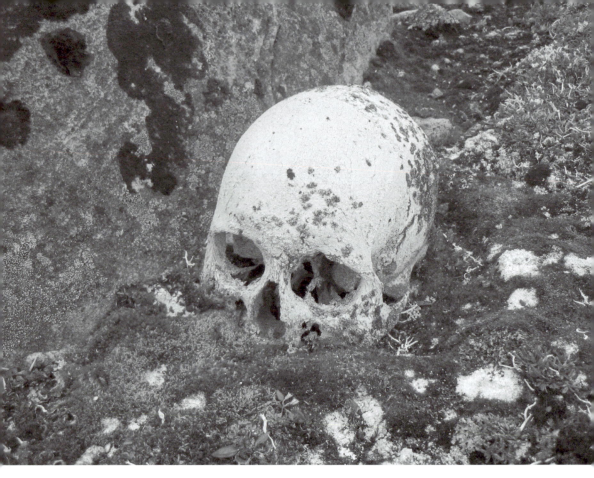

Figure 33 Franklin expedition skull, near the Todd Islets.
Photo by Tom Gross, used with permission.

The Erebus Bay sites – NgLj-1, NgLj-2, and NgLj-3 – have recently been re-examined by old Franklin hands Anne Keenleyside and Doug Stenton; they found the reburial consistent with the one described by Schwatka. Encouraged by the three relatively intact human crania at the site, they've been working on possibly identifying individuals using either their DNA or facial reconstruction, or both. This could also be attempted with other remains; partial DNA has even been extracted from Neanderthals, so other Franklin expedition bones, despite having spent more than 160 years in mostly sub-zero conditions, may well be identified this way.

And there are additional sites on land that have received only cursory examination; the original campsite south of Cape Felix, recently re-located by Tom Gross, was missed by most post-1859 searchers and has never been excavated. Beechey Island may yet have secrets to tell – no record was ever found there, although Franklin almost certainly deposited one. Then there's Matty Island off the eastern coast of King William, near which Inuit testimony suggests a ship may have foundered, as well as nearby Qiqiqtarjuaq Island, on whose shores television personality Bear Grylls and his crew claimed in 2010 to have located and photographed graves that might date to the Franklin era. The possibility exists that searches here may, indeed, discover the wreck of the *Terror*, whose route – if both ships were remanned after the 1848 abandonment – is unknown. Might the two ships, against their general orders, have separated in the hopes that at least one would manage to find its way to safety? There's Inuit evidence, collected by Dorothy Eber, that one ship may have tried the eastern route. In any case, I have a feeling that the *Terror* is unlikely to be found anywhere near its original location as given in the Victory Point record.

Beyond all this, there's a wealth of physical evidence that's never been properly looked at. An enormous number of Franklin relics, including nearly all those recovered by Rae, McClintock, and Schwatka, are in storage off-site at the National Maritime Museum; most have not been on public display since the Royal Naval Exhibition of 1891. There, in a building designed on the outside to resemble an enormous iceberg, the public was last treated to a complete look; many of the artifacts still bear the tags that were attached to them for that exhibit. There are hairbrushes containing human hair (and thus also DNA); canisters and tins that might be checked for traces of their contents; utensils whose provenance and scratched initials are imperfectly documented; pieces of wood and rope that have never been analyzed for what they can tell. There are also dozens of books – who knows what stories they might contain, in their annotations, dog-eared pages, or notes, and the "Peglar Papers," which still have never been examined with modern imaging techniques.

This last omission is perhaps the most striking, since the technology available to recover text from such manuscripts has advanced in remarkable ways. When David Livingstone, who, living in the town of Ujiji on the shores of Lake Tanganyika, lost all contact with the "Western" world for six years, he resorted to writing his field journals in berry juice on old newspapers, the only paper available to him. Not only were these journals written crosswise to the print, but the berry juice faded over time, leaving only faint traces half-obscured behind the bars of print, unlikely – or so it seemed – to ever be readable. However, in 2010–11 these diaries were finally published, after a years-long project of imaging and analysis undertaken at UCLA. This new process scanned the originals with reflected light of several different visible (and invisible) ranges of the spectrum, then merged the resulting imagery into a multilayered digital image that could be tweaked and retweaked to amplify the faded ink and fade away the lines of newsprint. Such a system has yet to be tried on the "Peglar" manuscript but could doubtless make many currently illegible passages readable once more.

Of course, even imagining any number of "friendly millionaires," and any number of willing hands, there's no way to completely "solve" the Franklin mystery. The best that we might hope for is to assemble a rough timeline and connect each known set of human remains to the likely routes the men took. It remains possible that some written records might be recovered from a cache on land; as David Woodman has noted, a letter left by Willem Barents at Ice Haven on Novaya Zemlya in 1595 was recovered in 1871, more than 250 years later, and it was still intact and legible. Written materials may also be recovered from the *Erebus*, and between them these two sort of records might at last give us a more complete sense of how the final years and months of the Franklin disaster unfolded. Surely, though, each man and group of men endured their own individual dramas, and of these we will never know the tale; our jigsaw puzzle will never have all its pieces, and some will remain orphaned, disconnected from the rest.

As long as even the slightest portion of the unknown remains, we will have searchers. One of the most persistent of these is surely Hay River resident Tom Gross, a member of several of David Woodman's Project Supunger teams. To this day, he's returned each year on his own to continue the search. Gross has set his sights high – he hopes to find Franklin's grave, and with it a cache of other materials, including documents, that he feels confident must have been deposited there. Having searched the area along the coast near Victory Point, Gross is now convinced that the features described by Supunger aren't to be found there. He points out that there were at least two places with the large piles of abandoned goods, the second on the shores of Erebus Bay; the large cook-stoves would make more sense there – the ships may well have been just a short distance offshore, and reachable by open water (thus the boats).

There are difficulties with this view: Su-pun-ger clearly stated that the site was farther north, near the tip of the island – but, as Gross notes, he was only about seventeen at the time and may have mistaken the long shore of Erebus Bay for the northern coastline. Gross also doubts that Su-pun-ger had ever seen something like a white man's map. A few years back, Gross heard a fascinating account from an Inuk in Gjoa Haven who described how his father told him about finding a "house of stone" a ways inland from Erebus Bay, one that answers in many respects to Su-pun-ger's description. This house was made with large, smooth stones, had a stone "doorway," and was built into the side of a natural ridge. It's possible that, despite the many searches closer along the coast, somewhere farther inland this stone house still stands.

It's a possibility Tom Gross is willing to stake his time and money on. And so, each summer, he returns to search again. I think we should all wish him luck.

APPENDIX

Franklin Searches, 1854–2015

NOTE: I've worked to make the criteria for this list as consistent as possible. Setting aside the searches of Rae and McClintock – the most significant among dozens undertaken in the 1850s – all the listed expeditions commenced after the discovery of the Victory Point record and meet the following criteria: (1) they were planned, in whole or in part, either to search for traces of Franklin's men or to visit known Franklin sites (this includes impromptu searches, where someone in the area for other reasons decided to make a side trip for either of the above purposes); and (2) the individual or group reached the target area. Thus, the list includes some very short trips that ended with little opportunity to search, so long as at least some members of the expedition reached the vicinity of their goal.

1854: Dr John Rae returned with the first detailed Inuit testimony as to the fate of Franklin's men, along with a wide array of relics; he was given the £10,000 reward for "ascertaining the fate" of Franklin.

1858–59: Francis Leopold McClintock, private expedition, later counted as Royal Navy service. McClintock and his lieutenant Hobson were the first to reach Franklin sites along the southern and western coasts of King William Island; among the numerous artifacts they brought back were the Victory Point record, the "Peglar Papers," and numerous books including *The Vicar of Wakefield.*

1865–69: Charles Francis Hall, private expedition, reaching King William Island, with "Hannah" (Tookoolito) and "Joe" (Ebierbing). Numerous Franklin relics were recovered and hundreds of interviews with Inuit conducted. The skeleton of an officer, originally believed to be Le Vesconte, was recovered and sent back to Great Britain for reburial.

1878–79: Frederick Schwatka, private expedition, sponsored by the American Geographical Society; searched the western and northwestern coasts of King William Island. Numerous graves and human remains were located, including that supposed, by the finding of a mathematics medal near the grave, to be that of Lieutenant John Irving, whose remains were returned to Great Britain for reburial.

1921–24: The Fifth Thule Expedition, led by Knud Rasmussen, private. This ambitious trek, chronicled in Rasmussen's *Across Arctic America* as well as in a detailed, ten-volume report, included visits to several Franklin-related sites, among them King William Island, and interviews with Inuit whose testimony showed a robust survival of oral tradition up to that point.

1925–26: L.T. Burwash, private expedition, to Gjoa Haven and King William Island, with a visit to Jenny Lind Island and Hat Island.

1928–29: L.T. Burwash, private expedition, to Matty Island and other locations. Owing to snow and ice at the Matty Island site, Burwash was unable to follow up on his theory that one of Franklin's ships foundered there.

1930: L.T. Burwash and Dick Finnie, private expedition to northwest coast of King William Island. On 6 September 1930 Burwash and Finnie located a Franklin "camp" between Cape Jane Franklin and Victory Point. See Burwash's reports published by the NMT/Department of the Interior, as well as "The Franklin Search," *Canadian Geographical Journal* 1 (November 1930): 587–603.

1931: "Paddy" Gibson with William Skinner of the HBC, private expedition to the Todd Islets (three+ remains found, including a complete skeleton; all reburied) and to an island in Douglas Bay (seven skulls and many other bones, all reburied). See Gibson, "Some Further Traces of the Franklin Retreat," *Geographical Journal* 79, no. 5 (1932): 402–8.

1933: "Paddy" Gibson, private expedition to Cape Herschel. See Gibson, "The Dease and Simpson Cairn," *The Beaver*, September 1933.

1936–42: L.A. Learmonth and D.G. Sturrock, private expeditions. Located the remains of three individuals, almost certainly Franklin's men, at "Tikeraniyou" between twelve and fifteen miles west of the reputed location of "Starvation Cove." With the remains were an 1820 George IV half-crown and a sailor's large ivory button. In 1942 they found a skull and some bones near Washington Bay on King William Island; they also found two skulls on the beach near Tulloch Point, and others near Richarson Point. Some of these remains were sent to Hudson's Bay House, others were said to have been reburied in Gjoa Haven "under the beacon."

1949: Henry A. Larsen of the RCMP, with officers Seaforth Burton and John Biench, searched the coast between Cape Felix and Cape Jane Franklin, as well as the area near "Starvation Cove," on foot. He found a skull (figure 21), identified in the lab as that of a white man, at Cape Felix; at "Starvation Cove" he found a leather-boot sole. See Cyriax, "Recently Discovered Traces of the Franklin Expedition," *Geographical Journal*, June 1951.

1950: L.A. Learmonth, private expedition to the North Magnetic Pole following up on Wright's theory that remains of Franklin's men – and perhaps his own grave – would be found there. They weren't.

1954 and 1955: Paul Fenimore Cooper, private expeditions to King William Island, researching what would eventually be his book *Island of the Lost* (New York: Putnam 1961). He was accompanied by his wife, who collected plant specimens; his (brief) reports were published in the *Arctic Circular*. Cooper also brought back one significant artifact, a board that almost certainly formed part of the decking of one of Franklin's ships; it was identified in 2015 by Karen Ryan at the Canadian Museum of History.

1962: Robert Cundy led the private "Cape Britannia Expedition" to the mouth of Back River to search for any record left by Franklin's men at Cape Britannia. It was intended to follow up on Noel Wright's theory that, if Franklin's men had begun an ascent of the river, they would certainly have deposited a record at the cairn at this site erected by Thomas Simpson in 1839; Wright believed the cairn had not been visited since. After a difficult journey during which one of their canoes was lost, they finally reached the cairn, only to find a note left there two years previously as part of "Operation Back River"; signed by B.G. Craig for the Canadian Geological Survey, the note stated that no Franklin relics had been found there.

1965: Dr E.F. Roots of the Canadian Department of Mines and Technical Surveys conducted a survey, using a sledge-mounted magnetometer, over a region north of O'Reilly Island to check out a magnetic anomaly detected in earlier surveys. Press accounts at the time credited B.F. Ackerman and D.J. Kidd of the Royal Canadian Navy, who had served aboard icebreakers in the vicinity, with having persuaded Roots to make the more detailed survey since they were convinced that the wreck of one of Franklin's ships was in the area. Roots concluded that the anomaly was much too large to be anything but a natural feature and was caused by formations of iron and manganese – but his team did find some shore debris, including a spike with the broad arrow, which gave "Nail Island" its name.

1967: "Project Franklin," Canadian military exercise to King William Island and "Starvation Cove." See the article by William C. Wonders in *Canadian Geographical Journal* 76 (1968). The expedition commenced on 4 August 1967 with forty-two men aboard an RCAF helicopter. They searched the same area as Larsen in 1949 and retrieved notes left by him in cairns there; they also found the sole and heel of an old boot. Other areas were searched via aerial fly-overs and by divers near O'Reilly Island; some shore debris found – a belaying pin, copper, and a piece of wood retained by one of the divers.

1971: Bob Pilot, with Mike Moore, private expedition. Ground search of the area between Collinson Inlet and Cape Felix; they relocated the Schwatka cairn and a note left there by Larsen.

1973 (1): "Franklin Probe" – Bob Pilot, Stu Hodgson (then the commissioner of the Northwest Territories). Searched area of the Boothia peninsula inland from Pattinson Harbour, finding a series of freshwater lakes, the second of which they dubbed "Probe Lake." They stated that the search was based on Inuit accounts of the burial of a Franklin officer in the area. No traces of Franklin's party were found.

1973 (2): 1st Royal Canadian Regiment, "Operation Northern Quest," one of whose goals was searching for "artifacts and information" about the Franklin expedition. Between Tulloch and Gladman points, one party (led by Sergeant Ron Eddy) uncovered a nearly complete human skeleton, along with shirt and jacket buttons (this may or may not have been the "Peglar" skeleton). A cairn was erected on the site, and the bones and artifacts were reportedly brought back to the Museum of Man (now the Canadian Museum of History) in Ottawa.

1974: Second "Franklin Probe" search, with multiple parties – one to Beechey Island (which included May Fluhmann, who was to write the first biography of Crozier two years later); one to Resolute Bay, where they relocated the grave of one of the *Resolute*'s crew; one to Dealy Island, where they found a roofless shed containing undisturbed provisions left for Franklin; one to "Starvation Cove"; and one to Fury Beach.

1975: While on a seal-hunting expedition, self-described historian John Goldi followed the southern coast of King William Island, recovering a human jawbone near one of the caches left behind by "Paddy" Gibson. He regarded its lack of teeth as a sign of scurvy and speculated it was that of a "cabin boy."

1981: Owen Beattie, private expedition. Land search, concentrated on southern and western coasts of King William Island.

1982 (1): Owen Beattie, private expedition. Second land search on King William Island results in recovery of remains and an article "A Report on Newly-Discovered Human Skeletal Remains from the Last Sir John Franklin Expedition," *The Musk-Ox* 33 (1983). These same remains were retrieved from storage in 2014 for a fresh study by Beattie along with Simon Mays; their analysis indicated signs of "pot polish," a rounding of the ends of the bones produced by their having been cooked in a pot.

1982 (2): Clifford J. Hickey, James M. Savelle, and George B. Hobson, private expedition. Searched the west shore of McClintock Channel for Franklin expedition-related materials. See their report in *Arctic* 46, no. 1 (1993) 79–81.

1984: First exhumation at the Beechey Island camp, private expedition led by Owen Beattie, with John Geiger. The body of John Torrington was exhumed and autopsied; photos of his uncovered face were widely reproduced in the press and inspired the James Taylor song, "The Frozen Man."

1985: Second exhumations at Beechey, uncovering the bodies of Harrington and Braine, both of which were autopsied. Toxicological analysis showed elevated lead levels in all three bodies, though subsequent studies have cast doubt on whether these levels were atypical of Victorian-era individuals. The Beechey exhumations were detailed in Beattie and Geiger's book *Frozen in Time in* 1987, which has since become a touchstone for Franklin searchers and aficionados around the world.

1989: Stephen J. Trafton, "Franklin Search Expedition," private. Located remains of the Franklin cairn at the site of their camp 3.3 miles south of Cape Felix. Recovered pencilled note by Schwatka left in a corked bottle in another Franklin-era cairn "located on a prominent ridge 1.7 miles south of Cape Felix and 0.8 miles inland." They also identified what they believed to be Crozier's cairn "1.8 miles south of Victory Point and 500 feet inland from the shore of Back Bay." Their report states that they believed this to be the same cairn located by L.T. Burwash in September 1930 and by Larsen in August 1949. The report by Trafton in *Mariner's Mirror* 77, no. 4 (1991), mentions eight searchers in two parties but gives no names.

1992: Woodman – "Project Ootjoolik," private expedition. Airborne survey of area west of Grant Point with long-range patrol aircraft (Aurora) from Canadian military. Result: sixty+ significant magnetic anomaly "hits," five of which were deemed to be possible wreck evidence. Detailed photo-reconnaissance helped update and correct charts of area.

1992 (1): Ernie Coleman and Margaret Bertulli ("Lady Franklin Memorial Expedition"), private. Identified two mounds, one of which appeared as though it could be a grave, on the northwestern coast of King William Island. Later excavation showed that it was merely some flat stones over natural features (see below 1993 [3]).

1992 (2): Barry Ranford with Mike Yarasavich, private expedition along the western coast of King William Island. Discovered the site later tagged as NgLj-2.

1993 (1): Barry Ranford, 13 July to 7 August, "The Franklin Recovery Expedition," private. Spent two weeks excavating NgLj-2, the site that Ranford discovered the year before. Personnel included Ranford, John

Harrington, Jennifer Ranford, Margaret Bertulli, Anne Keenleyside, and Jimmy Porter of Gjoa Haven. The remains of eleven of Franklin's men were gathered and sent to McMaster University for analysis. Cannibalism was confirmed. A further ten days was spent in the Terror Bay area, looking for the remains of a "hospital tent," without result.

1993 (2): MacInnis-Woodman Franklin expedition, private. Jointly organized by Dr Joe MacInnis and David Woodman. The plan was to use a small ski plane to land on sea ice and use "lightbulb" sonar through augured holes in the ice to investigate the targets from 1992. The expedition briefly landed at one spot in bad weather but did not get an accurate position. They drilled a hole and lowered sonar but discovered only "mud, mud, and more mud." They noted that "the water depth was approximately 20 meters, which was encouraging."

1993 (3): Peter Wadhams and Maria Pia Casarini, with Wayne Davidson, "Lady Franklin Memorial Expedition," private. Investigated Coleman's mounds and found they were natural features (see above 1992 [1]). Also found remains of what appeared to be a Franklin-era whaleboat at Back Bay on Prince of Wales Island.

1994: 15 July to 3 August, "The Franklin Survey Expedition," Barry Ranford, John Harrington, John MacDonald (archeologist), private expedition. Excavated a site discovered the year before (NgLj-3). They were accompanied by a crew of four from CBC television with host Carol Off, including cameraman Andrew Gregg; the resulting documentary, *The Mysterious Franklin Disappearance*, aired on 14 September of that year and included interviews with Pierre Berton, Margaret Atwood, and Rudy Wiebe.

1994 (2): Canadian Geographic Franklin Expedition, "Project Supunger," private. David Woodman organized a team to search for Su-pun-ger's vault between Victory Point and Collinson Inlet as far east as Cooper Lake. Result: found some new small traces of metal, cloth, etc. at "Crozier's Landing" and discovered one burial site (later determined to be of Inuit origin). GPS mapped all significant structures (Irving's grave, etc.). No trace of Supunger site found.

1995: David Woodman's second "Project Supunger," search, private. Landed at Cape Felix as one of three parties working loosely together. One went to rediscover Cape Felix campsite (Bertulli, Gross, Hobson); one (under Steve Trafton) went to Clarence Islands to locate cairn (it did not reach its destination, defeated by sea ice); and Woodman, with Rick Hammer and Jim Garnett, travelled down west coast to Crozier's Landing in search of Su-pun-ger site. Result: Cape Felix campsite archaeologically mapped for the first time by Bertulli, which led to the discovery of a Franklin campsite near Cape Maria Louisa.

1995 (1): Harrington and two others, private expedition to the Erebus Bay area where they investigated the coastline for about ten miles on either side of the prime Erebus Bay site. They located three "boat places" where the scattered wood remains and artifacts clearly showed that lifeboats had been abandoned. Barry Ranford was camped in the area that season as well (he and Harrington had decided on separate searches).

1995 (2): Ernie Coleman, private expedition. Landed near Cape Jane Franklin and spent time searching area between Collinson Inlet and Victory Point. Hampered by bad weather, nothing found.

1996: "Cape Crozier Expedition." John Harrington and four others, including John MacDonald (the archeologist from 1994), private expedition. Their party was dropped off near Franklin Point and explored every inch of coastline from (and including) Franklin Point to familiar territory at Erebus Bay, with the hope of finding Franklin's grave at Franklin Point. The search proved inconclusive.

1997: John Harrington, 17 to 30 July. Harrington and two others were flown to the "Schwatka Site" to place the remains of the three individuals he and Barry had discovered in 1993 and 1994 in weatherproof containers. They "gathered the bones, said a prayer and then flew west to the other side of a large inlet just west of Erebus Bay." They then explored the west coast of the Crozier peninsula as far as Fitzjames Island; several cairns were found but nothing related to Franklin.

1997 (2): "Eco-Nova Franklin 150 Expedition," private. Woodman served as search coordinator for this group, doing both sidescan work from survey boats and shore searches of islands. They searched the Grant Point area and finds of some copper items and wood from a small boat led them to move on to O'Reilly Island, where little was accomplished because of bad weather. Results: copper items initially thought to be Franklinian were later determined to be modern. Margaret Bertulli discovered one human skull on nearby islet that was thought from later photographic analysis to be of a Franklin crew member. Personnel included archaeologists Dr Robert Grenier and Margaret Bertulli.

1998 (1): Cameron Treleaven and Louie Kamookak, private expedition to Victory Point to place commemorative plaque on 150th anniversary. By Cameron's account, they arrived by travelling overland from Gjoa Haven, and it was *they* who had the kitchen tent described in Harrington's account (see below); they hosted Harrington's party and served them a dinner of Arctic char, departing the next day before the onset of the storm described by Harrington.

1998 (2): John Harrington, 21 April–1 May, private expedition. Also planned to mark the 150th anniversary of Franklin's men coming ashore on 25 April. Included Ron Rust, along with three others including Doug Stern, a last-minute recruit from Cambridge Bay who was experienced at surviving winter conditions. "After landing on King William Island we quickly set up a fairly large kitchen tent and our smaller individual sleeping tents. We all agreed that the first night in our tents was dangerously uncomfortable and we all decided to hunker down in the kitchen tent. At that point a major storm hit that flattened our unoccupied sleeping tents and endangered our kitchen tent. Thankfully Doug Stern was with us and with his guidance we were able to build two igloos that probably saved our skins. Our plane could not land in such conditions and the storm did not abate until the 29th. It was our plan to get out of there on the 25th so our fuel and food supplies were at an end. Doug successfully shot ptarmigan for one of our meals. The whole experience gave us a small taste of what Franklin's men experienced!"

1998 (3): August. John Harrington, private expedition. Flew to Taloyoak (formerly Spence Bay) on the Boothia peninsula; hired Inuit to take them by boat up the west coast of the Boothia to explore. They found a cairn which they believed to be the one erected by James Ross at the point where he discovered the Magnetic North Pole in 1831.

1999 (1): 19–28 August, John Harrington, private expedition. Purpose: retracing the pre-Franklin trip of John Ross in 1829 up the east coast of the Boothia peninsula.

1999 (2): David Woodman and Tom Gross by snowmobile; private expedition to area around Cape Maria Louisa in search of Supunger site. Stormbound at Cape Sidney for five days in blizzard, nothing found.

2000: "*St Roch II* Voyage of Rediscovery." Organized by James Delgado of the Vancouver Maritime Museum and Ken Burton of the RCMP. Woodman again served as coordinator. Continued search of area west of Grant Point, without result. Shore searches of nearby islands found no Franklin relics.

2000 (2): 22–30 August, private expedition. "This was a boat trip out of Cambridge Bay eastwards up the coast of Victoria Island to follow up on a lead that some ship wreckage was observed in the Albert Edward Bay area. It was hazardous at times with quickly changing weather up and down the coast. We did discover the rumoured site but concluded that it was likely an old fishing camp several decades old."

2001: New "Ootjoolik" search (now spelt *Utjulik* in accord with modern orthography), private expedition. David Woodman led team to do sledborne magnetometer survey. This expedition was assisted by support from Canadian Forces Rangers, including Doug Stern (see 1998 [2] above). Result: surveyed remaining northern area (Grant Point) at 200m spacing for magnetic anomalies. Later analysis revealed seven high-probability hits.

2001: John Harrington 6–13 August, private expedition. His final trip: "Ron Rust and I planned to take a floatplane to the Royal Geographical Islands to explore the coastline for boat debris. We did not set foot on land as the weather was continuously bad and our one and only flight to the area was thwarted by no place to land in the ice-filled choppy waters."

2002: "Irish-Canadian Franklin Expedition," private. Parts of this were filmed by Irish filmmaker John Murray for his *Franklin's Lost Expedition* documentary. David Woodman led team to continue sled-borne magnetometer survey. Result: resurveyed previously discovered northern area (Grant Point) hits at 50m spacing for enhanced resolution, surveyed southern (O'Reilly) area at 200m spacing. Later analysis revealed a total of fourteen high-probability hits in both areas.

2003: "American Express Franklin Memorial Expedition," private. More properly a retracing of Franklin's route than a search per se; the expedition leader was Rebecca Harris. Motto: "Long Live Dreams."

2004: "Irish-Canadian Franklin Expedition 2," private. David Woodman led a team to investigate highest-probability targets in both areas using a drop sonar through holes in the ice. Result: All targets identified with obvious geological anomalies (stone outcrops, etc.).

2004–present: Tom Gross (annually when possible), private expeditions.

2007: *Outpost* Magazine's "opXpedition," Evan Solomon, Chris Christie, Kevin Vallely, and Stephen Smith, guided by Louie Kamookak with Paul Ikuallak. They visited known remains along the southern coast of King William Island, including Gladman Point and the Todd Islets.

2008: First Parks Canada search. Led by Robert Grenier and Ryan Harris, with Louie Kamookak as consultant.

[2009: no Parks Canada search funded; no private searches]

2010: Parks Canada – led by Ryan Harris, Marc-André Bernier, and Jonathan Moore. Divers rediscovered the wreck of the Franklin search vessel HMS *Investigator* in Mercy Bay, as well as conducting ground archaeology on nearby sites.

2011: Parks Canada – Bernier and Harris.

2012: Parks Canada – Bernier and Harris.

2013 (1): Parks Canada – Bernier and Harris.

2013 (2): Excavation at Ng-Lj3 of grave established by Schwatka in 1879, conducted by Anne Keenleyside, Doug Stenton, and Robert W. Park. They found seventy-nine bones, representing the remains of three individuals, including three largely intact crania; some faunal bones were also found. The bones had been carefully stacked together in a square pit, consistent with what is known about Schwatka's reburial; stones belonging to the monument he had erected were found adjacent. One skull was recovered from the aluminum box left there at this site by Harrington in 1997. Evidence was found that suggested that two of the bodies may have been identical with those in the boat found by McClintock.

2014: Parks Canada – Bernier and Harris, with the support of the government of Nunavut, the Royal Canadian Geographical Society, Shell Canada, One Ocean, the W. Garfield Weston Foundation, and the Arctic Research Foundation. HMS *Erebus* located and the ship's bell brought to the surface for conservation.

2015 (1): April. Parks Canada – second dives (first ice dives) to HMS *Erebus* – Bernier and Harris, with divers from the Canadian Armed Forces. Additional imagery was acquired, and close observation found part of a leather sea boot, along with glass illuminators, plates, and marine buttons. One of the ship's cannons was also raised.

2015 (2): September. Third dives on HMS *Erebus*. Artifacts so far identified as retrieved during these dives include a strap buckle, the basket of a naval officer's sword, an ointment container, and additional china plates and a glass fragment thought to be from the window of the "great cabin."

Notes

Citations are indicated by page number

xiv: Notes to Thoreau's *Walden*: in "Of Maps and Men: In Pursuit of a Northwest Passage," Princeton University Libraries, http://libweb5. princeton.edu/visual_materials/maps/websites/northwest-passage/ thoreau.htm.

3: This description of the announcement draws from Alistair McDonald, "Canadian Search Finds Legendary Lost Franklin Ship in Arctic," *Wall Street Journal*, 9 September 2014.

3: "dozens of showmen": see my *Arctic Spectacles: The Frozen North in Visual Culture, 1818–1875* (Montreal and Kingston: McGill-Queen's University Press 2007).

5: "pleasure cruise": Sir John Barrow, *Voyages of Discovery and Research within the Arctic Regions, from the Year 1818 to the Present Time: under the Command of the Several Naval Officers Employed by Sea and Land in Search of a North-West Passage from the Atlantic to the Pacific: with Two Attempts to Reach the North Pole …* (London: John Murray 1856), 54.

6: "there goes the fellow in the panorama": Sir John Franklin to his sister, 12 April 1819, quoted in Henry Duff Traill, *The Life of Sir John Franklin, R.N.* (London: John Murray 1896), 69–70.

6: The incident is described by Sir John Richardson and quoted in Sir John Franklin's *Narrative of a Journey to the Shores of the Polar Sea, in the Years 1819, [18]20, [18]21 and [18]22 …* (London: John Murray 1823), 455–9.

7: "the name Franklin alone is, indeed, a national guarantee": Sir Roderick Murchison, president of the RGS, quoted in John Brown, *The North-West Passage and the Plans for the Search for Sir John Franklin* (London: E. Stanford 1860), 47.

7: "knights-errant of the sea": Joseph Conrad, "The Heart of Darkness," *Blackwood's Edinburgh Magazine*, February 1899, 194.

7: "the Northwest passage of that day": Mark Twain, *A Connecticut Yankee in King Arthur's Court* (New York: Harper and Brothers 1889), 70.

8: "utterly useless": Captain Sir John Ross, from "Minutes of Evidence before the Select Committee on the Expedition to the Arctic Seas," *Selections of Reports and Papers of the House of Commons*, vol. 32 (Literary and Scientific) (1836), 18.

9: "more chilling than Madame Tussaud's": William Makepeace Thackeray, "The Sights of London," *Punch*, April 1850.

9–10: "A long tirade against the lying, savage 'Esquimaux'": Charles Dickens, "The Lost Arctic Voyagers," *Household Words*, 2 and 9 December 1854, 362–5, 387–93.

10: *Harper's Weekly* 3, no. 148 (29 October 1859); see figure 4, p. 34.

11: "So far it is satisfactory to know …": *The Times*, quoted in the Bedfordshire *Times and Independent*, 27 September 1859, 4.

11: "Our English Penelope": Sometimes attributed to *The Times*, but Pierre Berton cites the *Daily Telegraph* in his *Prisoners of the North* (Toronto: Anchor Canada 2005), 126.

12: "This monument was erected by Jane …": Westminster Abbey Memorials List, http://westminster-abbey.org/our-history/people/sir-john-franklin.

12: "where someone got axed in the snow: Margaret Atwood, "Concerning Franklin and His Gallant Crew," in *Strange Things: The Malevolent North in Canadian Literature* (Oxford: Clarendon Press 1995), 12.

13: "Frozen Man": lyrics by James Taylor, published by Country Road Music.

13: "internal organs had disintegrated" … "puddle of yellow, granular liquid": Roger Amy, Department of Pathology, University of Alberta, "Report on the Exhumation of John Torrington, Deceased January 4, 1846." See the detailed discussion of the lead hypothesis on 74–6.

15: "the Canadian government had repeatedly balked at the offer": on this see Shelagh Grant, *Polar Imperative: A History of Arctic Sovereignty in North America* (Toronto: Douglas and McIntyre 2010), esp. chapter 7, "British Transfer of the Arctic Islands, 1870–1900."

16: "seems to meet the definition of an international strait": this is the current view of the United States. However, as Ana G. López-Martin notes in her *International Straits: Concept, Classification, and Rules of Passage* (Heidelberg: Springer-Verlag 2010), current conditions make the Passage more a series of sometimes-navigable straits, none of which are – individually at least – "international." She also observes that global warming may change this situation substantially, if it leads to the entire Passage becoming routinely navigable (59).

19: Permission was provided by the family of Gwendolyn MacEwen for the quotation from *Terror and Erebus*.

21: "Bones – no need to ask which bones": for this and other reactions to Landseer's painting, see *Reynolds's Newspaper*, 8 March 1864, 5 (*Times* review quoted); *Westmoreland Gazette*, 14 May 1864 (the *Athenaeum* quoted); and *The Examiner* 30 April 1864, 30.

22: "several issues of his own magazine, *Household Words*": Dickens, "The Lost Arctic Voyagers."

22: Dickens to W.H. Wills, 20 November 1854: *Letters of Charles Dickens*, Pilgrim ed., (Oxford: Clarendon Press), vol. 7 (1853–55).

24: *Under the Management of Mr. Charles Dickens: His Production of "The Frozen Deep,"* edited and with an introduction by Robert Louis Brannan (Ithaca, N.Y.: Cornell University Press 1966), 121.

24: "the crying of two thousand people": Dickens to Burdett Coutts, 5 September 1857: "I have been very much excited by the crying of two thousand people over the grave of Richard Wardour." *The Letters of Charles Dickens*, Pilgrim ed., vol. 8 (1856–58), 432.

24: What critic Harry Stone has called his "night side": see Harry Stone, *The Night Side of Dickens: Cannibalism, Passion, Necessity* (Columbus: Ohio State University Press 1994).

25: Charles Francis Hall, *Narrative of the Second Arctic Expedition Made by Charles F. Hall: His Voyage to Repulse Bay, Sledge Journeys to the Straits of Fury and Hecla and to King William's Land, and Residence among the Eskimos, during the Years 1864–'69*, edited by J.E. Nourse (Washington, DC: Government Printing Office 1879), 419–20.

26–7: This account is based on Huw Lewis-Jones, "'Nelsons of Discovery': Notes on the Franklin Monument in Greenwich," *Trafalgar Chronicle: Yearbook of the 1805 Club*, no. 19 (2009).

28–9: This account on this event is based on my own personal experience attending it, as well as on the printed program given out on the occasion.

29–30: S. Mays et al., "New Light on the Personal Identification of a Skeleton of a Member of Sir John Franklin's Last Expedition to the Arctic, 1845," *Journal of Archaeological Science* 38, no. 7 (2011): 1571–82.

30: "German forensic scientist Richard Helmer's identification of the Skull of Nazi 'Angel of Death' Josef Mengele": see "How They Identified the Angel of Death," *New Scientist*, no. 1463 (July 1985): 19.

32: Margaret Bertulli, "NgLj-2, A Franklin Site on Erebus Bay, King William Island, Field Work in 1993." Yellowknife: Prince of Wales Northern Heritage Centre 1994.

32–3: A. Keenleyside, M. Bertulli, and H.C. Fricke, "The Final Days of the Franklin Expedition: New Skeletal Evidence," *Arctic* 50, no. 1 (1997): 36–46.

33: Dr Keenleyside, personal communication (e-mail).

35–6: Joseph Conrad, "Geography and Some Explorers," *National Geographic Magazine* 45, no. 3 (1924): 252–3.

37: Colin Field, personal communication (e-mail).

39: "a second record": see Richard J. Cyriax, "The Two Franklin Expedition Records found on King William Island," *Mariner's Mirror* 44, no. 3 (1958): 179–89.

40–51: This is adapted from my own article, "The 'Peglar' Papers Revisited," *Trafalgar Chronicle: The Yearbook of the 1805 Club*, 2014, 202–15.

40: "the Captain's party found a human skeleton": [Allen Young], "The Search for Sir John Franklin (from the Private Journal of an Officer of the *Fox*)," *Cornhill Magazine* 1 (January 1860): 117.

41–2: "More recent research by Glenn M. Stein": see Glenn M. Stein, "Scattered Memories and Frozen Bones Revealing a Sailor of the Franklin Expedition, 1845–48," http://www.ric.edu/faculty/rpotter/aglooka/Scattered_Memories.pdf.

43ff.: R.J. Cyriax and A.G.E. Jones, "The Papers in the Possession of Harry Peglar, Captain of the Foretop, HMS Terror, 1845," *Mariner's Mirror* 40, no. 3 (1954).

50: *Axel and Valborg, a Tragedy, and Other Poems, Translated by Pierce Butler, Edited by Professor Palmer, M.A., St. John's College, Cambridge* (London: Trübner and Company 1874) 84.

53: Program transcript of NOVA episode, "Arctic Passage: Prisoners of the Ice," http://www.pbs.org/wgbh/nova/transcripts/3307_arctic.html.

54: "as far back as William Edward Parry's second Arctic expedition": M. Ross, *Polar Pioneers: John Ross and James Clark Ross* (Montreal and Kingston: McGill-Queen's University Press 1994), 83.

54: English Wikipedia, entry for Charles Sylvester, retrieved 17 December 2015.

54: "execrable machinery": Sir John Ross and James Clark, *Narrative of a Second Voyage in Search of a North-West Passage: and of a Residence in the Arctic Regions* (London: A.W. Webster 1833), 9, 204–5.

54: I use the amounts as given in R.J. Cyriax, *Sir John Franklin's Last Arctic Expedition* (1939), repr. 1997 by the Arctic Press.

55: All details about tinned food here are based on the booklet "Historic Tinned Foods" (Greenwich: International Tin Research and Development Council 1939).

55: "by one writer": see Scott Cookman, *Ice Blink: The Tragic Fate of Sir John Franklin's Lost Polar Expedition* (New York: Wiley 2001). His botulism argument has not been widely accepted; see my original review in the *Arctic Book Review* at http://www.ric.edu/faculty/rpotter/cookman.html as well as pp. 72–3 below.

55: On Franklin and daguerreotypes, see William J. Schultz, "Images of Colonial Empire: British Military Daguerreotypes, Part I: The British Sea Services," *Daguerreian Annual* 2005, 145–98, esp. 161–8.

55: On Francis Russell Nixon, see my blog post at the New Bedford Whaling Museum's "Arctic Visions," http://whalingmuseum-arcticvisions. org/francis-russell-nixon/.

55–6: On the Goodsir Talbotype, see Graham Smith, "'Dr. Harry Goodsir,' by Dr. Adamson of St. Andrews," *History of Photography* 10, no. 3 (1986): 229–36.

56: "'Fortnum and Mason have done their part well, and we find all of their stores of the best description'": quoted in James Delgado, *Across the Top of the World: The Quest for the Northwest Passage* (New York: Checkmark Books, 1999), 108.

56: "the re-use of hot water": In 2012 Franklin researcher Peter Carney conducted an impromptu experiment in which he sought to duplicate this process; see his post on his "Erebus & Terror files" blog, http://erebu sandterrorfiles.blogspot.com/2012/01/captain-backs-patent-poison-producer.html.

57: "tins of Goldner's meats were examined at the Clarence Victualling-yard": see "The 'Preserved' Naval Stores," *Illustrated London News*, 17 January 1852.

57: See also Constantin Areleanu, "A British Meat Cannery in Moldavia, 1844–52," *Slavonic and East European Review* 90, no. 4 (2012): 671–704.

58: "first featured in a woodcut": *Illustrated London News*, 4 October 1851, 409, "Traces of the Franklin Expedition" (see headpiece of this book's Introduction).

58: Roger Amy, Department of Pathology, University of Alberta, "Report on the Exhumation of John Torrington, Deceased January 4, 1846."

59: John Gieger and Owen Beattie, *Frozen in Time: The Fate of the Franklin Expedition*, 3rd ed. (Vancouver: Greystone Books 2014), 246.

59: K. Millar, A. Bowman, and W. Battersby, "A Re-Analysis of the Supposed Role of Lead Poisoning in Sir John Franklin's Last Expedition, 1845–1848," *Polar Record*, 7 January 2014.

59–60: "Soup can reopens mystery of doomed Franklin Expedition": McMaster University Daily News, 10 September 2014, http://dailynews.mcmaster.ca/article/soup-can-reopens-mystery-of-doomed-franklin-expedition/.

60: William Battersby and Peter Carney, "Equipping HM Ships Erebus and Terror," *International Journal for the History of Engineering & Technology* 8, no. 12 (2009): 192–211; blog post, "Archimedes and Croydon: The Engines of Erebus and Terror?" on Peter Carney's "Erebus and Terror Files," http://erebusandterrorfiles.blogspot.com/2010/07/archimedes-and-croydon-engines-of.html.

61: "the *Thomas*, a 700-ton barque": see my blog post, "Railway Engines at the Bottom of the Sea," http://visionsnorth.blogspot.com/2009/07/railway-engines-at-bottom-of-sea.html.

62: "a catalogue made of all our books": see *Nautical Magazine* 21 (1852): 163.

62: "Weekly Summary of Maritime Casualties": see my post "A Fateful Clipping," 12 June 2015, http://visionsnorth.blogspot.com/2015/06/a-fateful-clipping.html.

62: I've gathered these titles from Cyriax, along with some of the private letters sent home by the officers. My longer, partly conjectural list of the libraries of *Erebus* and *Terror* is among the "Legacy Libraries" at Library Thing.com, http://www.librarything.com/catalog/ErebusTerror.

62–3: John Leopold McClintock, *The Voyage of the 'Fox' in the Arctic Seas: A Narrative of the Discovery of the Fate of Sir John Franklin and His Companions* (London: John Murray 1859), 252.

63: *Bickersteth's Scripture Help*: see C. Stuart Houston, *To the Arctic by Canoe 1819–1821: The Journal and Paintings of Robert Hood* (Montreal and Kingston: McGill-Queen's University Press 1994), xxxi and 161–2.

63: "Comforter, where, where is your comforting?": this is from Gerard Manley Hopkins's poem "No worst, there is none. Pitched past pitch of grief."

63: *Student's Manual*: see my *Arctic Spectacles: The Frozen North in Visual Culture, 1818–1875* (Seattle and London: University of Washington Press 2007), 101. The book in question is the Reverend John Todd's *The Student's Manual, Designed by Specific Directions, to Aid in Forming and Strengthening the Intellectual and Moral character and Habits of the Student* (Northampton, UK, 1835), 386.

65: See the entry for "Poctes Bay" in Alan Day's *Historical Dictionary of the Discovery and Exploration of the Northwest Passage* (Lanham, MD: Scarecrow Press 2006), 224.

66: My thanks to Glenn M. Stein for the suggestion of "Poets Bay," which I am now convinced is correct. The name "Poctes" is exceedingly scarce in texts of the period, and there's no indication that Ross knew any one, or any thing, of that name.

66: Dease and Simpson's latitude and longitude is taken from the table at the end of Simpson's *Narrative of the Discoveries on the North Coast of America*, 419; Rae's from his "Arctic Exploration, with Information Respecting Sir John Franklin's Missing Party," *Journal of the Royal Geographical Society of London* 25 (1855): 253. There is some inconsistency even within Rae's account; in the 1953 edition of his letters and journals, he initially gives 93° 20′ (278) as the longitude of the Castor and Pollux River, but a short while later he refers to it as 93° 42′ (279), a more accurate figure. It's possible that Rae kept more than one set of figures, since at times he distinguishes those obtained "by the chronometer" from others. See *Rae's Arctic Correspondence, 1844–55* (London: Hudson's Bay Record Society 1953).

68–9: Discussion of Arnold 294, and the discovery that Gore had used it aboard HMS *Beagle*, can be found in my "Visions of the North blog" from May 2009 in two posts: 1) "A Horological Mystery," http://visions

north.blogspot.com/2009/05/horological-mystery.html; and 2) "The Missing Chronometer," http://visionsnorth.blogspot.com/2009/05/missing-chronometer-part-2.html.

70: David C. Woodman, *Strangers among Us* (Montreal and Kingston: McGill-Queen's University Press 1995).

71: In-nook-poo-zhee-jook's map: in Charles Francis Hall (ed. Nourse), *Narrative of the Second Arctic Expedition*, facing 398.

71: Qaqortingneq's map: from Knud Rasmussen, *The Netsilik Eskimos: Social Life and Spiritual Customs* (Copenhagen: Gyldendalske Boghandel Nordisk Forlag 1931), facing 100.

71–3: Godfred Hansen's map, from Rasmussen, ibid., facing 102.

73: The name *umiartalik* can be regarded as singular *or* plural in Inuktitut, which complicates matters still further. Some have identified "Crenchel Island" with "O'Reilly Island," but, since it appears to be roughly halfway between the Adelaide peninsula and the Royal Geographical Society Islands (#27), Hat Island seems a better match, and the shape is closely similar.

74ff.: Details about Gould's career are from Jonathan Betts's *Time Restored: The Harrison timekeepers and R.T. Gould, the Man Who Knew (Almost) Everything* (New York: Oxford University Press 2011).

74–5: "later editions of McClintock's account of his search included one of 'Franklin's Line of Retreat'": this map first appeared in the fifth edition of 1881, along with a new chapter describing Hall's and Schwatka's searches (my thanks to Regina Koellner for checking this against her copies).

78: "not altogether trustworthy": note in the legend at the bottom of the published map.

78: The map was dated 11 May 1927, which makes the omission of Hat Island, visited by Burwash the year before, more notable. For the Inuit testimony about this island, see Dorothy Eber, *Encounters of the Passage: The Inuit Meet the Explorers* (Toronto: University of Toronto Press 2008), 132–3.

81: Permission was provided by the family of Gwendolyn MacEwen for the quotation from *Terror and Erebus*.

84: Portions of Rae's report were published – without his authorization – by *The Times* of London shortly after his arrival in England.

85–6: "We were now joined by another one of the Natives": the text of the report here is taken from its republication in full in "Sir John Franklin and His Crews," *Household Words* 11 (3 February 1855): 12–20.

87: On the matter of Rae's HBC salary, see *Rae's Arctic Correspondence*, 291–7.

88: Rae obituary: *Journal of the American Geographical Society of New York* 25 (1893): 481.

88–9: Pierre Berton, *The Arctic Grail: The Quest for the North-West Passage and the North Pole, 1818–1909* (Toronto: McClelland and Stewart 1988).

89: Ken McGoogan, *Fatal Passage: The Untold Story of John Rae, the Arctic Adventurer Who Discovered the Fate of Franklin* (Toronto: Harper-Flamingo 2001).

90–1: Patrick Toomey, personal correspondence (e-mail), quoted in my "Visions of the North" blog post, "A Navigable Northwest Passage," 29 September 2012, http://visionsnorth.blogspot.com/2012/09/a-navigable-northwest-passage.html.

91: William Barr, personal correspondence, quoting in part his own statement published in "Misinterpretation and Obfuscation," *Polar Record* 51, no. 2 (2015): 221–2.

92–3: William Barr, personal correspondence.

92: "a discovery must be reported home in order to count": in this, Barr concurs; see his "Misinterpretation and Obfuscation," 222.

94: An almost direct quote from one of his letters. See Dickens to W.H. Wills, 20 November 1854: "It has occurred to me that I am rather strong on Voyages and Cannibalism, and might do an interesting little paper for the next No. on that part of Dr. Rae's Report." *The Letters of Charles Dickens*, Pilgrim ed., vol. 7 (1853–55), 470.

94: On their wealth at death, see the *Oxford Dictionary of National Biography Online*, entries for John Richardson and Charles Dickens.

95–7: Tagak Curley's and Gerald Dickens's comments are transcribed by me from John Walker's *Passage*.

99ff.: General details about Hall's early life and career are from Chauncey Loomis's *Weird and Tragic Shores: The Story of Charles Francis Hall, Explorer* (New York: Alfred A Knopf 1971).

101–2: "Esquimaux in Cincinnati": undated newspaper clipping, Hall Papers, Smithsonian Museum of American History.

106: Joe's surviving letter, Hall Papers, Smithsonian Museum of American History.

107–8: "The Pelly Bay men described the Esh-e-mut-a": Hall (ed. Nourse), *Narrative of the Second Arctic Expedition*, 256–7.

108: "On "teyma," "tima," or "*taima*," or as it is now rendered, see Kenn Harper's 2011 guest post on my "Visions of the North" blog, "Tima and Chimo," http://visionsnorth.blogspot.com/2011/12/tima-and-chimo.html.

108: "to judge by contemporary portraits": by 1845, Crozier appears to have been, at least, balding if not mostly bald; an early oil portrait now at the Royal Geographical Society (dated to 1830) shows him at least *balding*, and in his birthplace of Banbridge, Northern Ireland, both the memorial plaque in the Seapatrick church and the statue in the town centre depict him as largely bald.

109–10: "what Inuit historian Louie Kamookak calls a 'mixed' story": personal communication (Facebook message) with Louie Kamookak.

110–11: "She says that Nuk-kee-the-uk ...": David C. Woodman, *Unravelling the Franklin Mystery: Inuit Testimony*, 2nd. ed. (Montreal and Kingston: McGill-Queen's University Press 2015; 1st ed., 1991), 250, citing Hall Collection, Field Notes, book no. 28.

111: "the party on getting aboard": Woodman, *Unravelling the Franklin Mystery*, 2nd ed., 251.

111–12: "Far out on the ice": quoted in Woodman, *Unravelling the Franklin Mystery*, 2nd ed., 219, who in turn is quoting Rasmussen, *Report of the Fifth Thule Expedition*, 130.

112: "There was a man out hunting ...": Eber, *Encounters of the Passage*, 96.

114: "I will never forget the happy hours ...": quoted in Edward S. Cooper, *Vinnie Ream: An American Sculptor* (Chicago: Academy Chicago Publishers 2004), 159. While this book appeared five years before Chauncey's death, neither he nor I were aware of it at the time. I am most grateful to Mr Cooper for this discovery.

114: "Your notes, flags, & other valuables ...": quoted in Cooper, *Vinnie Ream*, 160. This and the previous letter are in the Vinnie Ream and R.L. Hoxie Papers at the Library of Congress.

117–18: "Many winters previous ...": *Journal of the American Geographical Society of New York* 12 (1880): 238.

120: "The white men are said to have been ...": ibid., 282.

120: "I know Thomas F. Barry ...": ibid., 280.

121 "I went in May and June with Captain Hall ...": ibid., 281.

121: On James Gordon Bennett and newspaper-sponsored expeditions, see Michael F. Robinson, *The Coldest Crucible: Arctic Exploration and American Culture* (Chicago: University of Chicago Press 2006), esp. 86–9.

122: "experienced seaman": see Ronald Savitt, "Frederick Schwatka and the Search for the Franklin Expedition Records, 1878–1880," *Polar Record* 88, no. 3 (2008): 193–210.

122: "Punny go to school every day": see Joe's letter, Hall Papers.

123: "His father, many years ago": see William Gilder, *Schwatka s Search: Sledging in the Arctic in Quest of the Franklin Records* (New York: Charles Scribner's Sons 1881), 29–31.

124: "Captain Potter further said": Gilder, *Schwatka's Search*, 38.

124: "Barry's own testimony": see "Thomas F. Barry's Statement," *Journal of the American Geographical Society of New York* 12, 275–9.

126: "We gave them a chart": ibid., 276.

128: "The next time he saw a white man": Schwatka, *The Long Arctic Search*, 62–3.

129–30: "When the white men were first seen": ibid., 69–70. Gilder's account of this story is slightly different, and he renders the woman's name as *Ahlangya*.

130–1: "This board": Woodman, *Unravelling the Franklin Mystery*, 255.

131: "ETERNAL GLORY," Schwatka, *The Long Arctic Search*, 72.

131: "another elderly eyewitness," named as "Tuktoocheeah" in ibid., 73–5.

132: "Rubbing off the tarnish": ibid., 80. The medal was made much of, and was passed on to Irving brother, a major-general in the British Army, who presided over the reinternment of the remains in Edinburgh's Dean Cemetery. A relief of this coin was even included in the gravestone as part of an ornamental border.

134: "The view alone": Heinrich Klutschak (translated and edited by William Barr), *Overland to Starvation Cove: With the Inuit in Search of Franklin, 1878–1880* (Toronto: University of Toronto Press 1987), 133.

135: "was granted US Patent #20,832": Google patent search, Frederick Schwatka of Rock Island, Illinois, "Design for a Spoon," SPECIFICATION forming part of Design No. 20,832, dated 16 June 1891: http://www.google.com/patents/USD20832?dq=Schwatka&hl=en&sa=X&ved=0CCQQ6AEwAWoVChMI8tOb2NjjxwIVESyICh1R5wDL.

138: "reproduced mimeographically": see Rauner Special Collections, Burwash Papers, Dartmouth College Library, http://ead.dartmouth.edu/html/stem12.html.

139: "The unknown, with its eternal lure": L.T. Burwash, *Report of Exploration and Investigation along Canada's Arctic Coast Line from the Delta of the Mackenzie River to Hudson Bay, 1925–1926* (NWT: Branch of the Interior [1927]), 1.

139: "When they were both young men": Woodman, *Unravelling the Franklin Mystery*, 77–8 and ff.

141: "In 1930 Burwash made one final effort": see *Canada's Western Arctic: Report on Investigations in 1925–26, 1928–29, and 1930* (Ottawa: F.A. Acland, Printer to the King's Most Excellent Majesty 1931), 90–8. This cumulative report, unlike Burwash's earlier productions, was printed at the expense of the Department of the Interior and included numerous photographic halftones.

141: "not previously examined": ibid., 92.

141: "reports from pilots" among these was one by Captain James Cuthbert in 1957; see "Notes from Calumet: Excerpts from the Journal and Letters of Captain Harold Wood, USCG, during the transit of the Northwest Passage by US Coast Guard Cutters *Storis*, *Bramble*, and *Spar*, 1957, compiled and edited by Lucinda Wood Langjahr," http://www.uscg.mil/history/docs/NWPassageJournal.pdf.

145: "'It was with a feeling of deep regret'": McClintock, *The Voyage of the 'Fox,'* 215.

146: "'In the dim and uncertain light'": William Gibson, "The Dease and Simpson Cairn," *The Beaver*, September 1933, 44–5.

146: "From his station at Gjoa Haven": for a general account of Gibson's searches, see his article "Sir John Franklin's Last Voyage," *The Beaver* 48 (1937): 45–75.

147: "Larsen's search took place in the summer of 1949": for this and other details, I draw on a personal communication from Doreen Larsen Riedel (his daughter).

148: "'definitely that of a white man, and a fairly young one at that'": typescript by retired RCMP superintendent V.A.M. Kent, who was at one point collaborating with Henry Larsen on an account of his career; copy supplied by Doreen Larsen Riedel. R.J. Cyriax is more specific, stating that the skull was that of a man of approximately twenty-five years of age: R.J. Cyriax, "Recently Discovered Traces of the Franklin Expedition," *Geographical Journal* 117 (June 1951).

148: "R.J. Cyriax's article": "Recently Discovered Traces of the Franklin Expedition," *Geographical Journal* 117 (June 1951): 4.

150: "One of the last of this line of succession is Robert Pilot": personal communications (e-mail) with Mr Pilot, October 2014, along with "Arctic Search" (Montreal *Gazette*, 23 August 1973) and "Franklin Probe Tries to Unravel Arctic Mystery" (Montreal *Gazette*, 16 August 1974).

151: "In 1981 Beattie began": Owen Beattie, "A Report on Newly Discovered Human Skeletal Remains from the Last Sir John Franklin Expedition," *The Musk-Ox* 33 (1983): 68–77.

155: "a photographer and a high school art teacher": these and other details on Ranford's background are from personal communications with John Harrington and Andrew Gregg, with additional information from Andrew Gregg's page at http://www.andrewgregg.ca/2011/04/18/searching-for-franklin/.

156: "Ranford and his former photography student Mike Yarasavich": for this and other information on Ranford's first search, see his "In Franklin's Footsteps," *Equinox* 69 (May/June 1993): 46–53.

156: "'Retracing a line for a second time … it was deeply embedded in moss'": ibid., 51–2.

157: "even when he took them to the exact spot": Personal communications with Margaret Bertulli and John Harrington, October 2014. See also Ranford's "Bones of Contention," *Equinox* 74 (spring 1994): 69–87.

158: "Keenleyside would confirm": Keenleyside, Bertulli, and Fricke, "The Final Days of the Franklin Expedition: New Skeletal Evidence," *Arctic* 50, no. 1 (1997): 36–46.

159: "Inuit testified to having seen elsewhere": cf. Woodman, *Unravelling the Franklin Mystery*, 143: "One man's body when found by the Innuits flesh all on & not mutilated except the hands sawed off at the wrists."

159: "Several bones of Franklin's men": from an information card accompanying the former Franklin exhibit at the National Maritime Museum in Greenwich.

160: "calcification of third molars": Keenleyside, Bertulli, and Fricke, "The Final Days of the Franklin Expedition," 38. In a personal communication to me (e-mail) from 1998, Keenleyside commented that "I should emphasize that my original age estimate of 12–15 years was based on the stage of formation of the third molars, which are extremely variable in the timing of their formation. Therefore the estimate could be off by a few years."

160: "Ranford kept searching, checking baptismal records": personal communication from Anne Keenleyside, 1998: "As I recall, Barry Ranford told me that he checked the baptism records of three of the individuals listed in the crew records as being 18 years of age and found that all three were in agreement with this. I don't think he was able to locate the baptism record of the fourth individual."

161: "'He just had this personal sense of ownership": personal communication (phone call) with Andrew Gregg, October 2014.

162: "[They] came to a place where they found a skeleton of a Kob-luna," Hall Collection, Smithsonian Institution, Hall's Journal for May–July 1866 (transcription by David C. Woodman).

163: "The pillar of wood stood by one side of it": ibid.

163: "After a while they concluded to go & make other attempts": ibid.

164: "He assumed": e-mail from David C. Woodman, 1994.

165: "As Andrew Gregg recalls it": personal communication with Andrew Gregg (phone call), October 2014.

165: "Barry Ranford took his own life": personal communication (e-mail) with John Harrington. The account that follows is based both on e-mails with Harrington and on the archived version of the Franklin Trail website, where all of the original descriptions and blog posts covering Harrington's searches are stored: http://web.archive.org/web/20000712140454/http://www.franklintrail.com/index.htm.

167: "'I made known to the party this gratifying result of all of our joint labours'": Ross's journal, quoted in Peter Lund Simmonds, *The Arctic Regions, and Polar Discoveries during the Nineteenth Century* (London and New York: George Routledge and Sons 1875), 112.

172: "His eye chanced upon a reprint of McClintock": e-mail, from David C. Woodman, 2015.

176: "The fact that Irving was buried here": personal letter from David C. Woodman, online at http://www.ric.edu/faculty/rpotter/temp/Woodman_letter.pdf.

177–8: "'Bye and bye, he [the Innuit] went again to the ship'": Woodman, *Unravelling the Franklin Mystery*, 205–6.

178: "'This evening a well-got-up procession sallied forth'": McClintock, *Voyage of the 'Fox,'* 50.

182: The trader was Roderick MacFarlane. See Woodman, *Unravelling the Franklin Mystery,* 314.

182: Image of sword and text from the Hudson's Bay Company archives; see my detailed blog post at http://visionsnorth.blogspot.com/2015/09/solomon-tozer-royal-marine.html.

182: For the details on the Royal Marines and Sergeant Tozer, I'm indebted to Ralph Lloyd-Jones's definitive research in "The Royal Marines on Franklin's Last Expedition," *Polar Record* 40 (2004): 319–26, esp. 323–4.

182: "sounded similar enough to Crozier's": personal correspondence (e-mail) with David C. Woodman.

183ff: personal communications with David C. Woodman over the years, along with his reports, available online at http://www.ric.edu/faculty/rpotter/woodman/mainpage.html.

184: "mowing the lawn": this phrase is commonly attributed to Robert Ballard, discoverer of the wreck of RMS *Titanic.*

189–91: This account of Fritz Koerner's interview is my own; I was present during the day it was shot on the ice at Resolute Bay, and took notes on the flight back.

189: "His study, published years ago": see B.T. Alt et al., "Arctic Climate during the Franklin Era, as Deduced from /Ice Cores," in Patricia D. Sutherland: *The Franklin Era in Canadian Arctic History, 1845–1869* (Ottawa: National Museum of Man, Archaeological Survey of Canada Paper no. 131, 1985).

191–2: "taken by the nip at 4:30 p.m.": *Illustrated London News,* 22 October 1853, 341 (also the source for the image).

194: "The ship was found not to have sustained any very material damage": from the account reprinted in *Family Mirror,* no. 7 (for the week ending 17 January 1857), 103.

194–5: "As regards the arrangement of the furniture": *Illustrated London News,* 27 December 1856, 648.

197: "When near the east edge of the bank": from "The Ships Seen in the Ice in the Spring of 1851," *Nautical Magazine,* May 1852, 265–76, as well as Joe O'Farrell's excellent guest post on my "Visions of the North" blog, "On the search for HM Ships Erebus and Terror," http://visionsnorth.blogspot.com/2009/10/guest-blogger-joe-ofarrells-on-search.html.

198: "found by Joe MacInnis": see his *The Breadalbane Adventure* (Montreal: Optimum Publishing 1982).

199: "CBC comedy show *This Hour Has 22 Minutes*," Season 22, airdate 14 October 2014.

201ff.: details based on my own notes from my 2004 visit to Gjoa Haven.

207: "What would you do if I told you": personal communication (e-mail) from Wally Porter.

207–8: "the 'sufferings' Franklin and his men endured": see Roald Amundsen, *My Life as an Explorer* (Garden City, NY: Doubleday, Page and Company 1927), 2.

209: "Kenn Harper … tracked down Eric Mitchell": see Kenn's guest post on my blog, "Visions of the North," "Alleged Franklin Records in Gjoa Haven," 3 September 2010, http://visionsnorth.blogspot.com/2010/09/alleged-franklin-records-in-gjoa-haven.html.

210: "This accession consists": text from artifacts database, Prince of Wales Northern Heritage Centre.

212: "I'm the only Louie Kamookak in the world": *Canadian Geographic*, December 2014, "Leading Inuit Historian discusses Franklin ships," http://www.canadiangeographic.ca/magazine/dec14/franklin-discovery-inuit-importance.asp.

217: "When David Livingstone": see "Livingstone's 1871 Field Diary: A Multispectral Critical Edition," web version of the report, with technical background, at http://livingstone.library.ucla.edu/1871diary/.

218: "Hay River resident Tom Gross": all information from telephone interviews with Tom Gross, December 2014.

Bibliography

BOOKS

Alexander, Alison. *The Ambitions of Jane Franklin: Victorian Lady Adventurer.* Crow's Nest, Australia: Allen and Unwin 2013.

Anderson, James. *Searching for Franklin: The Land Arctic Searching Expedition, 1855,* edited by William Barr. London: Hakluyt Society 2001.

Barrow, John. *Voyages of Discovery and Research within the Arctic Regions, from the Year 1818 to the Present Time: under the Command of the Several Naval Officers Employed by Sea and Land in Search of a North-West Passage from the Atlantic to the Pacific: with Two Attempts to Reach the North Pole ...* London: John Murray 1856.

Battersby, Willliam. *James Fitzjames: The Mystery Man of the Franklin Expedition.* Stroud, UK: History Press 2010.

Berton, Pierre. *The Arctic Grail: The Quest for the North-West Passage and the North Pole, 1818–1909.* Toronto: McClelland and Stewart 1988.

Bertulli, Margaret. "NgLj-2, A Franklin Site on Erebus Bay, King William Island, Field Work in 1993." Yellowknife: Prince of Wales Northern Heritage Centre.

Betts, Jonathan. *Time Restored: The Harrison Timekeepers and R.T. Gould, the Man Who Knew (Almost) Everything.* New York: Oxford University Press 2011.

Brown, John. *The North-West Passage and the Plans for the Search for Sir John Franklin.* London: E. Stanford 1860.

Burwash, L.T. (Laughlin Taylor). *Canada's Western Arctic, Report on Investigations in 1925–26, 1928–29 and 1930.* Ottawa: F.A. Ackland 1931.

– *Report of Exploration and Investigation along Canada's Arctic Coast Line from the Delta of the Mackenzie River to Hudson Bay, 1925–1926.* NWT: Branch of the Interior [1927].

Collins, Wilkie (ed. Robert Louis Brannan). *Under the Management of Mr. Charles Dickens: His Production of "The Frozen Deep."* Ithaca, NY: Cornell University Press 1966.

Cookman, Scott. *Ice Blink: The Tragic Fate of Sir John Franklin's Lost Polar Expedition.* New York: Wiley 2001.

Cooper, Paul Fenimore. *Island of the Lost.* New York: G.P. Putnam's Sons 1961.

Cyriax, Richard J. *Sir John Franklin's Last Arctic Expedition* (originally published in 1939 by Methuen). Plaistow and Sutton Coldfield, UK: Arctic Press 1997.

Davis-Fisch, Heather. *Loss and Cultural Remains in Performance: The Ghosts of the Franklin Expedition.* London: Palgrave Macmillan 2012.

Delagado, James. *Across the Top of the World: The Quest for the Northwest Passage.* New York: Checkmark Books 1999.

Eber, Dorothy. *Encounters of the Passage: The Inuit Meet the Explorers.* Toronto: University of Toronto Press 2008.

Galaburri, Richard. Lost! *The Franklin Expedition and the Fate of the Crews of H.M.S. Erebus and Terror.* New York: Black Raven 2011.

Geiger, John, and Alana Mitchell. *Franklin's Lost Ship: The Historic Discovery of HMS Erebus.* Toronto: HarperCollins Canada 2014.

Geiger, John, and Owen Beattie. *Frozen in Time: The Fate of the Franklin Expedition.* New York: Dutton 1988.

Gilder, William. *Schwatka s Search: Sledging in the Arctic in Quest of the Franklin Records.* New York: Charles Scribner's Sons 1881.

Grant, Shelagh. *Polar Imperative: A History of Arctic Sovereignty in North America.* Toronto: Douglas and McIntyre 2010).

Hall, Charles Francis (ed. J.E. Nourse). *Narrative of the Second Arctic Expedition Made by Charles Hall.* Washington, DC: US Government Printing Office 1879.

Irving, John, with Benjamin Bell. *Lieutenant John Irving, of H.M.S. Terror, in Sir John Franklin's Last Expedition to the Arctic Regions: A Memorial Sketch with Letters.* Edinburgh: David Douglas 1881.

Klutschak, Heinrich. *Overland to Starvation Cove: With the Inuit in Search of Franklin, 1878–1880,* edited and translated by William Barr. Toronto: University of Toronto Press 1987.

Lambert, Andrew. *Franklin: Tragic Hero of Polar Navigation*. London: Faber and Faber 2009.

Loomis, Chauncey. *Weird and Tragic Shores: The Story of Charles Francis Hall, Explorer*. New York: Alfred A. Knopf 1971.

MacInnis, Joe. *The Breadalbane Adventure*. Montreal: Optimum Publishing 1982.

McClintock, Francis Leopold. *The Voyage of the 'Fox' in the Arctic Seas: A Narrative of the Discovery of the Fate of Sir John Franklin and His Companions*. London: John Murray 1859.

McGoogan, Ken. *Fatal Passage: The Untold Story of John Rae, the Arctic Hero Time Forgot*. Toronto: HarperFlamingo 2001.

Neatby, Leslie. *The Search for Franklin: The Story of One of the Great Dramas of Polar Exploration*. New York: Walker and Company 1970.

Owen, Roderic. *The Fate of Franklin: The Life and Mysterious Death of the Most Heroic of Arctic Explorers*. London: Hutchinson 1978.

Potter, Russell. *Arctic Spectacles: The Frozen North in Visual Culture, 1818–1875*. New York and London: University of Washington Press; Montreal and Kingston: McGill-Queen's University Press 2007.

Rae, John. *John Rae's Correspondence with Hudson's Bay Company on Arctic Exploration, 1844–1855*. London: Hudson's Bay Record Society 1953.

Rasmussen, Knud, *The Netsilik Eskimos: Social Life and Spiritual Customs*. Copenhagen: Gyldendalske Boghandel Nordisk Forlag 1931.

Robinson, Michael. *The Coldest Crucible: Arctic Exploration and American Culture*. Chicago: University of Chicago Press 2006.

Savours, Ann. *The Search for the North West Passage*. New York: St Martin's Press 1999.

Schwatka, Frederick. *The Long Arctic Search*. Mystic, CT: Marine Historical Association 1965.

Stone, Harry. *The Night Side of Dickens: Cannibalism, Passion, Necessity*. Columbus: Ohio State University Press 1994.

Sutherland, Patricia, ed. *The Franklin Era in Canadian Arctic History 1845–1859*. Ottawa: National Museum of Man 1985.

Traill, Henry Duff. *The Life of Sir John Franklin, R.N.* London: John Murray 1896.

Williams, Glyn. *Arctic Labyrinth: The Quest for the Northwest Passage*. Berkeley: University of California Press 2010.

Woodman, David C. *Strangers among Us*. Montreal and Kingston: McGill-Queen's University Press 1995.
– *Unravelling the Franklin Mystery: Inuit Testimony*. Montreal and Kingston: McGill-Queen's University Press 1991; 2nd ed. 2015.

ARTICLES

Areleanu, Constantin. "A British Meat Cannery in Moldavia, 1844–52." *Slavonic and East European Review* 90, no. 4 (2012).
Battersby, William, with Peter Carney. "Equipping HM Ships Erebus and Terror." *International Journal for the History of Engineering & Technology* 8, no. 12 (2009): 192–211.
Battersby, William, with S. Mays et al. "New Light on the Personal Identification of a Skeleton of a Member of Sir John Franklin's Last Expedition to the Arctic, 1845." *Journal of Archaeological Science* 38, no. 7 (2011): 1571–82.
Bayliss, Richard. "Sir John Franklin's Last Arctic Expedition: A Medical Disaster." *Journal of the Royal Society of Medicine* 95, no. 3 (2002): 151–3.
Burwash, L.T. "Across Arctic Canada, 1925–1926." *Geographical Journal* 74, no. 6 (1929): 553–68.
– "The Franklin Search." *Canadian Geographic Journal* 1 (1930): 587–603.
Craciun, Adriana. "The Franklin Relics in the Arctic Archive." *Victorian Literature and Culture* 42 (2014): 1–31.
– "Writing the Disaster: Franklin and *Frankenstein*." *Nineteenth-Century Literature* 65, no. 4 (2011): 433–80.
Cyriax, R.J. "Captain Hall and the So-Called Survivors of the Franklin Expedition." *Polar Record* 4, no. 287 (1944): 170–85.
– "A Historic Medicine Chest." *Canadian Medical Journal* 57 (1947): 295–300.
– "A Note on the Absence of Records." *Scottish Geographical Magazine* 75, no. 1 (1959): 30–40.
– "The Position of Victory Point, King William Island." *Polar Record* 44, no. 6 (1952): 496–507.
– "Recently Discovered Traces of Sir John Franklin's Expedition." *Geographical Journal* 117, no. 2 (1951): 211–14.

– "The Two Franklin Expedition Records Found on King William Island." *Mariner's Mirror* 44, no. 3 (1958): 179–89.

– "The Unsolved Problem of the Franklin Expedition Records Supposedly Buried on King William Island." *Mariner's Mirror* 55, no. 1 (1969): 23–32.

Cyriax, R.J., with A.G.E. Jones. "The Papers in Possession of Harry Peglar, Captain of the Foretop, HMS Terror, 1845." *Mariners Mirror* 40, no. 3 (1954): 186–95.

Durey, Michael, "Exploration at the Edge: Re-Assessing the Fate of Sir John Franklin's Last Arctic Expedition." *The Great Circle* 30, no. 2 (2008): 3–40.

Galaburri, Richard, "The Franklin Records: A Problem for Further Investigation." *Musk-Ox* 32 (1983): 62–5.

Gibson, William. "The Dease and Simpson Cairn." *The Beaver*, September 1933, 44–5.

– "Sir John Franklin's Last Voyage." *The Beaver* 48 (1937): 45–75.

Gillies-Ross, W. "The Type and Number of Expeditions in the Franklin Search 1847–1859." *Arctic* 55, no. 1 (2002): 57–69.

Keenleyside, A., M. Bertulli, and H.C. Fricke. "The Final Days of the Franklin Expedition: New Skeletal Evidence." *Arctic* 50, no. 1 (1997): 36–46.

Koerner, Roy, et al. "Arctic Climate during the Franklin Era, as Deduced from Ice Cores." In Patricia Sutherland, *The Franklin Era in Canadian Arctic History* (Ottawa: National Museum of Man 1985).

Kowal, Walter, et al. "Source Identification of Lead Found in Tissues of Sailors from the Franklin Arctic Expedition of 1845." *Journal of Archaeological Science* 18, no. 2 (1991): 193–203.

Kowal, Walter, P.M. Kranh, and Owen Beattie. "Lead Levels in Human Tissues from the Franklin Forensic Project." *International Journal of Environmental Analytical Chemistry*, 35, no. 2 (1989): 119–26.

Learmonth, L.A. "Notes on Franklin Relics." *Arctic* 1 (1948): 122–3.

Lewis-Jones, Huw. "'Heroism Displayed': Revisiting the Franklin Gallery at the Royal Naval Exhibition, 1891." *Polar Record* 41, no. 3 (2005): 185–203.

– "'Nelsons of Discovery': Notes on the Franklin Monument in Greenwich." *The Trafalgar Chronicle: Yearbook of the 1805 Club*, 2009.

Lloyd-Jones, Ralph. "The Men Who Sailed with Franklin." *Polar Record* 41 (2005): 311–18.

– "The Royal Marines on Franklin's last expedition." *Polar Record* 40 (2004): 319–26.

Millar, K., A. Bowman, and W. Battersby, "A Re-Analysis of the Supposed Role of Lead Poisoning in Sir John Franklin's Last Expedition, 1845–1848." *Polar Record* 51, no. 3 (2015): 224–38.

Notman, Derek N.H., et al. "Arctic Paleoradiology: Portable Radiographic Examination of Two Frozen Sailors from the Franklin Expedition (1845–1848)." *Journal of the American Journal of Roentgenology* 149 (August 1987): 347–50.

Parkinson, Edward, "'All Well': Narrating the Third Franklin Expedition." In John Moss, ed., *Echoing Silence: Essays on Arctic Narrative* (Ottawa: University of Ottawa Press, 1997). 43–52.

Potter, Russell A. "The 'Peglar' Papers Revisited." *Trafalgar Chronicle: The Yearbook of the 1805 Club*, 2014.

– "'Those Wrecked or Stranded Ships': Unresolved Aspects of the Franklin Expedition." *Trafalgar Chronicle: The Yearbook of the 1805 Club*, 2010.

Pyragius, Ramona. "Journey into White Hell: Canadian Expedition Attempts to Unravel Arctic's Greatest Mystery." *Canadian Motorist*, February 1974, 12–23.

Rae, John. "Arctic Exploration, with Information Respecting Sir John Franklin's Missing Party." *Journal of the Royal Geographical Society of London* 25 (1855): 253.

Ranford, Barry. "Bones of Contention (Franklin Expedition Special Report)." *Equinox*, March/April 1994, 69–87.

– "In Franklin's Footsteps." *Equinox* (June 1993) 46–53.

– "More Pieces of the Franklin Puzzle." *Up Here Magazine* 2, no. 4 (1995): 36–9.

Smith, Graham. "'Dr. Harry Goodsir,' by Dr. Adamson of St. Andrews." *History of Photography* 10, no. 3 (1986): 229–36.

Stenton, Douglas R. "A Most Inhospitable Coast: The Report of Lieutenant William Hobson's 1859 Search for the Franklin Expedition on King William Island." *Arctic* 67, no. 4 (2014): 511–22.

Stenton, Douglas R., with Anne Keenleyside and Robert W. Park. "The 'Boat Place' Burial: New Skeletal Evidence from the 1845 Franklin Expedition." *Arctic* 68, no. 1 (2015): 32–44.

Stenton, Douglas R., et al. "Faces from the Franklin Expedition? Cranio-facial Reconstructions of Two Members of the 1845 Northwest Passage Expedition." *Polar Record* 52, no. 1 (2016): 76–81.

Wadhams, Peter, and Maria Pia Casarini. "Signs of Life." *Geographical Magazine* 66, no. 4 (1994): 26–7.

Wonders, William C. "Search for Franklin." *Canadian Geographical Journal* 76 (1968): 116–27.

Woodman, David C. "Inuit Accounts and the Franklin Mystery." In John Moss, ed., *Echoing Silence: Essays on Arctic Narrative* (Ottawa: University of Ottawa Press 1997).

Index